Mediterranean Diet Cookbook for Beginners 2023

Discover Delicious Meals with Easy-To-Follow Instructions.

Build Healthy Habits and Lose Weight with the #1 Well-Balanced,

Tasty Mediterranean Cuisine.

Marina Lo Russo

Table of Content

Chapter 3 Main Courses 70

Introduction

Everyone mentions the Mediterranean diet, but few people understand what it entails to it with commitment. The Mediterranean diet is a typical eating pattern found in Mediterranean nations. It is full of good foods, with a focus on fruit, vegetables, and whole grains in particular. Its health benefits are well-documented and well-known, and we shall come to understand them as a group. The Mediterranean region, notably Italy, is well-known worldwide for its cuisine, and the term "Mediterranean diet" is frequently used to refer to the idea of a healthy, balanced diet.

What the Mediterranean diet entails

The earliest form of the Mediterranean diet, which restricted the consumption of animal fats and favored vegetables, was developed in 1939 by nutritional doctor Dr. Lorenzo Piroddi. He did this in response to a fictitious link between eating habits and the emergence of metabolic problems.

Dr. Anciel Keys, an epidemiology and nutritionist at the University of Minnesota's School of Public Health, was the first scientist to bring the Mediterranean diet to the scientific community's attention after he accidentally discovered its health benefits during the Second World War. In particular, he was struck by the eating patterns of the Cilento population and became convinced that the low incidence of cardiovascular disease in this population was due to their diet, typical of southern Italy and other Mediterranean countries; a diet rich in "poor" foods that were easily accessible to the non-poor population, such as pasta, bread, legumes, fruit, vegetables, olive oil, and wine. He was also struck by the eating patterns of the population of the Cilento.

Diet literally translates to "style of life" and has roots in ancient Greece. The Mediterranean diet is, therefore, unrelated to the numerous and well-known diets widely practiced in the never-ending search and pursuit of the "fit weight." Still, instead it suggests education on a proper diet based on the consumption of readily available foods because they are seasonal and local, as well as being rich in nutrients even in their simplicity. These nutrients, particularly, have a preventive and/or health-promoting effect. A very "holistic" view of nutrition that shares many similarities with the idea of nutraceuticals' regulatory physiology can correctly integrate various nutritional components in the event of food shortfalls or increased dietary requirements.

Speaking of the Mediterranean diet as the "elixir of life" makes more and more sense in modern times. This is supported by a study called "StudioH70" carried out by the University of Gothenburg and in which Gianluca Tognon, a researcher from the University of Pavia and a partner of the Swedish university, also participated. The research started in the 1950s and followed thousands of 70-year-olds in the Gothenburg area who followed a Mediterranean diet for more than 40 years. They were compared to a group of contemporaries who followed a diet high in animal fats. According to the findings, persons who consume a Mediterranean-style diet have a 20% higher chance of living longer.

As a result, the Mediterranean diet is an effective eating plan and way of life that can slow down the body's aging process. On the other hand, it is a proven fact that among the populations of the Mediterranean basin, who eat pasta, fruit and vegetables, whole grains, legumes, fish, olive oil, and wine, the percentage of mortality due to ischemic heart disease primarily is significantly lower than in nations like Finland and the United States, where the daily diet contains a lot of saturated fats and is deficient in Omega 3 fatty acids or polyphenols, which are typical of oil and wine, for example.

The Mediterranean Diet's Food Pyramid

Everyone has undoubtedly seen the food pyramid in one of its many forms. It provides a quantitative breakdown of the foods that make up the Mediterranean diet and serves as a visual reminder of what we should consume, how often, and how much. As we move down the Food Pyramid, we find items that should be consumed more frequently (daily), guiding people toward a balanced diet. At the top are foods that should be consumed less frequently (once a month).

The Pyramid has undergone several iterations over time due to ongoing study and improvements. The two that stand out the most are the American Pyramid and the Greek Pyramid, both created by Dr. Walter Willet of the Harvard School of Public Health in conjunction with Antonia Trichopolou and her husband Dimitrios, who are professors in Athens and epidemiology, respectively. It suggests:

-   Daily unrefined grains, legumes, fruits, nuts, olive oil, milk, and dairy products - and exercise.
-   Each week, fish, eggs, and lean meat
-   Red meat, wine with meals in moderation.

The Cretan, Greek, and Italian diets, with the lowest chronic illness spread rates ever recorded in the 1960s, were associated with the nutritional data used to build this Pyramid. The only exception from the Greek pyramid was the use of beans weekly instead of daily. The food pyramid of the Mediterranean diet has changed over time due to changes in eating habits and new information about food, despite the diet's lengthy history. When talking about fats, the distinction between polyunsaturated and saturated fats has been noted in particular.

Nowadays, it is advised to regularly take "good fats" or polyunsaturated fats. These foods include extra virgin olive oil, walnuts, unsalted almonds, and other veggies. A distinction has also been made between different types of carbohydrates, such as the simple sugars found in sweets that increase the glycemic index and should only be ingested in moderation, and the complex carbohydrates found in vegetables like potatoes. To sum up, we ought to make a daily effort to emphasize whole grains, vegetables, fruits (fresh and dried in moderation), extra virgin olive oil, milk, yogurt, and goods manufactured from soy. It's recommended to consume eggs, fish, and meat in moderation. At the base, there is a lot of water where people usually engage in physical activity.

Do you want some figures? Thus, we can conclude that the following division of the optimal daily dietary requirements is appropriate:

-   80 percent of the carbs are complex (whole-grain bread, pasta, rice, and corn), whereas 20 percent are simple sugars.
-   just 15% of proteins
-   25% of the diet should consist of fruits, vegetables, and polyunsaturated fats like those found in olive oil.

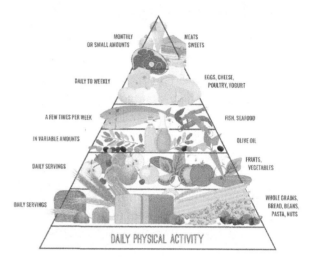

MEDITERRANEAN DIET

The advantages: numerous diseases are prevented.

Numerous studies have been published in recent years proving the direct link between the Mediterranean diet's dietary components and a decline in the incidence of cardiovascular diseases, tumors, neurological disorders, etc. Here are some of the more illustrative examples:

Demency

The Mediterranean diet is known for its consumption of foods that have a protective effect on the brain, such as fruit and vegetables (which are high in antioxidants), dried fruit (which is rich in polyunsaturated fatty acids), and fish (rich in Omega 3, which make up the membrane of the cells of the nervous system).

Infarct

The Mediterranean diet, full of foods high in antioxidant and anti-arteriosclerotic compounds, reduces the risk of heart attack by around one-third. A Mediterranean-style diet also lowers the risk of subsequent infarctions by roughly 40% after an episode of infarct, according to recent studies.

Sarcopenia

By following a complete and balanced Mediterranean diet and engaging in regular physical activity, it can be avoided from an early age.

Metabolic Syndrome

The Mediterranean diet restricts the consumption of foods high in saturated fats, is moderately calorie-dense, and includes fiber, olive oil, walnuts, and almonds, which are high in mono- and polyunsaturated fatty acids and vitamins that lower cholesterol and increase insulin sensitivity.

Chronic Inflammation

Strong anti-inflammatory and antioxidant effects are produced by the high content of unsaturated fats, fiber, vitamins, and trace substances with anti-free radical action.

Cereals in the Mediterranean diet

Cereals are a key component of the Mediterranean Diet Pyramid, which also emphasizes the regular consumption of fruits and vegetables. Which cereals, though? Whole grains are preferred because they contain complex carbs, essential nutrients for giving the body energy and have a low glycemic index. So yes to wholegrain bread, pasta, rice, etc., which have been wrongly stigmatized for a very long time by the main low-calorie diets. Therefore, let's not forget that according to their characteristics, whole grains can enhance our health by helping to prevent various diseases, as has already been well explored. Sadly, though, whole grains' outermost layers are most vulnerable to environmental contamination and pesticides.

Cereal properties

Whole grain cereals, in particular, are a great source of protein and B vitamins, vitamin E, and minerals like magnesium and selenium. They contain a lot of fiber, facilitating intestinal transit and lowering the chance of intestinal tumor development. Additionally, they often lack vitamins and minerals and, contrary to long-held belief, have a low-calorie content that suits them for slimming regimens. The bran portion of the wheat grain includes phenolic acids, which benefit the "good" gut bacterial fauna. This is an important final point to make.

Cereals' differences between whole and refined

Refining procedures that separate the three parts of the grain from whole grains produce refined cereals.

CRUSH (the protective shell that contains fiber, minerals, vitamins, antioxidants)

Kernel (the innermost part of the grain, rich in vitamins, unsaturated fats and antioxidants)

ENDOSPERM (the most energetic part of the germ, rich in starch and proteins).

The bran and germ are removed during the refining process, which results in flour that is highly rich in starch and can be used to make softer bread goods that taste better and hold up better to cookingr Unfortunately, they lack nutrients compared to products made from whole grains, have a higher glycemic index, and include a lot of gluten.

In contrast to processed grains, whole grains do not include bran or germ. As a result, there will be less starch and more fiber, vitamins, minerals, protein, and antioxidants. Additionally, because whole grains and their derivatives have a lower glycemic index and are consequently more satiating and "dietetic," they limit calorie intake by having more fiber in the bran.

Calories and dietary information

Wholegrain cereals come in a variety of varieties, and depending on the species, they have different nutritional and calorie contents. However, the calorie intake often falls between 310 and 390 kcal/100 gr For instance: While 100 gr of oats have 389 kcal, 100 gr of pearl barley have 319 kcal. Regarding nutrition, there are 70.5 g of carbohydrates, 10.4 g of protein, and 1.4 g of fats in 100 g of barley. 72.3 gr of carbohydrates, 12.6 gr of protein, and 7.1 gr of fats are found in 100 gr of oats. The nutritional values and caloric ranges of all species of whole grains are represented by the aforementioned extremes.

Benefits of whole grains

The foods of the Mediterranean diet, which include whole grains with fruits and vegetables, suggesting that this assumption is correct. These foods help to reduce the assimilation of lipids and cholesterol and, as a result, the incidence of many risk factors for the onset of various diseases affecting the cardiovascular, immune, and intestinal systems.

A final point relates to the selection of grains or flours. Consuming cereals made from grains rather than flour is preferred for a healthy diet, and the semi-integral variety can be similarly effective in terms of cooking efficiency.

Chapter 1
Appetizers

Italian Appetizer

Eggplant rolls with ricotta and basil

Ingredients: 4 servings

- ✓ 300 gr of eggplants
- ✓ 200 gr of ricotta cheese
- ✓ 6 basil leaves
- ✓ black pepper
- ✓ extra virgin olive oil
- ✓ salt

Directions: 35 min

Thinly slice eggplant lengthwise and grill on a cast-iron skillet over medium heat. Mix the ricotta in a bowl to soften it and add salt, pepper and chopped basil, continuing to stir. Spread the creamy ricotta over the eggplant slice and fold it over. Place the rolls on a baking sheet and bake at 200°C for about 10 minutes.

Rolls of salmon, cheese, and arugula

Ingredients: for 4 servings

- ✓ 8 slices of smoked salmon
- ✓ 180 gr of goat cheese

- ✓ 40 gr of rocket
- ✓ black pepper
- ✓ extra virgin olive oil
- ✓ parsley
- ✓ salt

Directions: 25 min

Wash and clean the arugula, removing the hardest parts. Chop it finely. Put the cheese in a bowl and mix, also adding the chopped arugula, a little 'oil, salt and pepper. Roll out the salmon and spread a tablespoon of cheese on each slice. Gently roll the salmon slices up to form rolls. Add some raw oil and chopped parsley to each roll. Serve.

Anchovies au gratin

Ingredients: 4 servings

- ✓ 800 gr of anchovies
- ✓ 3 garlic cloves
- ✓ parsley
- ✓ pepper
- ✓ breadcrumbs
- ✓ olive oil
- ✓ white wine vinegar
- ✓ salt

Directions: 25 min

Clean the anchovies well, taking care to remove the heads. Place a sheet of baking paper on a baking sheet and grease it with oil; lay the anchovies on top. Prepare a mixture of minced garlic, breadcrumbs, parsley, pepper, salt, and olive oil. Sprinkle the anchovies with plenty of olive oil and white wine vinegar. Bake in a preheated oven at 200° for about 20 minutes.

Lettuce rolls with asparagus and beef

Ingredients: for 2 servings

- ✓ 1 beef steak of about 350 gr
- ✓ 20 asparagus

16

- ✓ 6 large lettuce leaves
- ✓ the juice of half a lemon
- ✓ mustard
- ✓ 1/2 teaspoon chopped dried coriander
- ✓ 1 teaspoon chopped garlic
- ✓ salt
- ✓ black pepper
- ✓ chili

Directions: 45 min

Wash the asparagus, removing the tough parts with a knife. Lay a sheet of aluminum foil on a baking sheet and arrange the asparagus neatly. Add the steak cut into strips. Combine the following ingredients in a bowl: lemon juice, garlic, salt, coriander, pepper, and chili pepper; mix well and add to the baking dish. Close the aluminum foil and bake in preheated oven at 200° for about 30 minutes. When ready, gently open the foil, pour the cooking liquid into a bowl and add mustard. Place two lettuce leaves on a large plate, arrange the preparation and pour the sauce over them. Cover with the other two lettuce leaves, roll up and serve.

Mushroom croutons

Ingredients: for 6 people

- ✓ 600 gr of champignons
- ✓ 6 tomatoes
- ✓ 200 gr of croutons
- ✓ 3 yolks of hard-boiled eggs
- ✓ 10 pitted black olives
- ✓ basil
- ✓ lemon juice
- ✓ salt
- ✓ olive oil

Directions: 15 min

Wash and cut mushrooms into thin strips; chop tomatoes, chop olives and chop basil leaves. Mix ingredients and season with oil, lemon juice and salt. Lay the crostini on a serving plate, pour a drizzle of olive oil over them, spread the vegetables, decorate with the crumbled, hard-boiled egg yolks and serve.

Tartar with anchovies

Ingredients: for 6 people

- ✓ 600 g of beef tenderloin
- ✓ 2 egg yolks
- ✓ mustard
- ✓ 200 g of fresh gutted anchovies
- ✓ tabasco sauce
- ✓ capers in oil
- ✓ apple vinegar
- ✓ soy sauce
- ✓ 330 g of sunflower oil
- ✓ salt
- ✓ extra virgin olive oil
- ✓ black pepper
- ✓ pink pepper

Directions: 50 min

It's essential to use fresh, safe-sourced meat. Cut the anchovies by removing the bones, and divide into two fillets; put them in an ovenproof dish with a few grains of pink pepper and cover with vinegar. Leave to marinate for 10 minutes and dry with kitchen paper. In the meantime, whip the egg yolks adding a little mustard and sunflower oil a little at a time; add a teaspoon of vinegar, two teaspoons of soy sauce, a few drops of Tabasco, and continue to mix until the ingredients are completely blended.

Mince the meat with a knife and season with salt, extra virgin olive oil, and black pepper. Serve with the anchovies, a few capers in oil, and the mayonnaise.

Quinoa patties and yogurt sauce

Ingredients: 24 pieces

- ✓ 300 g of quinoa
- ✓ 300 g of potatoes
- ✓ 250 g of white yogurt
- ✓ 4 medium zucchini
- ✓ 100 g of pecorino cheese
- ✓ pecorino cheese
- ✓ sesame
- ✓ mint

- ✓ extra virgin olive oil
- ✓ salt

Directions: 1h 20min

Peel the potatoes cut them into cubes and pour them into a pot of boiling salted water until cooked. Rinse quinoa under running water to remove bitterness. Pour into a saucepan and add two cups of cold water; season with salt and cook for 10 minutes from the boiling point; turn off the heat and allow to rest. Mash the potatoes. Grate zucchini and cheese with a coarse-hole grater and add to quinoa and potatoes. Place the mixture back in the refrigerator until completely chilled. Then add the salt and work the mixture with your hands, forming small patties. Dip them in sesame seeds, place them on a baking sheet lined with baking paper and bake in a ventilated oven at 200 °C for about 20 minutes. Chop the mint and mix it with the yogurt, salt and one tablespoon of oil. Serve the patties with a yogurt sauce.

Codfish with artichokes and potatoes

Ingredients: for 4 servings

- ✓ 400 g 2 desalted cod fillets
- ✓ 4 artichokes
- ✓ 3 potatoes
- ✓ 60 g hard ricotta cheese
- ✓ marjoram
- ✓ parsley
- ✓ extra virgin olive oil
- ✓ salt
- ✓ butter
- ✓ pepper

Directions: 50 min

Peel the potatoes, cut them into chunks and boil them for 9 minutes in salted water before draining them with a skimmer. Clean the artichokes, cut them into four wedges each and boil them in the same water as the potatoes for 15 minutes. Dress the potatoes and artichokes with oil, salt and a sprig of chopped parsley. Over high heat, brown the cod fillets with a bit of oil and a knob of butter for 2-3

minutes per side. Let them cool before breaking them up with your hands to make petals. Garnish with shredded ricotta, pepper and a few marjoram leaves and serve with the potato and artichoke salad.

Melon skewers

Ingredients: for 4 servings

- ✓ Melon 1
- ✓ Watermelon 600 g
- ✓ Cooked ham 300 g
- ✓ Mozzarella (cherries) 350 g
- ✓ Balsamic vinegar

Directions: 20 min

Remove the skin and seeds from the melon and watermelon, then use the appropriate equipment to form them into balls. Cut each slice of ham in half and roll them up. Start by alternating a melon ball, a watermelon ball, a ham roll and a mozzarella roll on the skewers. Continue until all ingredients are used up. Arrange all skewers on a serving platter and drizzle with balsamic vinegar. Refrigerate until ready to use, then serve and enjoy.

Salmon canapés with avocado butter

Ingredients: for 6 servings

- ✓ Salmon (smoked) 250 g
- ✓ Brisèe dough (roll) 1
- ✓ Avocado 1
- ✓ Parmesan cheese 3 tablespoons
- ✓ Cheese (spreadable) 100 g
- ✓ Extra virgin olive oil
- ✓ Chives

Directions: 35 min

Begin by rolling out the Brisèe pastry and cutting it out with a round pastry cutter that is not too huge in diameter. Place the dough disks inside ramekins or silicone molds to make miniature bowls. Prick the bottom with fork prongs and bake at 180° C for 15 minutes, or until golden brown. Meanwhile, make the avocado cream by cutting the avocado in half, removing the stone, and scraping out the flesh with a spoon. If it's ripe, put it in a bowl; add the spreadable cheese, grated Parmesan cheese, a bit of salt, and a drizzle of extra virgin olive oil if it's harder. To make a homogenous cream, thoroughly combine the components. Begin assembling the canapés by cutting the salmon into strips. Fill the Brisèe pastry cups halfway with avocado cream, then top with salmon pieces arranged in the shape of a bit of rose and chopped chives. Allow cooling before servingr

Anchovies stuffed with dried tomatoes

Ingredients: for 8 servings

- ✓ Small anchovies 26
- ✓ 200 g Lettuce leaves
- ✓ Desalted capers 30 g
- ✓ 4 Chopped parsley
- ✓ Medium eggs 2
- ✓ Sundried tomatoes 6
- ✓ Grated Pecorino cheese 50 g
- ✓ Peanut seed oil
- ✓ Pepper
- ✓ Salt
- ✓ Breadcrumbs

Directions: *20 min*

Start by cleaning the anchovies: remove the head, open them and discard the bones. Rinse well and pat dry with paper towels. Remove the lettuce coarsely and wilt it in a frying pan over medium heat for one minute. Combine parsley, salt, pepper, capers, sun-dried tomatoes, garlic, grated pecorino cheese and half a beaten egg in a bowl. Chop until the mixture is smooth and the color is green. Half of the anchovies should have a teaspoon of filling and the other half should be closed. The stuffed anchovies should be dipped in the remaining beaten egg before being immersed in the breadcrumbs. Heat a large amount of oil in a skillet and cook the stuffed anchovies on both sides over medium heat. Using paper towels, drain the cooked anchovies. Serve with slices of sun-dried tomatoes as a garnish.

Octopus carpaccio

Ingredients: for 6 servings

- ✓ Octopus 1 kg
- ✓ Celery 3 ribs
- ✓ Onions 1
- ✓ Laurel 3 leaves
- ✓ Carrots 2
- ✓ Lemon 1
- ✓ Garlic 3 cloves
- ✓ Ginger 1 root
- ✓ Parsley as needed
- ✓ White wine 1 glass
- ✓ Extra virgin olive oil as needed
- ✓ Vinegar
- ✓ Pepper
- ✓ Salt

Directions: *40 min*

To make the stock, place the celery, carrots, and onion in a pot with plenty of water and bring it to a boil. Combine the bay leaves, garlic clove, and a glass of white wine in a large mixing bowl. Boil for at least 40 minutes after adding the octopus. Allow it to cool, remove it from the pot and drain on a dishtowel as soon as it reaches lukewarm. Remove any residual black from the octopus' tentacles and grate the ginger over it. Wet it with lemon juice and season it with salt. Using a knife, cut a plastic bottle in half. Put the octopus in it and push it down as far as you can with a meat tenderizer. Refrigerate the bottle for at least three hours or, if the octopus is prepared the night before, for the entire night, with the flesh tenderizer acting as a weight. Green beans should be blanched and boiled before slicing the peppers into cubes. Remove the octopus from the refrigerator, remove it from the bottle, and cut it into thin slices with a slicer, if possible. Season the pieces with salt, pepper, chopped parsley, a drizzle of oil, and a dash of vinegar on a tray. In the center of the carpaccio, arrange the green beans and peppers. Serve with a couple lemon slices on top.

Swivels of bread and eggplant

Ingredients: for 4 servings

- ✓ Sandwich bread 4 slices
- ✓ Eggplants 1
- ✓ Tomato sauce 200 g
- ✓ Extra virgin olive oil
- ✓ Salt
- ✓ Pepper

Directions: 35 min

Remove the green section of the eggplant and cut it into thin round slices, aiming for at least sixteen. Start cooking the eggplant in a nonstick frying pan with a little extra-virgin olive oil. Place four or five slices of eggplant in the pan at a time. Allow them to fry for about five minutes on both sides. Adjust the salt, then transfer the slices to a plate with tongs. Place the bread pieces on the workbench and use the rolling pin to flatten them slightly. Using a spoon, sprinkle a dollop of passata over each piece. Adjust the salt to taste. On each slice of bread, place four slices of cooked eggplant. Add another dollop of tomato sauce on top. Each stuffed slice of bread should be rolled upon itself until the filling is completely encased. Using a knife, cut the roll into three equal sections. Place all of the turnovers on a baking sheet lined with baking paper. Drizzle a little oil on top. Preheat the oven to 180°C and bake the pan for 15 minutes.

Tomatoes in peanut cream

Ingredients: for 4 servings

- ✓ Small tomatoes 16
- ✓ Onions 2
- ✓ Peanuts 120 g
- ✓ Extra virgin olive oil
- ✓ Celery 4 leaves
- ✓ Salt
- ✓ Chia seeds
- ✓ Pepper

Directions: 15 min

Place the peanuts in the glass container after rinsing them under running water. Peel the spring onion and cut it into half-moons, slices, and coarse chops. Add the spring onion, chopped, to the container. Drizzle with oil and season with salt and pepper. Using an immersion blender, finely combine everything until it's smooth and thin. Remove the stem from the cherry tomatoes and cut them in half along their circle. Place a teaspoon of peanut cream on top of each tomato and pack it down as much as possible. Toss in a few chia seeds into the cream. Place a few celery leaves in a serving dish after washing them. Serve the stuffed cherry tomatoes over a bed of celery.

Black sesame tofu pralines

Ingredients: for 4 servings

- ✓ Tofu 300 g
- ✓ Zucchinis 2
- ✓ Breadcrumbs 50 g
- ✓ Garlic 2 clove
- ✓ Basil 10 leaves
- ✓ Brewer's yeast 25 g
- ✓ Black sesame seeds 60 g
- ✓ Pepper
- ✓ Extra virgin olive oil
- ✓ Salt

Directions: 15 min

Wash two zucchinis, trim the ends, cut them into cubes, and place them in a glass jar. Rinse the tofu, drain it, and combine it with the zucchini in the container. Basil should be washed, dried, and thinly sliced. Combine the tofu and zucchini with them. Season with salt, pepper, and chopped garlic clove. Blend everything in a blender. Combine a little oil, nutritional yeast flakes, and breadcrumbs in a mixing bowl. Stir the ingredients with a spoon to combine them. Fill a small dish halfway with black sesame seeds. Make the patties ahead of time. Take a small bit of the mixture, run it between your fingers, and shape it into walnut-sized cakes. Roll them in black sesame seeds to ensure that the seeds have correctly adhered to the pralines. Serve the patties with a basil leaf and a zucchini slice threaded onto a stick.

Asparagus and ham with crumbs

Ingredients: for 4 servings

- ✓ Asparagus 900 g
- ✓ Grated bread 120 g
- ✓ Sweet raw ham 9 slices
- ✓ Grated Grana cheese 3 teaspoons
- ✓ Extra virgin olive oil 3 spoons
- ✓ Salt

Directions: 30 min

In a mixing bowl, combine the grated cheese and breadcrumbs. Heat the oil in a frying pan and add the breadcrumbs to the cheese. Stir for one minute over medium heat, or until a crumbly-looking mixture forms. The woody part of the asparagus should be removed, and the fibrous section should be peeled. Tie them up and cook them in lightly salted boiling water for 10 minutes, keeping the tips out. Drain the asparagus, pat dry with paper towels, and wrap with ham. Place them on a platter and top them with parmesan cheese and breadcrumbs. Before serving, bake for 5 minutes in a hot oven.

Mackerel meatballs with chickpeas and lemon

Ingredients: for 4 servings

- ✓ Mackerel in oil drained 250 g
- ✓ Canned chickpeas 450 g
- ✓ Extra virgin olive oil 3 tablespoons
- ✓ Untreated lemon 1
- ✓ Eggs 1
- ✓ Thyme
- ✓ Breadcrumbs
- ✓ Pepper
- ✓ Salt

Directions: 50 min

Combine the drained chickpeas, mackerel, a tablespoon of extra virgin olive oil, grated lemon rind, and half a lemon's strained juice in a blender. Blend until the mixture is smooth and compact. Add 4 tablespoons of breadcrumbs, salt, and pepper to the mixture in a mixing basin. Whisk together an egg and additional breadcrumbs in two separate bowls to taste. Form walnut-sized meatballs with damp hands, then coat in beaten egg and breadcrumbs. When they're done, spread them out on a baking sheet coated with baking paper, drizzle with oil, and bake for 15 minutes at 190°C, rotating halfway through. Mackerel meatballs with chickpeas and lemon are a variation. You may also replace the lemon with lime and add chopped fresh chili.

Shrimp tartare

Ingredients: for 4 servings

- ✓ Green apples 1
- ✓ Celery 1 stalk
- ✓ Fresh prawns as needed
- ✓ Extra virgin olive oil as needed
- ✓ Lemon
- ✓ Salt 1 pinch
- ✓ Mint
- ✓ Pepper

Directions: 15 min

Remove the peel off a green apple and cut it into small wedges. Celery and shrimp should be cut into small pieces. Mix in the extra virgin olive oil and extra virgin olive salt. Take a large pastry cup and lay the shrimp in pieces inside after squeezing the lemon on the apple. In small pieces, add celery and apple. Combine the extra virgin olive oil, pepper, and salt in a mixing bowl. Mint leaves can be added as a garnish.

Oysters gratin

Ingredients: for 4 oysters

- ✓ 4 oysters
- ✓ 4 spoons of breadcrumbs
- ✓ 3 tuft of parsley
- ✓ salt

- ✓ olive oil
- ✓ pepper

Directions: 20 min

Using a kitchen brush, clean the oysters. With a knife, cut them open. Combine breadcrumbs, minced parsley, salt, and pepper in a mixing dish. Place the oysters in the baking dish, top with breadcrumbs, and sprinkle with olive oil. In a vented oven preheated to 220ºC, bake for 10 minutes (for a crispier browning, turn on the grill in the last few minutes). Hot or warm oysters au gratin is ready to serve.

Lettuce rolls

Ingredients: for 4 servings

- ✓ 8 lettuce leaves
- ✓ 140 gr of smoked salmon
- ✓ 400 gr of Philadelphia
- ✓ 2 of avocados
- ✓ salt
- ✓ pepper

Directions: 15 min

The lettuce leaves should be washed and dried. Wash and split the avocado in half, giving special care to the huge central stone. Keep the half with the core in the fridge while cutting the other half into thin slices and peeling them. Begin creating your rolls. Spread a small amount of cheese on a lettuce leaf. Place a small salmon on top of the cheese, followed by a few avocado slices. Season the lettuce leaf with salt and pepper, then gently roll it around the stuffingr After securing the first with a couple of toothpicks, continue with the remaining rolls. After that, cut each roulade in half and serve.

Shrimp and squid skewers

Ingredients: for 4 servings

- ✓ 280 gr of shrimp tails
- ✓ 280 gr of squids
- ✓ 1 tablespoon of olive oil
- ✓ 1 pink grapefruit
- ✓ salt

- ✓ pink pepper

Directions: 20 min

Clean the shrimp, cut the squid into 2 cm broad rings, and assemble the skewers. Place a grapefruit slice on top of a shrimp and a piece of squid. Add another shrimp and a bit of squid to the mix. The calamari grits were used to close my skewers. Continue with the remaining skewers, then season with salt, oil, and pink pepper and drizzle with grapefruit juice. Cook the skewers on a hot grill for a few minutes on each side. Serve right away.

Caprese pops

Ingredients: for 4 servings

- ✓ 12 small mozzarellas
- ✓ 12 cherry tomatoes
- ✓ salt
- ✓ basil
- ✓ olive oil
- ✓ pepper

Directions: 10 min

After washing and drying the cherry tomatoes, remove the tops. Break up the basil leaves in a small dish and season with salt and pepper. Fill the cavity created by slightly emptying the cherry tomatoes with basil. A piece of mozzarella closes the cherry tomato. Finally, puncture the entire thing with a skewer and garnish with more basil. Place in the refrigerator until ready to serve.

Stuffed cucumbers

Ingredients: for 4 servings

- ✓ 2 cucumbers
- ✓ 2 radishes
- ✓ 200 gr of milk flakes
- ✓ 1 pinch of integral sea salt
- ✓ pepper
- ✓ oil

Directions: 10 min

Cucumbers should be washed, trimmed, and half of their skin removed. Each cucumber should now be cut into six cylinders. Then, to make a cavity, hollow out each one. Fill with milk flakes and serve. Season with pepper and whole-grain sea salt, and serve with radish as a garnish. Serve with a dab of olive oil, if desired.

Squid with lemon

Ingredients: for 4 servings

- ✓ 600 gr of squids already cleaned
- ✓ 2 garlic cloves
- ✓ 1 lemon
- ✓ parsley
- ✓ salt
- ✓ olive oil

Directions: 15 min

Cut the squid into rounds. In a nonstick skillet with oil, fry the garlic, then add the squid. Cook for a few minutes to allow the flavors to meld, then add the lemon juice. Allow it to decrease before gradually adding the grated lemon peel and chopped parsley. Allow cooling for a minute before serving the squid with lemon.

Tomato salad

Ingredients: for 4 servings

- ✓ 4 tomatoes
- ✓ 16 basil leaves
- ✓ 1 red onion
- ✓ 1 garlic clove
- ✓ olive oil
- ✓ pepper
- ✓ salt

Directions: 10 min

Tomatoes should be washed and sliced into small pieces. Cut the onion into thin slices after cleaning it. In a salad bowl, combine the tomatoes and onions. With knife-chopped basil, garlic, salt, pepper, and oil, make a fast pesto. Toss your tomato salad with some dressingr

Puff pastries stuffed with cheese and ham

Ingredients: for 4 servings

- ✓ 1 puff pastry roll
- ✓ 250 gr of cooked ham
- ✓ 250 gr of *caciotta* cheese
- ✓ 60 gr of grated parmesan cheese
- ✓ 1 egg

Directions: 30 min

Puff pastry should be rolled out and cut into 6 rectangles. Cooked ham should be cut into strips. In the center of each puff pastry rectangle, place a ham slice. Distribute the cheese among the cooked ham slices. Wrap the puff pastry around the filling to form dumplings, pressing down firmly on the sides to seal the borders. Brush the puff pastry with beaten egg and sprinkling grated Parmesan cheese on top. Preheat the oven to 190 degrees and bake it for 15 minutes. If the surface of the pastry becomes too brown, cover it with aluminum foil. Remove the puff pastries from the oven and top with cheese and ham. The puff pastries can be served hot or cold.

Spanish Appetizer

Homemade tuna patties

Ingredients: for 10 servings

- ✓ ½ red bell pepper
- ✓ ½ green bell pepper
- ✓ 4 cloves of garlic
- ✓ 4 onions
- ✓ 14 wafers dough
- ✓ 280 gr. canned tuna
- ✓ 1 egg for painting
- ✓ Salt
- ✓ Extra virgin olive oil

Directions: 60 min

Remove the seeds from the peppers by washing them, opening them, and removing them. Set aside the peppers, which have been cut into small cubes. Peel and dice the onions and garlic cloves in the same manner. In a large frying pan, heat 4 tablespoons of olive oil. Add the chopped vegetables and cook for about 20 minutes, or until they are tender. To avoid sticking and evenly distributing the cooking, we must stir from time to time. Crumble the canned tuna and add it to the pan. Cook for another 5 minutes before turning off the heat. On a baking dish, place a piece of greaseproof paper. Fill each dough wafer with 2 teaspoons of tuna filling, fold the dough over itself, and seal the open perimeter with a fork. Place the dumplings on the tray with the baking paper. Paint the dumplings with beaten egg while the oven is preheating to 180o C. Bake for 20 minutes, adjusting the heat as needed. Remove the pasties when this time has passed and serve hot or cold, as desired. These classic tuna patties can be served as an appetizer or beach lunch.

Garlic shrimp

Ingredients: for 4 servings

- ✓ 1 kgr of shrimps
- ✓ 10 cloves of garlic
- ✓ 2 dried chili peppers
- ✓ Extra virgin olive oil (about 20 tablespoons)
- ✓ Salt
- ✓ black pepper

Directions: 12 min

Clean the shrimps thoroughly by removing their head and tail. Wash the shrimps in a basin to eliminate any contaminants. Use a cotton cloth or absorbent paper to dry. Remove the intestine and season to taste with salt and pepper. Remove from the equation. Combine the extra virgin olive oil and chili peppers in a casserole dish. Garlic cloves should be peeled and thinly sliced. Heat the garlic cloves that have been cut. Remove and lay them away; they'll be added in the end. Toss the prawns into the oil after they've been drained. We increase the heat and season to taste with salt and pepper. The oil will change color in a minute; do not be alarmed; the shrimp will release its broth, emulsifying as the temperature rises. Add the garlic and chile peppers. Combine tastes by stirring them together. Serve right away.

Russian Salad

Ingredients: for 4 servings

- ✓ 1 kg potatoes
- ✓ 4 eggs
- ✓ 2 cans of tuna
- ✓ 3 carrots
- ✓ 700 g mayonnaise
- ✓ 250 g frozen peas
- ✓ Olives
- ✓ Salt
- ✓ Piquillo peppers

Directions: 35 m

Bring water to a boil in a casserole, add the eggs and cook for 10 minutes. Remove the shells and set them away after removing them from the water. Simultaneously, boil water with two teaspoons of salt in another casserole; add the whole potatoes and peel and the carrot, whole and peeled. Allow for 30 minutes of cooking time. After around 20 minutes, pierce the potato with a fork to see whether it is cooked. Remove the potatoes and carrots from the dish and set them aside to warm up before peeling and cutting them into cubes. Heat a teaspoon of extra virgin olive oil in a separate pan and sauté the peas with a pinch of salt until cooked. Combine the ingredients in a large mixing bowl. Toss the chopped potatoes and carrots in a large mixing dish. After that, add the eggs. Combine the peas, tuna, and mayonnaise in a mixing bowl. We thoroughly combine all ingredients, form our salad into the shape we choose, and top it with grated egg yolk, olives, and piquillo peppers. Refrigerate for at least one night.

Anchovies in vinegar

Ingredients: for 4 servings

- ✓ 1 kg of anchovies
- ✓ olive oil
- ✓ wine vinegar
- ✓ parsley
- ✓ garlic

Directions: Clean the anchovies thoroughly and remove the boneless loins. Each loin should be washed and dried. Bleed for 2 hours in cold water with ice cubes. Soak for 1 hour in a marinade of 1/3 water and 2/3 vinegar. To avoid anisakis, put the food in the freezer. Dress the anchovies with extra virgin olive oil, filleted garlic, and chopped parsley after they've been defrosted. Those that aren't eaten right away can be refrigerated in an airtight container with olive oil to keep them fresh for up to seven days.

Clams in marinara style

Ingredients: for 4 servings

- ✓ 600 gr of clams
- ✓ 1 onion
- ✓ 1 tablespoon of flour
- ✓ 2 cloves of garlic
- ✓ 1 chili pepper
- ✓ 1 tablespoon of sweet paprika
- ✓ 1/2 glass of sherry wine
- ✓ 2 tablespoons of tomato
- ✓ parsley
- ✓ extra virgin olive oil
- ✓ 1 bay leaf
- ✓ water

Directions: 15 m

Allow the clams to soak in the water for 2 hours, changing it every half hour. Set aside the steamed clams once they've been opened. Produce a sofrito by cooking half an onion, chile, and garlic over low heat, then adding the paprika and flour to make a paste or roux. Stir in the sherry wine until the alcohol has evaporated. Reduce for 5 minutes with the fried tomato and the previously drained water from opening the clams. Cook the clams in the sauce for another 3–4 minutes or until the sauce is to our likingr

Piquillo peppers stuffed with chicken

Ingredients: for 4 servings

- ✓ 5 tablespoons of Mayonnaise
- ✓ 1 jar of olives stuffed with piquillo peppers
- ✓ 8 pepper balls
- ✓ 1 small can of corn
- ✓ 1/2 chicken breast
- ✓ Salt

Directions: 20 min

Bring water to a boil with the bay leaf, pepper balls, salt, and 1/2 chicken breast in a pot. Cook until it is done, about 10 minutes. Remove it from the oven and shred it in a basin. Add the stuffed olives to the bowl and chop them up. Combine the corn and mayonnaise in a mixing bowl. Mix thoroughly and fill the peppers with a spoon.

Grilled vegetables with wine

Ingredients: for 4 servings

- ✓ 800 gr of a variety of vegetables to our taste (for ex.: zucchini, red bell pepper, eggplant, green beans, carrot, broccoli)
- ✓ 200 ml of white wine
- ✓ Extra Virgin Olive Oil
- ✓ Salt

Prepare the vegetables by chopping them into roughly the same size pieces. We separate the broccoli into saplings and the carrot; if we have one, we can use it to peel the carrot. Finally, we removed the tops from the green beans. Extra virgin olive oil is poured into the bottom of a large pan (with a lid). We add the vegetables and cook them for a few minutes over high heat. Cover after adding the white wine; allow the alcohol to evaporate. Allow it to simmer over high heat until the wine completely evaporates (about 5 minutes). Remove the cover and add another 6 tablespoons of Oil. Cook for 2 minutes, then season with salt and serve.

Artichoke Roses with Ham

Ingredients: for 4 servings

- ✓ 18 artichokes
- ✓ 18 thin slices of Iberian ham
- ✓ Salt
- ✓ Pepper
- ✓ Olive oil

Directions: 45 min

Wash the artichokes and cook them in water for 8-10 minutes without peeling them; they should be tender but entire. Cool them in water and ice before drainingr Cut the 'buds' almost in half and remove the stems and huge, complex, unattractive leaves. With a pick, carefully open the leaves and flatten them gently with your hands. In a frying pan, heat a little oil and cook them face down until golden brown, in batches; carefully flip them over, browning them with more oil if required, and arrange them on a dish. Open the artichoke hearts slightly and insert a rolled-up slice of Iberian ham in the center.

Puff Pastry Bites with Cream Cheese and Spinach Cream

Ingredients: for 4 servings

- ✓ 1 refrigerated puff pastry dough sheet
- ✓ 380 g spinach
- ✓ 140 g feta cheese
- ✓ 2 eggs
- ✓ Butter
- ✓ 120 g white cheese spread
- ✓ 1 teaspoon dried dill
- ✓ 3 tablespoons olive oil

- ✓ a few sprigs of dill
- ✓ Salt
- ✓ Pepper

Directions: 45 min

Clean the spinach, then wash, dry, and finely cut it. In a nonstick frying pan, heat a tablespoon of oil, add the spinach, and sauté for 4 to 5 minutes; remove and drain well. Feta cheese should be crumbled. In a mixing dish, crack the egg and add a tablespoon of oil, white cheese, and dried dill. Whisk until the mixture is smooth and uniform, preferably with a hand whisk. Season with salt and pepper, then stir in the spinach and feta cheese with a whisk until well combined. Preheat the oven to 185 degrees Fahrenheit. Butter the inside of an eight-cavity muffin tray. Roll out the puff pastry with a rolling pin and cut 8 squares somewhat larger than the holes in the pan. Fill these with the spinach mixture, lining them with dough, so the corners overhangr Fold the ends of the puff pastry pieces inwards to cover the filling, then lightly press them with your fingers to keep them together. Brush the puff pastry with melted butter and bake for about 20 minutes until golden brown and puffy. Remove them from the mold, let them aside to cool, and then remove them. Serve immediately with cleaned and sliced dill as a garnish.

Veal Carpaccio Rolls with Arugula and Dates

Ingredients: for 4 servings

- ✓ 100 g Carpaccio of veal
- ✓ Arugula
- ✓ 6 dates
- ✓ 30 g Parmesan cheese
- ✓ Black pepper
- ✓ Extra virgin olive oil
- ✓ Salt

Directions: 10 min

Separate the slices of carpaccio without breaking them. Cut the dates into pieces and grate the Parmesan cheese. Spread several slices of carpaccio on the bottom of the rolls, then top with arugula, grated Parmesan, and two or three pieces of dates. Season with salt and pepper, spray with oil, then secure the roll with a toothpick to prevent it from falling apart.

Tomato and mozzarella pintxos

Ingredients: for 4 servings

- ✓ 4 slices of bread
- ✓ 8 fillets of salted anchovies
- ✓ 12 cherry tomatoes
- ✓ 300 gr. of fresh mozzarella
- ✓ 1 tablespoon of honey
- ✓ 3 tablespoons of sherry vinegar
- ✓ thyme
- ✓ zest of a lime
- ✓ olive oil
- ✓ rosemary
- ✓ black pepper
- ✓ salt

Directions: 10min

To begin, toast the bread pieces and set them. Cut the cherry tomatoes in half and sauté them with a sprinkle of olive oil; after adding the sherry vinegar, honey, thyme, and rosemary, cook for one minute. Remove the pan from the heat and season with salt and pepper before adding the lime zest. Remove from the equation. Drain the whey from the mozzarella, on the other hand, and cut it into uneven pieces with your fingers. Drizzle olive oil on the toasted bread slices before assemblingr Season with salt and pepper after placing the tomatoes and mozzarella on top. Finally, grate a bit extra lime over the pintxo and add the salted anchovies.

Salmon sushi with mayonnaise

Ingredients: for 4 servings

For sushi:

- ✓ 1 spring onion, finely julienned
- ✓ 30 parsley leaves
- ✓ 30 rocket leaves
- ✓ 30 g mustard
- ✓ 30 chervil leaves
- ✓ 4 slices of fresh salmon

- ✓ 4 cooked prawns
- ✓ 80 g flaked Parmesan cheese

For the vinaigrette:

- ✓ 1 pinch of olive oil
- ✓ 1 pinch of Modena vinegar
- ✓ salt
- ✓ pepper

For the watercress mayonnaise:

- ✓ pinch of cider vinegar
- ✓ 1 egg
- ✓ 1 pinch of salt
- ✓ 2 dl olive oil
- ✓ 1 pinch of black pepper
- ✓ 60 g watercress

Directions: 20min

Wash the herbs and immerse them in ice water for sushi. Place the salmon slices on greaseproof paper and spread mustard on each one. Place a couple slices of Parmesan, some spring onion, and a cut shrimp on each slice. The herbs should be evenly distributed among the four slices.

Vinaigrette: combine all ingredients in a small glass and serve alongside the sushi.

Mayonnaise: In a mixing glass, combine the egg and the chopped watercress. The blender's arm is introduced, and the remaining ingredients are added. Beat at maximum power without moving the arm, gradually elevating it to emulsify the emulsion. Season with salt. Roll the slices gently into the shape of sushi for presentation. Serve with mayonnaise and vinaigrette.

Iberian ham tapa

Ingredients: for 4 servings

- ✓ Bread
- ✓ Tofu
- ✓ Extra virgin olive oil from Spain
- ✓ Chives
- ✓ Green asparagus
- ✓ Iberian ham

Directions: 10min

To begin, slice the bread and drizzle with a little extra virgin olive oil from Spain. It enhances the bread's flavor and gives the tapa a smooth, delectable scent. Place the tofu on top after cutting it. Sauté the asparagus in a frying pan with a couple of teaspoons of extra virgin olive oil. Roll them in ham and place them on the tofu when cooked and warm. To end, a smidgeon of chives is chopped and sprinkled on top.

Avocado appetizer

Ingredients: for 4 servings

- ✓ 350 g ripe avocado
- ✓ 20 g lemon juice
- ✓ 1 fresh chili pepper
- ✓ 1 tablespoon of red bell pepper
- ✓ 1 tablespoon red onion
- ✓ Salt
- ✓ Pepper
- ✓ Potato chips

Directions: 10min

Cut the bell pepper and red onion into small pieces. Cut the fresh chili pepper into small pieces. Mash the avocado with the chopped chili pepper and lemon juice in a food processor until it is very finely diced. Season with salt and pepper, then add the chopped onion and bell pepper. Serve the avocado appetizer on a big plate with chips and three dishes.

Fried onion rings

Ingredients: for 4 servings

- ✓ 2 eggs
- ✓ 2 sweet onions
- ✓ 80 g cornstarch
- ✓ 200 ml. milk
- ✓ 80 g plain flour
- ✓ 1 tablespoon of olive oil
- ✓ .1 pinch of flour
- ✓ Olive oil for frying
- ✓ Salt

Directions: 10min

In a frying pan, heat the oil for fryingr Toss the onions in flour and cut them into 0.5 cm thick rings. Separate the yolks from the whites and stiffen the whites. Combine the egg yolks, cornstarch, flour, milk, oil, salt, and whipped egg whites in a mixing bowl. Using the frying batter and oil, coat the floured onion rings. Fry them till golden brown over low heat. Place them in a paper-lined basket. Ready.

Banner with anchovies and pickled

Ingredients: for 4 servings

- ✓ 8 salted anchovies
- ✓ 8 breadsticks
- ✓ 8 marinated anchovies
- ✓ 8 small pickled chili peppers
- ✓ 8 small pickled gherkins
- ✓ 8 canned glass red peppers
- ✓ 8 pitted olives
- ✓ Salmorejo
- ✓ 1 pinch of tomato concentrate
- ✓ 1 ripe, peeled and deseeded tomato
- ✓ 120 g bread crumbs soaked in water
- ✓ 1 tablespoon of mayonnaise
- ✓ 1 pinch of tabasco
- ✓ 8 cheese triangles
- ✓ 2 piquillo peppers
- ✓ Virgin olive oil
- ✓ Cider vinegar
- ✓ Virgin olive oil
- ✓ Cider vinegar

Directions: 10min

In a blender, combine the salmorejo ingredients and blend until smooth. Assemble the contents on skewers made of wood. Place the chilled salmorejo, glass peppers, salt, and oil on each breadstick. Place a stick on each piece of bread. Ready.

Figs, mozzarella and ham toast

Ingredients: for 4 servings

- ✓ 1 ball of buffalo mozzarella (250 g)

- ✓ 12 ripe figs
- ✓ Bread toasts (cut in rectangles)
- ✓ 6 slices of Iberian ham
- ✓ 80 g sherry vinegar
- ✓ Pepper
- ✓ 2 finely chopped shallot
- ✓ 140 g extra virgin olive oil
- ✓ Basil sprouts
- ✓ Salt

Directions: 15min

To make the vinaigrette, combine the salt and vinegar in a mixing dish. To dissolve the salt, mix it vigorously. Whisk in the oil until it is completely emulsified. Before serving, stir in the finely chopped shallot with a spoon. The toast is as follows: cut the bread pieces into slices and bake them between two greaseproof paper-lined pans at 180°C. Cut the figs half from the tip to the base, then cut a small slice from each side to place on a greaseproof paper-lined tray. Cut the mozzarella into fig-sized pieces and arrange them on each figr To warm the figs, place them in the oven at 180°C for 3 minutes. Dress them with a few drops of vinaigrette and freshly ground black pepper when they come out of the oven. Arrange the figs on top of the heated mozzarella, bread, ham slice, and basil sprouts. Serve with a drizzle of vinaigrette on top.

Seasoned olives

Ingredients: for 4 servings

- ✓ 1 kgr of green olives
- ✓ 2 pinch of spring onion
- ✓ black pepper
- ✓ 8 cloves of garlic
- ✓ 2 bunch of rosemary
- ✓ 1 bunch of thyme
- ✓ 3 bay leaves
- ✓ few leaves of parsley
- ✓ 1 pinch of hot paprika
- ✓ 1 lemon
- ✓ 1 pinch of red pepper powder
- ✓ 1 dash of virgin olive oil
- ✓ 1 dash of sherry vinegar
- ✓ 1 dash of Pedro Ximénez wine

Directions: 20min

Pepper, chives, garlic, thyme, rosemary, and bay leaf are ground in a mortar. Mix parsley, lemon zest, juice, and paprika in a mixing bowl. Combine the red pepper powder, vinegar, Pedro Ximenez, and olive oil in a mixing bowl. Over the olives, pour the mixture. Allow plenty of time for them to soak.

Camembert and Iberian ham toast

Ingredients: for 4 servings

- ✓ 2 slices of loaf bread
- ✓ 6 slices of camembert
- ✓ 60 g of spring onion in fine julienne
- ✓ 6 peeled walnuts
- ✓ 40 g g gherkin in thin slices
- ✓ 6 cherry tomatoes
- ✓ 2 Parsley leaves
- ✓ 3 slices of Iberian ham
- ✓ 8 rocket leaves
- ✓ bacon in slices
- ✓ paprika
- ✓ Lemon juice
- ✓ Salt
- ✓ Olive oil

Directions: 15min

Brown the bacon cubes in a skillet. In the same pan as the bacon, toast the bread slices. Drizzle a little oil on each slice of bread before adding the gherkin slices, spring onion, bacon cubes, three slices of cheese, two split cherry tomatoes, and two walnuts. Preheat the oven to 200°F and bake for 5 minutes. Remove the parsley leaves, rocket leaves, olive oil, a pinch of paprika, and a few drops of lemon juice from the oven and top each with a slice of ham. Serve.

Cod and grapefruit carpaccio

Ingredients: for 4 servings

- ✓ 1 cod fillet
- ✓ 1 pink grapefruit
- ✓ 1 ripe avocado

- ✓ 3 chopped shallots
- ✓ Sesame oil
- ✓ Olive oil
- ✓ 1 pinch of soy sauce
- ✓ Tender sprouts
- ✓ 2 tablespoons toasted sesame seeds

Directions: 20min

In a basin, grate the grapefruit skin. Remove the grapefruit segments and peel the grapefruit. Add the avocado pulp after squeezing the grapefruit core over the grapefruit zest. Shallot, oils, soy, salt, and pepper are mashed together with a fork. On a dish, spread the avocado cream. On a cutting board, cut the cod into thin slices. Place them on top of the avocado. Season the fish with salt and pepper. Toss with olive oil, toasted sesame seeds, and grapefruit segments. Freshly cut sprouts can be sprinkled on top. Ready.

Greek Appetizer

Greek salad

Ingredients: for 2 servings

- ✓ 120 g cherry tomatoes
- ✓ 180 g feta cheese
- ✓ 30 g cucumber
- ✓ 10 g red onion
- ✓ 20 g rocket
- ✓ 10 ml extra virgin olive oil
- ✓ 30 g pitted black olives
- ✓ salt

- ✓ pepper
- ✓ oregano

Directions: 40min

Wash the vegetables and dry them with a cloth. Then take the feta and cut it into about 2 cm per side cubes. Repeat the operation with the vegetables, so you have all the ingredients almost the same size. Transfer them all to a bowl; add oil, salt, pepper, oregano, and mix; then cover with a sheet of plastic wrap and let rest in the refrigerator for about half an hour. Divide Greek salad among small bowls or plates and serve fresh if possible.

Chicken meatballs

Ingredients for 4 servings

- ✓ 1 kg of chicken in pieces
- ✓ 2 medium-sized eggs
- ✓ Parsley
- ✓ Carrot grated
- ✓ Mix of spices for chicken
- ✓ 3 slices of bacon
- ✓ 1 cup hard cheese or parmesan or feta
- ✓ Mushrooms (optional)
- ✓ Some olive oil
- ✓ flour for breading

Directions: 20min

Cut the chicken into pieces to cook it faster. After boiling the chicken, cut it into small pieces with your hand. Put them in a bowl with the eggs, spices, and the rest of the ingredients. Mix with your hands and add a little oil to make the flour mixture easier to bread the mixture. Lightly flour and fry. Put them on non-stick paper and serve.

Roasted courgette sticks

Ingredients for 4 servings

- ✓ 4 courgettes cut into sticks
- ✓ 3 egg whites, beaten
- ✓ 1/4 teaspoon salt

- ✓ 2 egg yolks, grated breadcrumbs
- ✓ 2 tbsp grated pecorino
- ✓ 1/4 tsp. garlic powder

Directions: 40min

In a small bowl, mix egg whites with salt and pepper. Mix the breadcrumbs, garlic powder, and cheese in a small bowl. Put parchment paper on a baking sheet and drizzle some olive oil. Dip the zucchini into the bowl of eggs and then into the bowl of breadcrumbs. Layer the zucchini on the baking sheet and bake for 20-25 minutes. Each serving is equal to one whole zucchini stick.

Canapés with cream cheese and pomegranate

Ingredients for 4 servings

- ✓ 1 cup of pomegranate seeds
- ✓ 200 g parmesan flakes
- ✓ 220 g cream cheese
- ✓ Balsamic cream
- ✓ 2 chopped lettuce leaves
- ✓ 1 baguette sliced

Directions: 10min

In a preheated oven, bake the bread slices for a few minutes until golden. Spread the baguette slices with the cream cheese, top with parmesan flakes, drizzle with balsamic cream, and top with pomegranate seeds and some chopped lettuce. Put them in the fridge for a while and after half an hour, serve them.

Cucumber rolls stuffed with vegetable sticks

Ingredients for 4 servings

- ✓ 10 long and thin slices of cucumber
- ✓ cream cheese
- ✓ vegetable sticks (carrots, colorful peppers)

Directions: 10min

Stuff the long and thin cucumber slices with vegetable sticks after spreading them with cream cheese. Then close them like a roll and place them upright on the plate.

Prosciutto wrapped in pear and blue cheese

Ingredients for 4 servings

- ✓ 2 ripe pears
- ✓ 8-10 slices of prosciutto
- ✓ 200 g blue cheese in slices

Directions: 10min

Wash the pear, remove the skin and cut it into thin slices half a centimeter thick. Spread the slices of prosciutto on a surface. Place a slice of blue cheese on one end and a piece of pear on top. Wrap the prosciutto around your pear and cheese and secure it with a toothpick.

Individual Salads in Nests

Ingredients for 4 servings

- ✓ 5 rusk cups
- ✓ 2 green salads
- ✓ 2 cups of pomegranate
- ✓ 1 package of croutons
- ✓ 200 g parmesan cheese in flakes
- ✓ Olive oil
- ✓ Balsamic cream
- ✓ Salt

Directions: 10min

Put the salad in the rusk cups and add the croutons and pomegranate. In a bowl, add the olive oil, the balsamic cream (as much as you want), salt and mix until combined. Add the dressing to your salad and use two spoons to mix it all over. Grate parmesan leaves and serve.

Festive stuffed bread

Ingredients for 4 servings

- ✓ 1 loaf of round bread, one kilo
- ✓ 1 can of roasted Florina peppers
- ✓ 2 eggplants, thinly sliced
- ✓ 2 sliced zucchini
- ✓ A few sliced mushrooms
- ✓ Basil leaves
- ✓ Half a cup of parmesan cheese
- ✓ 4 slices of cheese
- ✓ 4 slices of smoked ham or turkey
- ✓ 1 cup sun-dried tomato sauce
- ✓ A little oil
- ✓ Some oregano or thyme for the vegetables

Directions: 30min

Take a loaf of bread from the oven and remove the top of the loaf from the top of the loaf. Spread the sun-dried tomato sauce on the inside of the loaf of bread, as well as on the lid. Roast the vegetables with some oil on the oven grill until tender. Once your vegetables are ready, start filling the loaf and layering the ingredients. On top of the tomato sauce, put the eggplants, parmesan, zucchini slices, basil leaves, parmesan, mushrooms, oregano or thyme, the ham, a few more vegetables, and finally, the slices of cheese, leaving no gaps. Finally, put the lid on, press it down, close it with cellophane or foil, and put it in the fridge for a few hours to let the flavors meld. Take it out and bake it in a preheated oven at 220o for about half an hour to crisp up and melt the cheese. Serve on its own or with other snacks at the holiday table or as a main course with a salad.

Salmon roll with cream cheese

Ingredients for 4 servings

- ✓ 200g smoked salmon
- ✓ 25 dry toast rolls, round
- ✓ For the filling:
- ✓ 80g cream cheese at room temperature
- ✓ 2 - 3 tablespoons of chives finely chopped
- ✓ 3 - 4 tablespoons of chopped dill
- ✓ white pepper

Directions: 15 min

Execution: Mix the cheese with the chives. Spread the salmon slices on foil. Make sure that one slice covers part of the other without opening and that the filling comes off with the wrappingr This way, you form a rectangle of about 30 x 20 cm. Lay the cheese filling on top of the salmon. Leave a margin of uncovered cheese along the long side to start rolling the roll from there. Sprinkle the dill and pepper over the surface of the cheese. Using the foil, turn the salmon with the filling; on the side, leave a margin on the salmon to make a roll that forms a two-color spiral (pink of the salmon and white of the cheese) when viewed from the sides. As you roll up the roll, push the foil so that at the end, you enclose it and fold it into a tightly tied roll with a diameter equal to the diameter of the breadcrumbs you will make the sofas. Refrigerate the roll for 6-7 hours or from the day before. Unroll it and cut it with a sharp toothless or electric knife into 2 cm thick rounds.

Potatoes Au Gratin

Ingredients for 4 servings

- ✓ 1.5 kg of medium potatoes
- ✓ 200 g of bacon
- ✓ 4 tablespoons of Cow Butter
- ✓ 3 tablespoons of flour
- ✓ 250 g of cream
- ✓ 150 g of a variety of grated cheese with Graviera or grated Long Matured Graviera
- ✓ 1 pinch of nutmeg
- ✓ Salt, pepper

Directions: 25min

Peel the potatoes from the skins and black specks. Put them in a pot and cover them with water. Season lightly with salt and add 1 tablespoon of Village Cow Butter. Boil the potatoes for ½ hour (they do not need to be completely cooked). Drain them and let them cool, then cut them into slices. Place them on a baking tray like cherry tomatoes, one touching the other in rows. Finely chop the bacon into small pieces the size of small beans; place them in a pan without oil and sauté until crispy. Scatter them over the potatoes. In a small saucepan, heat the remaining Village Cow Butter. Once melted and thoroughly heated, pour the flour and stir until the flour darkens. Pour in the cream and stir well until a thick béchamel gel forms. Remove it from the heat, and pour in the cheese, stirring constantly, add a little grated nutmeg, pepper and a little salt. Pour the delicious béchamel over the potatoes and bacon. Cover the baking tray with aluminum foil and bake in a preheated oven at 180o for 1 hour. Uncover the baking tray and continue baking at 200o for 15 minutes. Remove the baking tray from the oven, let it cool, cut the food into square pieces and serve on plates.

Christmas Salad

Ingredients for 4 servings

For the dressing:

- ✓ 2 tablespoons of olive oil
- ✓ 1 teaspoon of chopped mint
- ✓ 1 tablespoon of mayonnaise
- ✓ 1 cup cottage cheese
- ✓ 3 tablespoons Worcestershire sauce

For the salad:

- ✓ arugula (enough for each person) cut into medium-sized pieces
- ✓ 1 tablespoon of chopped parsley
- ✓ 10 chestnuts, boiled and shelled (cut into 4 pieces)
- ✓ 3 tablespoons of chopped walnuts
- ✓ 2 diced avocados
- ✓ ¼ grated mozzarella cheese

Directions: 10 min

Spread the arugula on a large platter and season lightly with salt. Spread the chestnuts and walnuts on top. Sprinkle with parsley and spread the mozzarella cheese. Mix the dressing ingredients, drizzle over the salad and rub pepper over the top.

Broccoli pie

Ingredients for 4 servings

- ✓ 350-400 g broccoli in florets, scalded, drained
- ✓ 1 sheet of puff pastry

- ✓ 1 dry onion, finely chopped
- ✓ 2 leeks, finely chopped
- ✓ 250 g chopped cream cheese
- ✓ 50 g feta cheese
- ✓ 80 g blue cheese melted with a fork
- ✓ 2-3 tablespoons of olive oil
- ✓ 1 beaten egg
- ✓ salt, pepper nutmeg

Directions: 40 min

Sauté the onion and leeks in a spoonful of oil in a high-sided pan. Add the broccoli and the remaining oil and continue to sauté. Remove from the heat and allow to cool for a while. Add the cheese, salt, pepper, and nutmegr Stir the filling to mix the ingredients well. Roll out the puff pastry sheet and spread the filling on top. Fold the pastry sheet into a roll to enclose the filling and wet the edges to make them stick. Brush the surface with the eggr Place the baking tray with the roll in a preheated oven at 200° C and bake for 30 minutes or until golden brown. Notes: Try the broccoli pie by replacing the two suggested cheese slices with grated Parmesan cheese. Sprinkle the top with sesame seeds or black sesame seeds if desired. If you are not following a vegetarian diet, add 5 slices of chopped bacon, sautéed with the onion and leeks.

Easy appetizer with plums and bacon

Ingredients for 4 servings

- ✓ 20 plums
- ✓ 10 slices of bacon
- ✓ a little oil

Directions: 10 min

Cut each slice of bacon in half. Wrap each plum with half a slice of bacon and secure with a toothpick. Brush an ovenproof dish with a little oil and bake in a preheated oven at 180 °C until the bacon is golden brown.

Stuffed fried olives

Ingredients for 4 servings

- ✓ 40-50 large pitted green olives
- ✓ 50 g butter or lard
- ✓ 200 g mixed pork and beef, finely chopped
- ✓ 3 tablespoons of grated head cheese
- ✓ 2 eggs
- ✓ 1/2 cup bread crumbs, soaked
- ✓ some grated breadcrumbs
- ✓ 1 tablespoon of tomato paste
- ✓ salt, pepper, nutmeg
- ✓ flour and oil for frying

Directions: 15 min

Melt the butter or lard in a saucepan. Add the chopped meat and brown it for 5'-6'; add the tomato paste, salt, pepper, and 1-2 tablespoons of hot water. Allow the mixture to cool and mash.

Mix the pureed meat mixture with the bread crumbs well beaten and 1 egg with the head cheese and nutmegr Knead everything together very well until it becomes a soft and thick dough.

Fill the olives with the mixture, flour them and pass them through the second, beaten egg and the crushed breadcrumbs. Leave them in the fridge for at least 30 minutes. Fry them in plenty of hot oil and leave them on a paper towel to drain before serving them as a snack.

Roasted cherry tomatoes in oil with garlic and basil

Ingredients for 4 servings

- ✓ 250 g cherry tomatoes
- ✓ 2-3 tablespoons of olive oil
- ✓ 2-3 cloves of garlic, finely chopped
- ✓ 1 large sprig of basil
- ✓ salt, a little sugar and a little oregano

Directions: 20 min

Lay the cherry tomatoes on a baking tray lined with parchment paper and drizzle with olive oil. Sprinkle with a bit of salt, a little sugar, a little oregano, and chopped garlic. Place the basil sprig in between. Bake in a preheated oven at about 170°C until they are wilted outside but still juicy. Remove the basil and keep them

in the fridge in olive oil. Serve them on toasted bread or pies with cheese curds, fresh cream cheese mixed with herbs, or cottage cheese.

Moroccan Appetizer

Chickpea Hummus

Ingredients for 4 servings

- ✓ 400 g chickpeas (cooked, drained weight)
- ✓ 2 tbsp. tahini (sesame paste)
- ✓ 2 tablespoons olive oil
- ✓ Juice of 1 lemon
- ✓ 1 pinch of salt
- ✓ 1 tsp. cumin powder
- ✓ 1 clove garlic (optional)
- ✓ Cayenne pepper to taste
- ✓ Sesame seeds (optional)

Directions: 20 min

Blend the chickpeas and lemon in a blender on high speed until a creamy consistency. Chickpea Hummus recipe step 1 picture Add the olive oil, tahini, garlic, cayenne pepper and cumin and blend until the mixture is emulsified. Chickpea Hummus recipe step 2 photo Serve with crudités, bread, or crackers. Store in the refrigerator for up to 5 days.

Beet hummus

Ingredients for 4 servings

- ✓ 400 gr of chickpeas
- ✓ 200 gr of beets
- ✓ 1 garlic clove
- ✓ 1 lime
- ✓ Extra virgin olive oil
- ✓ Tahini
- ✓ Cumin powder
- ✓ Cinnamon powder
- ✓ Peppermint
- ✓ Salt

Directions: 15min

Start by cooking the 200 gr of beets for 1 hour in a pot full of boiling water. When it is tender, remove it from the water and let it cool.

Cook the 400 gr of chickpeas in boiling water or use some from a jar. In the latter case, wash them with plenty of tap water by putting the chickpeas in a mesh strainer.

Put the cooked chickpeas in a blender or food processor with the peeled garlic clove and the lemon juice. Grind until you have a homogeneous paste.

Moroccan melon salad

Ingredients for 4 servings

- ✓ 1 large melon
- ✓ 30 gr of white sugar
- ✓ 1 tablespoon ginger
- ✓ 1 tablespoon lemon (juice)
- ✓ Cardamom seeds
- ✓ Walnuts (shells)
- ✓ 3 mints (leaves)
- ✓ Orange (zest)

Directions: 2 hs

Peel the melon. Open it, remove the seeds and cut it into small square cubes, only the white part.

We introduce in a big bowl all the pieces of melon. We put together the rest of the recipe ingredients: orange zest, lemon juice, a few strips of mace, a couple of fresh mint leaves, some natural cardamom seeds, half a tablespoon of ginger, and 50 gr of white sugar. We mix well all the ingredients. Once this is done, cover it and let it macerate for two hours in the refrigerator. And we will have it ready after that time, and we will only need to take it out of the fridge and serve the dessert.

Moroccan olive pâté

Ingredients for 4 servings

- ✓ 1 cup / 200 gr of cured black olives such as Kalamata or use green olives.
- ✓ 2 tablespoons of capers, rinsed and drained
- ✓ 1 or 2 cloves of garlic, pressed or finely chopped
- ✓ 1 tablespoon harissa
- ✓ 1 tablespoon lemon juice or to taste
- ✓ Optional: 1 tablespoon of fresh parsley, chopped
- ✓ 1/4 cup olive oil or more to taste

Directions: 15 min

Rinse olives and remove pits. Combine olives with capers. Chop the olives and capers as finely as possible by hand, or place them in a food processor and pulse several times until the mixture is almost a paste. If you're using a processor, be careful not to over-blend because you want to maintain some consistency. Blend the chopped olives with the remaining ingredients by hand or in the food processor again by pulsing several times until combined. Taste and adjust the harissa, garlic, and lemon juice as desired. For a thinner pâté, increase the amount of olive oil, adding a teaspoon or two at a time, until desired consistency is achieved.

Moroccan crunchy salad

Ingredients for 4 servings

- ✓ Red bell pepper 1
- ✓ Green bell pepper 1
- ✓ Red onion 1
- ✓ Chilli pepper 1
- ✓ Celery 1
- ✓ Fresh parsley
- ✓ Fresh mint

- ✓ Extra virgin olive oil 40 ml
- ✓ Lemon juice
- ✓ Ground black pepper
- ✓ Salt

Directions: 10 min

Wash well and dry all the vegetables. Finely chop the peppers, discarding the seeds. Finely chop the red onion and celery, peeling the filaments if necessary. Open the chili pepper, remove the seeds and chop finely. Mix all the vegetables in a large bowl. Finely chop the parsley and mint, previously washed and dried, and add them to the mixture. Season with salt and pepper to taste and dress in olive oil and freshly squeezed lime or lemon juice.

Moroccan Carrot Salad

Ingredients for 6 servings

- ✓ 400 ml of water
- ✓ 500 g of chopped peeled carrots
- ✓ 1 clove of garlic
- ✓ 1 teaspoon of sweet paprika
- ✓ 1 teaspoon of ground cumin
- ✓ 1 pinch of cinnamon
- ✓ 1 teaspoon of cayenne
- ✓ 1 pinch of sugar
- ✓ 100 ml of extra virgin olive oil
- ✓ 30 ml of lemon juice
- ✓ 1 teaspoon of salt

Directions: 10 min

Steam the carrots and place them in a bowl. Crush the garlic, paprika, cumin, cinnamon, cayenne pepper, sugar, and cinnamon with a blender. Add the oil, lemon juice, and salt and mix. Pour this mixture over the carrots and mix well with a spoon. Let it macerate while it cools and serve.

Moroccan Eggplant Salad

Ingredients for 4 servings

- ✓ 2 eggplants

- ✓ 3 tomatoes
- ✓ 2 cloves of garlic
- ✓ 1 teaspoon sweet paprika
- ✓ 1/2 teaspoon ground cumin
- ✓ 1/4 teaspoon cayenne
- ✓ 2 teaspoons chopped coriander
- ✓ 40 ml lemon juice
- ✓ extra virgin olive oil
- ✓ salt

Directions: 30 min

Remove a few strips of skin from the eggplants. Cut them into 1 cm thick slices, sprinkle them with salt and put them in a colander to drain the water they release. Leave them for about 20 minutes and then dry them with kitchen paper. Peel the tomatoes and cut them into small cubes. Heat the olive oil in a frying pan and fry the eggplants until golden brown on both sides; remove them and place them on a plate with kitchen paper to absorb the excess oil. In the remaining oil, we fry the chopped garlic cloves without letting them toast, add the tomato, the paprika, the cumin and the cayenne. Put the eggplants back in and cook, lightly crushing the eggplants and the tomato with a spoon. Cook until almost all the liquid has evaporated. When the oil separates, remove the excess, add the coriander and lemon juice, and season with salt and pepper. Serve warm or cold.

Chickpeas with Moroccan sausage

Ingredients for 4 servings

- ✓ 400 g cooked chickpeas
- ✓ 1 red or white onion
- ✓ 2 cloves garlic
- ✓ 175 g chorizo sausage
- ✓ 2 bay leaves
- ✓ 2 teaspoons of sweet paprika
- ✓ 1 teaspoon thyme
- ✓ 1 little sage (optional)
- ✓ 5 ml lemon juice
- ✓ extra virgin olive oil
- ✓ black pepper and salt

Directions: 30 min

Rinse and drain the chickpeas cooked al dente, or drain a jar of cooked chickpeas. Remove any skins that may have come off or peel them. Chop the red onion into pieces that are not really small, chop the garlic cloves and chop the chorizo, removing the skin. Heat a couple of tablespoons of olive oil in a good frying pan or casserole and cook the onion and garlic for about 5 minutes, until transparent. Add the chorizo and bay leaf and sauté for a few minutes. Add the chickpeas, paprika, thyme, and sage, stirring well. Lower the heat, cover, and cook for about 15-20 minutes to integrate all the flavors nicely. In the end, season with lemon juice, salt, pepper, and add a little more paprika, if desired

Moorish lamb skewers

Ingredients for 4 servings

- ✓ 1 Kg of lamb meat
- ✓ 1 onion
- ✓ 2 cloves of garlic
- ✓ Hot paprika
- ✓ Freshly ground black pepper
- ✓ Ginger powder
- ✓ Ground cumin
- ✓ Turmeric
- ✓ Olive oil
- ✓ Salt
- ✓ Wooden or metal skewer sticks

Directions: 25hs

As I have already mentioned, the trick to making these skewers tasty is to leave the meat in marinade for a day. To prepare the marinade, we are going to mix in a bowl a cup of olive oil, the previously peeled and chopped onion, the peeled and chopped garlic cloves, a quarter of a spoon of pepper, ginger, cumin, turmeric, another of hot paprika and a pinch of salt. Once the marinade is ready, cut the lamb meat into medium-sized cubes and put them in the container with the marinade. Mix well so that all the meat is impregnated and put it in the refrigerator, where it will have to be for 24 hours. Every 8 hours, stir the lamb meat to absorb the spice mixture well. The following day we prick the pieces of meat in therods forming the Moorish skewers. Then we pass them through the griddle or a frying pan with a few dropsolive oil until the meat is to our taste. Remove and serve.

Chapter 2 First Courses

Italian First Courses

Spaghetti Carbonara

Ingredients for 4 servings

- ✓ 100 gr of bacon
- ✓ 2 eggs
- ✓ 1 yolk
- ✓ 3 tablespoons fresh cream (optional)
- ✓ 4 tablespoons pecorino romano cheese
- ✓ to taste salt
- ✓ to taste black pepper
- ✓ 320 gr of pasta (durum wheat)
- ✓ 1 garlic clove
- ✓ 3 tablespoons extra virgin olive oil

Directions: 35 min

Cut the guanciale into cubes. Pour the oil into a large pan, crush the garlic clove, peel it, put it in the pan, let it brown over medium heat, and then remove it. Add the guanciale and fry it. Remove the pan from the heat and set it aside for the next steps. Bring the water to a boil in a second pot, adding two teaspoons salt. Whisk some eggs in a bowl, with a pinch of salt and half of the pecorino cheese. Pour the spaghetti into the boiling water and stir with a fork, calculating the cooking time indicated on the pasta package. One minute before draining, put the pan with the guanciale for the carbonara back on the heat. Drain without draining too much, and pour into the pan, stirring quickly for a few moments with a wooden spoon. Add the eggs, turn off the heat, stir quickly to prevent them from congealing, and distribute your spaghetti carbonara on plates; garnish with the remaining pecorino cheese and freshly ground pepper.

Bucatini all'amatriciana

Ingredients for 4 servings

- ✓ 1 tablespoon extra-virgin olive oil
- ✓ 60 gr of pecorino romano cheese
- ✓ hot pepper to taste
- ✓ salt to taste
- ✓ 6 tomatoes
- ✓ 100 gr of bacon
- ✓ 400 gr pasta (durum wheat)
- ✓ 1/4 white onion

Directions: 35 min

Work the tomatoes by incising the skin of the tomatoes with a well-sharpened knife, blanch them in boiling water for about one minute, drain them, and run them under cold water. Peel them, remove the seeds, and cut the pulp of the tomatoes into fillets. Dice the guanciale, place it in a pan with a drizzle of hot oil and let it brown. Once crispy, drain with a slotted spoon and keep warm. Add the finely chopped onion, the whole piece of chili pepper, and the sliced tomatoes to the cooking juices in the pan. Salt and cook the sauce for the bucatini amatriciana for 10 minutes. After this short time, remove the chili pepper and add the guanciale kept aside. Cook the bucatini in plenty of boiling salted water for the time indicated on the package, drain them al dente and transfer them to the pan with the sauce. Allow the bucatini to season with the sauce for about a minute on heat. Finally, as a final touch, sprinkle the bucatini amatriciana with pecorino cheese and serve it immediately.

Tagliatelle with Bolognese sauce, the traditional recipe

Ingredients for 6-8 servings

- ✓ 400 g tomato puree
- ✓ 250 g minced pork meat
- ✓ 200 g ground beef muscle
- ✓ 150 g ground diaphragm
- ✓ 150 g bacon
- ✓ 150 g carrot
- ✓ celery
- ✓ onion
- ✓ tomato paste
- ✓ white or red wine
- ✓ milk butter
- ✓ extra virgin olive oil
- ✓ salt
- ✓ pepper
- ✓ tagliatelle

Directions: 3h 30min

Heat 3-4 tablespoons of oil and a knob of butter in a saucepan, add chopped celery, carrot, and onion, and cook over medium heat. Add the diced bacon and all the meat after 2-3 minutes. Raise the heat and deglaze it, stirring continuously. Deglaze with 80 g of wine and let the alcoholic part evaporate. Lower the flame and let the liquid reduce, continuously stirringr Add salt and pepper. Add the passata and 2 tablespoons of tomato paste, boil again, stirring, cover, and let simmer over low heat for 2-3 hours, adding broth if necessary; towards the end, add 200 g of milk. Cook the tagliatelle in boiling salted water, drain, and season.

Spaghetti with Seafood

Ingredients for 4 servings

- ✓ Mussels: half a kilo
- ✓ Spaghetti: 350 Gr
- ✓ Clams: half a kilo
- ✓ Sea Turtles: 250 Gr
- ✓ Shrimps: half a kilo
- ✓ Tomatoes: 50 Gr of Pulp
- ✓ Garlic: 2 Slices
- ✓ Parsley: 1 Tuft
- ✓ Extra Virgin Olive Oil: 2 Spoons

Directions: 40 min

Clean and open the clams and mussels. In a large saucepan, brown the garlic in the oil, then reduce the tomato pulp to which you have added a little cooking water from the mussels and clams. Add the shrimp and then the flesh of the cicadas. Boil the pasta in the water to which you have added the rest of the cooking water from the mussels and clams. Use a large pot because it tends to "foam" a lot. Add the clams and shelled mussels (except for a few for garnish), as well as shelled shrimp if you do not want to serve them in the dish whole, to the fish sauce and stir well. Drain the pasta and toss it in the sauce, adding the chopped parsley. Mix well and serve.

Spaghetti Garlic Oil and Chilli

Ingredients for 2 servings

- ✓ Spaghetti: 160 Gr
- ✓ Garlic: 2 Cloves
- ✓ Chilli Pepper: 1 Fresh Spicy
- ✓ Extra Virgin Olive Oil: 20 Ml
- ✓ Maizena: 1 Spoonful
- ✓ Parsley: 1 Spoonful Optional
- ✓ Parmesan Cheese: 40 Gr

Directions: 16 min

Boil the spaghetti in a pot of salted water. Dissolve the cornstarch in a teaspoon of cold water: this little trick will allow the spaghetti to take the sauce better. Chop the garlic you need to feel in this dish, and gently brown it in the oil. Wash the chili pepper well and remove the top. Chop the hot chili pepper finely, leaving some seeds if you like very hot flavors; brown the chili pepper as well; while draining the pasta, which should be very al dente, pour the spaghetti into the pan with the garlic and chili pepper and add the cornstarch, mix well and adjust the salt, if you want to add the parsley, serve the spaghetti oil garlic and chili immediately, accompanying the dish with grated cheese to be added at will.

Spaghetti with White Clams Without Tomato

Ingredients for 2 servings

- ✓ Spaghetti: 160 Gr
- ✓ Fresh Clams: 500 Gr
- ✓ Chopped Parsley: 1 Spoonful
- ✓ Garlic: 1 Spike
- ✓ Olive Oil: 2 Spoonfuls
- ✓ Cornstarch: 1 Spoonful

Directions: 110 min

Purge the clams and open them, saving the cooking water. Boil the spaghetti, adding the cooking water from the clams that will not be used for the sauce. Be careful not to salt the water too much because the clam cooking water is already salty. Fry the garlic in a pan where we will sauté the spaghetti, and add clams, parsley, and cooking water. Let the sauce thicken. Add the cornstarch dissolved in cold water when the spaghetti is almost ready, and the sauce is no longer liquid. Stir and add the spaghetti. Stir well and serve. In this way, the sauce will stick well to the spaghetti.

Penne All'Arrabbiata

Ingredients for 2 servings

- ✓ Penne: 150 Gr
- ✓ Tomato Pulp: 150 Gr
- ✓ Tomatoes: 150 Gr Fresh
- ✓ Hot Chili Pepper: 1 Fresh
- ✓ Onion: Half
- ✓ Oregano: 1 Sprig
- ✓ Garlic: 1 Clove
- ✓ Extra Virgin Olive Oil: 2 Spoonfuls

Directions: 13 min

Wash the tomatoes and remove the seeds. Peel the garlic and onion and chop them with the chili pepper. Fry the vegetables in the oil, add the tomatoes and oregano, cover, and let it cook. Drain the pasta al dente, toss it in the sauce along with the fresh tomatoes, and season with salt and chili.

Risotto with Asparagus

Ingredients for 2 servings

- ✓ Rice: 150 Gr
- ✓ Asparagine or Asparagus: One Small Bunch
- ✓ Garlic: 1 Clove
- ✓ Saffron: 1 Sachet
- ✓ White Wine: Half (Glass)
- ✓ Raw Ham In Chunks: 50 Gr At Least
- ✓ Butter: 50 Gr
- ✓ Parmesan Cheese: 4 Spoons
- ✓ Vegetable Broth: 1 (2 Liters)

Directions: 13 min

Wash and clean the asparagus, removing the hard stalks. Boil them for 8 minutes in salted water. Set aside the cooking water we will use to cook the rice; toast the rice in a pan with butter and garlic clove. Add a little white wine, wait for it to evaporate, add the asparagus stalks cut into small pieces. The tips will be added later. Cook the rice, using the water from the asparagus, and add, little by little, ladles of vegetable stock. Meanwhile, cut the prosciutto into cubes. Halfway through cooking the risotto, add the asparagus tips. One minute before turning off the flame, add the saffron, and, finally, the Parmesan in cream form with the flame off. After 1 minute, add the diced prosciutto, keeping some aside to decorate the risotto. Serve.

Tagliatelle With Porcini Mushrooms

Ingredients for 2 servings

- ✓ Tagliatelle (fresh pasta): 200 Gr
- ✓ Porcini Mushrooms: 200 Gr
- ✓ Parsley: 1 Tuft
- ✓ Garlic: 1 Spike
- ✓ Olive Oil: 2 Spoons

Directions: 20min

Clean the porcini mushrooms with a wet cloth. Slice the mushrooms. Wash the parsley and chop it together with the garlic. Trifle the mushrooms with a bit of light oil, adding the parsley. Cook the tagliatelle in plenty of salted water. Drain the tagliatelle, and toss them in the sauce for a couple of minutes. Serve.

Fisherman's Risotto

Ingredients for 2 servings

- ✓ Cuttlefish: 30 Gr
- ✓ Shrimp Tails: 30 Gr
- ✓ Squid: 60 Gr
- ✓ Octopus: 60 Gr
- ✓ Fresh Clams: 250 Gr
- ✓ Fresh Mussels: 250 Gr
- ✓ Rice: 160 Gr
- ✓ Fish Broth: 1 Lt
- ✓ Garlic: 1 Spike
- ✓ Olive Oil: 3 Spoons
- ✓ White Wine: 1 Glass

Directions: 115 min

Wash the octopus and remove the entrails. Place it in a pot with the bay leaf and half a lemon. Add the water and boil for about half an hour over low heat. Drain the octopus and slice them thinly. Soak mussels and clams in salted water for a few hours to remove sand. Clean the mussels. In two separate pots, open the mussels and clams: put 1 tablespoon of oil in the bottom of the mussel pot, cover and cook over high heat until they feel open (4 or 5 minutes). Shell the shrimp tails and set them aside, along with the cleaned and sliced squid. Shell the mussels and clams. Boil, the cuttlefish in the fish broth to which you have added the filtered broth from the mussels and clams. Cut them into strips. Pour the oil into a thick-bottomed pan, add the finely sliced garlic, and let it wilt; add the rice and toast the grains briefly; deglaze the rice with the white wine, and let it evaporate over high heat. Add the fish stock a little at a time, and cook the rice for 15 minutes. Raise the heat and add the fish you have prepared; add a tablespoon of chopped parsley. Serve the risotto.

Champagne Risotto

Ingredients for 2 servings

- ✓ Rice: 160 Gr
- ✓ Onion: 1
- ✓ Champagne: 2 Glasses
- ✓ Butter: 1 Walnut
- ✓ Parmesan Cheese: 2 Spoons
- ✓ Vegetable Broth: Half a liter

Directions: 35 min

Finely chop the onion. Melt the butter in a saucepan, add the onion and rice and mix well. Add the champagne, keeping half a glass to one side. Add the vegetable stock a little at a time and cook. Add the Parmesan cheese and stir in the rice. Transfer the risotto with the champagne to plates forming a cavity in the center. Pour a little champagne ice cream into the hole. Serve.

Risotto with Artichokes

- ✓ Rice: 150 Gr
- ✓ Artichokes: 3
- ✓ Vegetable Broth: Half a liter
- ✓ Grana Padano cheese: 30 Gr
- ✓ Garlic: 1 clove
- ✓ Parsley: 1 Spoonful
- ✓ Olive Oil: 2 Spoons
- ✓ White Wine: One Glass

Directions: 30 min

Cook the vegetable stock. Clean the artichokes by removing the tips and tough leaves. Cut the artichokes into four parts. Chop the garlic and parsley in a risotto pan together with the oil; add the rice and the artichoke hearts. Deglaze rice with white wine and stir. Cook by adding the stock a little at a time. Stir in the cheese, salt, and pepper to taste.

Boscaiola style penne

Ingredients for 4 servings

- ✓ 450 gr ribbed penne
- ✓ olive oil
- ✓ 2 garlic clove
- ✓ 1 shallot
- ✓ 120 gr of diced bacon
- ✓ 300 gr sausage
- ✓ half a glass of white wine

- 260 gr mushrooms
- 120 gr peas
- 8 Piccadilly tomatoes
- 150 ml cream
- salt
- parsley
- grated cheese
- pepper

Directions: 30 min

Pour a drizzle of olive oil into a saucepan and add 2 cloves of garlic and 1 chopped shallot. Add the diced bacon and brown it. Crumble the sausage into the saucepan and brown it. Add the wine and let it evaporate. Add the mushrooms and peas and stir. After a few minutes, add the tomatoes as well. Cover everything with a cup of hot water. Add the chopped parsley and let it cook, with the lid on, for about 20 minutes. Add the cream and stir; let thicken for 1-2 minutes and remove from heat. Add plenty of grated cheese.

Pasta with sausage and mushrooms

Ingredients for 2 servings

- medium-sized pasta: 250 gr
- sausage: 240 gr
- champignon mushrooms: 6
- Piccadilly tomatoes: 6
- white wine: 35 ml
- olive oil
- 1 white onion
- garlic: 1 clove
- chili pepper: 1 piece
- salt and pepper
- parsley
- grated cheese

Directions: 30 min

Clean mushrooms and remove stems, and cut them into small pieces. Pour a drizzle of olive oil into a saucepan. Add the chopped onion, garlic, and chili pepper and sauté over low heat. Crumble the sausage and add it, browning it for a couple of minutes. Add the

chopped stalks and stir. Deglaze with white wine and add the chopped tomatoes. Let it cook for a couple of minutes, and add the mushrooms and chopped parsley. Dilute with a glass of hot water and cook for about 10 minutes. Adjust the salt at the end of cookingr Cook the pasta until al dente and transfer it to the casserole with the sausage and mushroom sauce. Stir and add a little pasta cooking water to combine. When ready, add the grated cheese and stir to make it creamy. Decorate with a bit of parsley.

Baked pasta

Ingredients for 4 servings

- 150 g of mortadella
- 150 g fresh or semi-matured cheese
- 300 g of egg pasta
- 60 g of grated parmesan cheese
- 250 g of tomato puree
- 2 tablespoons of extra virgin olive oil

Directions: 45 min

Cut the mortadella and cheeses into cubes. Boil plenty of salted water and pour the pasta. Drain when not fully cooked. Pour it into an oven dish and dress it in the oil, tomato, and part of the parmesan. Add the cold cuts and cheeses. Mix well and add the rest of the parmesan cheese on top. Bake in a preheated oven at 200° C for about 20 minutes.

Pasta with speck and walnuts

Ingredients for 2 servings

- 50 g of speck
- 6 walnuts
- 1 shallot
- 2 spoons of extra virgin olive oil
- 2 spoons of dry white wine
- Black pepper
- 3 spoons of cream
- 200 g of pasta

Directions: 45 min

Cut the speck into 2-inch strips. Shell and chop the walnuts. Chop shallot and sauté in oil over medium heat. Add a few tablespoons of water and wait a couple of minutes. Add bacon and a little pepper, and leave on fire for a few minutes. Add the white wine and let it evaporate. Turn off the heat, add the cream and walnuts. Stir and cover. In the meantime, cook the pasta in salted water, and when it is done, drain it, add the sauce, and stir over high heat.

Pasta with meatballs sauce

Ingredients for 2 servings

- ✓ 1 onion
- ✓ 2 tablespoons of extra virgin olive oil
- ✓ 60 ml vegetable broth
- ✓ fine salt
- ✓ 300 g of tomato puree
- ✓ 4 Baked meatballs
- ✓ 200 g of pasta
- ✓ Grated Parmesan cheese

Directions: 45 min

Clean and chop the onion and let it brown in oil for a few minutes. Add a couple of tablespoons of broth salt and leave on the fire for 10 minutes with a lid. Add the tomato, salt and mix well. After a few minutes, add the meatballs. Cook the sauce over low heat, with a lid, for about twenty minutes, stirring occasionally. Boil the pasta in plenty of salted water and, just before draining, add half a ladleful of the cooking water to the saucepan, then turn on the heat. Saute the drained pasta over high heat in the saucepan for a few minutes, turning often. Serve by placing a meatball on each plate and sprinkling with plenty of grated Parmesan cheese. Saute the drained pasta over high heat in the saucepan for a few minutes, turning often. Serve immediately.

Broccoli and sausage pasta

Ingredients for 2 servings

- ✓ 400 g of broccoli
- ✓ 200 g of sausage
- ✓ 2 garlic cloves
- ✓ 3 tablespoons of extra virgin olive oil
- ✓ Freshly ground black pepper
- ✓ Salt

- ✓ 200 g of pasta

Directions: 30 min

Wash the broccoli and select the most tender parts (the florets). Mince the sausage. Cut the garlic into small pieces and fry in plenty of oil.

Add the sausage and let it cook, stirring occasionally. Turn off the heat and set it aside. Cook the pasta in plenty of salted water together with the broccoli. They will cook together, and the pasta will have more flavor. When they are cooked, drain them and add them to the sauce. Turn the heat back on and saute for a few minutes over high heat, adding some of the cooking water you've set aside until the ingredients mix well and thicken. Serve immediately.

Pasta with ham and peas

Ingredients for 2 servings

- ✓ 150 g of peas
- ✓ 60 g of diced raw ham
- ✓ 150 ml vegetable stock
- ✓ 2 small onions
- ✓ 1 tablespoon of extra virgin olive oil
- ✓ Salt
- ✓ black pepper
- ✓ 200 g of pasta

Directions: 45 min

Bring the broth to a boil while you cut the ham into cubes. Finely chop the onion and fry it in a pan with plenty of oil. Add a little stock and continue cookingr Add the peas and cook over high heat; add the broth, a pinch of salt, and a grind of pepper, and let it cook over medium heat, with the lid on, for about 10-12 minutes. The exact cooking time will depend on the size of the peas and the texture of their skins. If the cooking liquid becomes too dry, add more broth. After the indicated time has elapsed, add the ham and continue cooking for another 2-3 minutes. At the end of the cooking time, remove the lid, turn up the heat and leave to dry out, stirring continuously, then turn off the heat, adjust the salt and cover. Boil the pasta in plenty of salted water and, just before draining, add half a ladleful of the cooking water to the saucepan, then turn on the heat.

Saute the drained pasta over high heat in the saucepan for a few minutes, turning often. Serve immediately with a drizzle of raw oil.

Pumpkin and sausage pasta

Ingredients for 2 servings

- ✓ 200 g of pumpkin
- ✓ 150 g of sausage
- ✓ 2 sprigs of rosemary
- ✓ Freshly ground black pepper
- ✓ 1 shallot
- ✓ 2 tablespoons of extra virgin olive oil
- ✓ 80 ml of dry white wine
- ✓ 230 ml of vegetable broth
- ✓ Salt
- ✓ 200 g of pasta
- ✓ 30 g of Parmesan cheese

Directions: 45 min

Cut the flesh of the pumpkin into cubes. Crumble the sausage. Wash and chop the rosemary and shallot. Brown the shallot in plenty of oil. Add the sausage, rosemary, and a pinch of pepper and brown over a high flame. Add the wine and let it evaporate. Add the pumpkin, cook for 3-4 minutes, and then add 3 tablespoons of vegetable stock. Let it cook over medium heat with a lid for 6 minutes. When the pumpkin is cooked, adjust the salt, turn off the heat and set aside. Cook the pasta in salted water according to the cooking time indicated on the package and when it is cooked, drain it. Add the pasta to the sauce, turn off the heat, and stir. Add the parmesan shavings and serve.

Polenta with meat sauce

Ingredients for 2 servings

- ✓ 300 g of Bolognese meat sauce
- ✓ 600 ml water
- ✓ 4 g of salt
- ✓ 2 tablespoons of extra virgin olive oil
- ✓ 130 g of quick-cooking polenta

- ✓ 40 g of grated Parmesan cheese
- ✓ Black pepper

Directions: 30 min

Heat the meat sauce in a small pan. Meanwhile, prepare the polenta. Boil a large pot with water, checking the exact proportion on the package of the type of flour used. Add the coarse salt, and the oil and pour in the flour, stirring continuously with a whisk to avoid lumps formingr Use a wooden spoon and cook, stirring continuously over medium heat, for the time indicated for the type of flour used. Toward the end of cooking, add the grated Parmesan cheese. When the polenta is ready, divide it between two plates, flatten it with a spoon and place a portion of meat sauce in the center of each. Sprinkle with slivers of Parmigiano Reggiano, a grinding of pepper, and serve immediately.

White Truffle Risotto

Ingredients for 2 servings

- ✓ 200 g of risotto rice
- ✓ 50 g of white truffle
- ✓ 2 onions
- ✓ 2 celery stalks
- ✓ 30 g of butter
- ✓ 4 tablespoons of cooking cream
- ✓ 50 g of grated parmesan cheese
- ✓ 1 glass of dry white wine
- ✓ 1 liter of chicken broth
- ✓ Salt
- ✓ pepper

Directions: 30 min

Finely chop the onion, clean and finely chop the celery, and brown them in a saucepan with butter. Add rice and often stir for 3 minutes. Add the wine, raise the flame and let it evaporate. Lower the flame and add a couple of ladles of boiling broth. As soon as the broth is absorbed, add more, stirring often. Turn off the heat, add the cream and cheese, adjust the salt, and cover, allowing to rest for 3 minutes. Sprinkle the rice with truffle shavings using pepper.

Pappardelle with wild boar

Ingredients for 2 servings

- ✓ 400 g of wild boar meat
- ✓ 300 g of pappardelle
- ✓ white wine
- ✓ red wine
- ✓ carrots
- ✓ onion
- ✓ celery
- ✓ garlic
- ✓ laurel
- ✓ rosemary
- ✓ juniper berries
- ✓ black pepper
- ✓ extra virgin olive oil
- ✓ salt

Directions: 1 hour plus the marinating time of the meat (12 hours)

Wash the meat in cold salted water, drain it and cut it into large pieces. Wash and chop the carrots, celery, and half an onion. Add one clove of garlic, three bay leaves, rosemary, juniper berries, and black pepper. Cover the meat with red wine and marinate for 12 hours. Drain the meat and chop it, along with the carrot and celery. Cut half the onion into julienne strips. Pour three tablespoons of oil into a non-stick pan, add the chopped vegetables, rosemary, and a few bay leaves; sauté, then move the vegetables to the edges and pour the meat in the center salt and brown it. Add the white wine and let it fade away. Continue cooking with hot water or broth. Bring plenty of water to a boil, add salt and cook the Pappardelle for 5 minutes; drain "al dente" and dress them with the freshly prepared sauce.

Orecchiette pasta with turnip tops

Ingredients for 2 servings

- ✓ 600 g of turnip tops
- ✓ 3 tablespoons of extra virgin olive oil
- ✓ 2 fillets of anchovies in oil
- ✓ 2 garlic cloves
- ✓ Chilli pepper
- ✓ 200 g of orecchiette-type pasta
- ✓ Salt
- ✓ Olive oil
- ✓ Freshly ground black pepper

Directions: 45 min

Select turnip greens by removing the toughest leaves and branches, keeping the leaves separate from the flowers. Rinse with plenty of water. There is plenty of oil in a saucepan, brown oil, garlic, anchovies, and chili pepper. Cook the pasta in plenty of salted water brought to a boil. Add the leaves and flowers to the pot five minutes before the pasta is cooked. Drain everythingr Turn on the heat under the pan with the oil and add the pasta with the turnip tops and a little cooking water. Saute for a couple of minutes and serve with a generous grinding of pepper and a drizzle of raw oil.

Pasta alla Norma

Ingredients for 4 servings

- ✓ 400 gr of medium-sized pasta
- ✓ 450 gr of eggplants
- ✓ 800 gr of fresh tomatoes
- ✓ 180 gr of grated salted ricotta cheese
- ✓ 3 tablespoons of extra virgin olive oil
- ✓ 1 garlic clove
- ✓ fresh basil
- ✓ salt

Directions: 30 min

Cut the eggplant into thin slices a few millimeters. Fry them in a pan with plenty of oil for a few minutes. Pass peeled tomatoes through a vegetable mill. Fry the garlic in plenty of oil and add the tomato sauce and basil. Cook for 20 minutes over medium heat and season with salt.

Meanwhile, cook the pasta in plenty of salted water, drain and pour it directly into the tomato sauce. Turn on the heat and stir to combine all the ingredients. Add the fried eggplant and grated salted ricotta to each plate. Decorate with a basil leaf and serve.

Salmon Risotto

Ingredients for 2 servings

- ✓ 160 gr of rice for risotto
- ✓ 250 gr of salmon
- ✓ extra virgin olive oil
- ✓ white wine
- ✓ vegetable stock
- ✓ butter
- ✓ one shallot
- ✓ parsley

Directions: 35 min

Finely chop the shallot and brown it in plenty of olive oil, add the rice and often stir to toast it well without burning it, add the white wine, let it fade, and add a few ladlefuls of vegetable stock. Add more ladles of broth when the previous one is absorbed. Meanwhile, cut the salmon into thin strips, and a few minutes before the rice is cooked, add it to the rice. Continue cookingr Add the butter and stir. Also, add the chopped parsley and let it stand a few minutes before servingr

Spaghetti Cacio e pepe (Spaghetti, Cheese and pepper)

Ingredients for 2 servings

- ✓ 400 g of spaghetti
- ✓ 250 g of pecorino romano
- ✓ plenty of black pepper
- ✓ cooking water

Directions: 35 min

Boil plenty of salted water, taking care to salt it less than usual because the pecorino is already salty. Add the pasta and in the meantime, prepare the sauce. Grate the pecorino and set it aside. Add a little of the pasta cooking water and stir until the cheese is completely dissolved and transformed into a cream. Drain and pour it into the pot over low heat when the pasta is cooked. Add the cream cheese and plenty of black pepper. Serve.

Greek First Courses

Greek Moussaka

Ingredients for 4 servings

- ✓ 2-3 well-cleaned medium-sized eggplants
- ✓ 450 g lamb or veal meat
- ✓ 2 potatoes, peeled and cut into half-centimeter slices
- ✓ 1 onion, chopped
- ✓ 1 chopped garlic clove
- ✓ 2-3 ripe tomatoes, peeled and chopped.
- ✓ 1/2 small glass of white wine
- ✓ 1 beaten egg
- ✓ pinch of salt
- ✓ thyme and ground pepper
- ✓ For the béchamel sauce
- ✓ 25 g flour
- ✓ 25 g butter OR you can use olive oil
- ✓ 500 ml of whole milk or semi-skimmed milk
- ✓ grated cheese for gratin and mozzarella slices
- ✓ pinch of nutmeg

Directions: 1 hour 10 minutes

Wash the eggplants first, then slice them into half-centimeter pieces. We lay them out on absorbent paper and sprinkled them with salt. While they drain, we softly fried the potatoes in oil until they are tender inside. We will have seasoned them with a bit of salt beforehand. Remove, drain, and set aside when ready. Remove most of the oil from the pan at this point, leaving only a small quantity. . Cook the eggplants in batches after drying them thoroughly on both sides. We fry with oil added. We take them out and put them in a colander to drain the extra oil. In the leftover oil from the cooked potatoes and eggplants, we fry the onion and garlic before adding the meat and seasoning it with salt and pepper. Once the tomato has been sautéed, add the thyme. We completely sauté it, cover it, and cook it for about 20 minutes at medium heat. After that, add the wine and continue to cook in the pan for an additional 10 minutes. Until the drink has completely been absorbed. While the meat is frying, we will build the béchamel sauce in a saucepan by melting the butter, thoroughly frying the flour to prevent it from tasting raw, and then quickly combining the milk to create our béchamel sauce.

Add salt and a dash of nutmegr Remove the meat from the fire after it has finished cooking, then stir in a beaten egg to thoroughly combine the sauce. We heat the oven to 160 degrees in the meanwhile. After greasing an oven-safe baking dish, put the meat sauce on top of the base of potato slices, then the first layer of eggplant, and finally another layer of meat. Till you've dealt with them in this way all you can. Béchamel sauce should be applied on top, then grated mozzarella or Parmesan cheese can be added as desired. The dish should be baked for 15 to 20 minutes. Following this, we increase the oven's heat to 200° to finish the gratin for 3–4 minutes.

Greek style pasta

Ingredients for 2 servings

- ✓ perforated fusilli: 200 gr.
- ✓ Piccadilly tomatoes: about 15
- ✓ black olives
- ✓ basil
- ✓ capers
- ✓ pepper
- ✓ olive oil
- ✓ chilli (optional)
- ✓ salt

Directions: 20 min

A piece of chile pepper and a whole or minced garlic clove are added to a big frying pan with olive oil. The tomatoes should be added as soon as the garlic starts to cook. Add a few fresh basil leaves, black olives, and capers. Considering how salty the feta and olives are already, use salt sparingly. Allow the Greek sauce to simmer for five minutes or so. While the pasta cooks, add the sauce to a separate pan, then add the pasta three minutes before it's finished. If additional cooking water is required, complete the cookingr Finally, whisk in the feta cheese that has been chopped into little pieces. Serve the Greek-style pasta with basil leaves, feta that has been crumbled, and some oil.

Garides pilafi

Ingredients for 4 servings

- ✓ Shrimp 1 Kg
- ✓ Rice 340 Gr
- ✓ Tomato Sauce Ready 300 Gr
- ✓ Parsley 1 Sprig
- ✓ Onions 1
- ✓ Black Pepper
- ✓ Salt

Directions: 30 min

The shrimp should be thoroughly cleaned of their whiskers. Let them drain after saltingr Place the pan containing the onion and oil over the flame. Add the tomato puree, salt, and pepper as soon as the onion is cooked. Boil the sauce for ten to fifteen minutes. Then add the rice and 4 ladles of the seafood stew. Shrimps should be added when it is almost done. Depending on how you want your rice cooked, let the mixture simmer for 15 minutes or until the water has gone. Serve warm.

Soupies pilafi

Ingredients for 4 servings

- ✓ rice 360 gr
- ✓ seeds 1 kg
- ✓ tomato sauce, ready 1,5 cups
- ✓ extra-virgin olive oil 6 tablespoons
- ✓ onions 2
- ✓ salt to taste
- ✓ black pepper to taste

Directions: 80 min

Carefully remove the ink sacs before cleaning the cuttlefish. In a container, dilute the ink with water. Cuttlefish should be sliced into strips and well-washed. Cook the cuttlefish in the oil after browning the chopped onions. Cook for approximately an hour after adding the tomato sauce, salt, and pepper. Add another glass of water and then the ink diluted in it. Add the rice to the sauce in the pan as soon as it starts to boil, then turn the heat down to let the rice cook.

Greek style pasta

Ingredients for 3-4 servings

- ✓ 300 gr. of celery or fusilli
- ✓ 1 eggplant
- ✓ 2 peppers of different colors
- ✓ 150 gr. cherry tomatoes
- ✓ 60 grs. black olives without stone
- ✓ 150 grs. feta cheese cut into cubes
- ✓ extra virgin olive oil
- ✓ 50 grs. pine nuts
- ✓ 3 tablespoons dry white wine
- ✓ 3 tablespoons white wine vinegar
- ✓ salt
- ✓ pepper

Directions: 1h

After cooking the pasta until it is al dente, drain it, and then quickly cool it with cold water. Transfer to a bowl and combine well with 2 tablespoons of oil. The eggplant should be diced, salted, and allowed to drain in a strainer for 30 minutes. The peppers are sautéed in the same skillet for 5 minutes while the eggplant cooks in 2 tablespoons of oil over high heat for 5 minutes with the vinegar and wine. The peppers are sautéed in the same skillet for 5 minutes while the eggplant cooks in 2 tablespoons of oil over high heat for 5 minutes with the vinegar and wine. In a nonstick skillet, toast the pine nuts until they are golden. Refrigerate the pasta after adding the feta cheese, peppers, eggplant, olives, cherry tomatoes, pine nuts, and seasonings of salt, pepper, and oil. Serve your food in Greek

Moroccan First Courses

Moroccan couscous

Ingredients for 6-8 servings

- ✓ 1 leg or shoulder of lamb (1½ kg without bones
- ✓ 500 gr. couscous
- ✓ 200 gr. chickpeas
- ✓ 1 eggplant
- ✓ 2 onions
- ✓ 4 carrots
- ✓ ½ kgr cabbage
- ✓ 2 potatoes
- ✓ 300 gr. turnips
- ✓ 1-2 hot peppers
- ✓ 5 ripe tomatoes, peeled
- ✓ 200 gr. cleaned pumpkin
- ✓ 4 zucchini
- ✓ 3 garlic cloves
- ✓ 1 stick of celery
- ✓ 1 bunch of coriander
- ✓ 1 teaspoon black pepper
- ✓ 1 teaspoon ground cumin
- ✓ 1 bunch of parsley
- ✓ 1 cinnamon stick
- ✓ 1 teaspoon ras el hanout
- ✓ Ground saffron
- ✓ Olive oil
- ✓ Salt

Directions: 1.30 h

In the lower pan, finely chopped celery, onions, and garlic are sautéed in olive oil. Five minutes later, add the chopped coriander, parsley, cinnamon, ras el hanout, black pepper, and a dash of saffron. Brown the meat for 10 minutes after adding it in chunks. Add the chickpeas, pre-soaked for 12 hours, and cover them with hot water. Allow the mixture to simmer. After washing, draining, and seasoning with salt, black pepper, ground cumin, and a touch of oil, the couscous. Pour the steam into the strainer pot as soon as it emerges from the holes. Pour the steam into the strainer pot as soon as it emerges from the holes. Transfer the couscous to a bowl, toss it with a fork while moistening it with water and oil, and then transfer it back to the strainer pot. Three times, repeat the action every 15 minutes. Add the cabbage, slice it into large pieces, and continue simmering for another 45 minutes. Cook for 20 minutes before adding optional chile peppers and chopped onion. Add the diced potatoes, turnips, tomatoes, peppers, eggplant, and peppers. Cook for an additional 20 minutes after tasting the salt and pepper. On a dish, spread the couscous and top with the meat, chickpeas, and vegetables. After serving, put the broth in a tureen.

Cous cous with Moroccan style lamb

Ingredients for 8 servings

- ✓ 500 gr cous cous
- ✓ 1 kgr of lamb
- ✓ 400 gr cooked chickpeas
- ✓ 3 carrots
- ✓ 300 gr pumpkin
- ✓ 2 zucchini
- ✓ 1 tomato
- ✓ 2 onions
- ✓ ½ small cabbage
- ✓ 1 tsp. turmeric
- ✓ 1 tsp. ground ginger
- ✓ 1 tsp. ground black pepper
- ✓ 1 tsp. saffron
- ✓ Bunch of fresh coriander
- ✓ 200 ml. extra virgin olive oil
- ✓ Salt
- ✓ 25 gr butter

Directions: 100 min.

To have everything ready to use, prepare all the components. The tomato should be chopped, the onion should be peeled and cut into small cubes, the carrot should be washed and sliced in half lengthwise, and the zucchini should be washed and cut into four equal pieces. In addition to cutting the cabbage into four pieces, we open the pumpkin and take out the interior seeds. We clean it and set aside all the prepared vegetables. It is necessary to wash the pumpkin and clean the inside by removing the seeds because we will utilize it with its skin on. Next, it's the zucchini turn, which we add to the casserole with a bunch of coriander and tie to remove it at the end of the cooking process. For an additional 25 minutes, the meat and veggies are cooked together. The meat needs to be very soft. Therefore, the stew will be cooked for a total of 2.5 hours. With great care to preserve the vegetable whole, arrange the meat on one side of the casserole and the vegetables on the other. The chickpeas should be cooked in the casserole at medium-low heat for 10 minutes. This is how we can make the sauce.

We'll prepare the couscous while the stew cooks. Given that we would need to handle the couscous, we put it in a large container with as many sides as possible. We add the salt to the couscous after stirring it with a spoon to dissolve it in half a glass of water. 100 cc of olive oil is added and thoroughly incorporated into the cous cous by hand-swirlingr

Before beginning the procedure, 20 minutes should have passed. Before putting the cous cous in a sieve, we use our hands to break up any lumps. You can use anything you currently have at home instead of the pasta strainer I used. We placed the colander on top of the pot of heated meat. Or, in the event of a fault, a casserole is cooked in boiling water.

25 minutes should pass before servingr After that, remove the strainer and transfer the couscous to the earlier-used hydration container. Distribute it evenly across the surface to chill it and let it breathe. We next

add 100 cc of water and thoroughly combine it with our hands.

Once the temperature permits, the cous cous is put back in the sieve on top of the casserole containing the stew or boiling water. We cooked it for a further 25 minutes. We repeat the process, including 100 ml of water, and put it back into the casserole to continue cookingr Thirdly, add the cous cous to the pan along with 100 ml of water and the butter. Absorption will be homogeneous thanks to stirringr

Place it back in the colander and cook it for 25 minutes on the casserole. Assemble the cous cous into a crown shape on the serving plate. Round in shape and hollow inside. The meat should be placed inside the couscous-made hole in the center. On the couscous, we evenly distribute the vegetables all over. The meal is given some chickpeas and stew sauce as water, and the issue is kept in a sauceboat. We now serve the food hot.

Fez Couscous of 7 Vegetables

Ingredients for 4 servings

- ✓ 750 g couscous
- ✓ 280 g of pumpkin
- ✓ 1 red bell pepper
- ✓ 2 carrots
- ✓ 2 zucchini
- ✓ 1 onion
- ✓ 200 g chickpeas
- ✓ 2 tomatoes
- ✓ 8 strands of saffron
- ✓ 1 tablespoon black pepper
- ✓ 2 cinnamon sticks
- ✓ 1 tablespoon ground turmeric
- ✓ 1 kg of lamb in pieces
- ✓ Salt
- ✓ Pepper
- ✓ Virgin olive oil
- ✓ 25 g raisins
- ✓ 2 tablespoons unsalted butter
- ✓ 1 bunch of parsley
- ✓ 1 bunch coriander

Directions:

The night before, the chickpeas need to be soaked. When preparing the dish, moisten the couscous by mixing it in a large bowl with 750 gr of boiling water. We put it on top of the couscous bowl. Set aside.

We cut the food into sizable pieces. 250 g each of pumpkin, tomatoes, red bell peppers, zucchini, onions, and carrots. A large pot of water should be filled with 200 g of chickpeas and pieces of pumpkin, red bell pepper, zucchini, onion, carrot, and tomato.

Add 2 cinnamon sticks, a little hot water, and 1 tablespoon each of black pepper and turmeric powder. Chop the lamb, then place it on a plate. To taste, add salt and pepper. One dab of extra virgin olive oil should be added. Add it to the stew along with the vegetables.

To the pot, add one bunch each of chopped parsley and coriander. Cover with water and boil before continuing to cook the lamb and chickpeas until tender. Place the couscous in the basin, cover it, and simmer it for 15 minutes. In the meantime, put 30 g of raisins in a bowl and pour boiling water over them.

We give them a 15-minute soak. We take out the couscous and manually stir it together. We put it back in the couscous cooker and simmered it for four more minutes. The couscous is removed and 2 teaspoons of unsalted butter are added. Pour the couscous into a tajine. Gradually remove the vegetables and meat, then top with the couscous. As a garnish, include the 30 g of soaked raisins. Serve.

Moroccan couscous with chicken and vegetables

Ingredients for 4 servings

- ✓ 350 g couscous
- ✓ 200 g soaked chickpeas
- ✓ 1 zucchini
- ✓ 2 cloves of garlic
- ✓ 2 carrots
- ✓ 2 onions
- ✓ A quarter of white cabbage
- ✓ A few pieces of green, red, yellow bell pepper
- ✓ 200 g of pumpkin
- ✓ 4 pieces of chicken (thighs, drumsticks, breasts)

- ✓ 1.5 liters of soft chicken broth or vegetable broth (we can use cubes)
- ✓ 1 level tablespoon of Ras el Hanout (the amount is to taste) or a mixture of assorted aromatic spices or Moroccan spices (cumin, cinnamon, ginger, cloves, black and cayenne pepper and turmeric).
- ✓ Salt
- ✓ Pepper
- ✓ Olive oil

Directions:

We prepare the chicken pieces in a deep enough casserole with plenty of olive oil, salt, and pepper. After golden brown, we add chickpeas, which must have been soaking since the night before. We prepare the chicken pieces in a deep enough casserole with plenty of olive oil, salt, and pepper.

After golden brown, we add chickpeas, which must have been soaking since the night before. If you decide to use canned cooked chickpeas, save aside some because you won't add them until you're ready to serve.

Once the stock has been added, occasionally stir for 30 minutes over medium heat or until the chickpeas are cooked. Add the finely chopped vegetables after draining the liquid and discarding the chicken and chickpeas. They all need to be cleaned and peeled, except the zucchini, which keeps its skin.

The vegetables shouldn't be stirred up to keep them from dissolvingr As you can see in the photo, vegetables are typically served in halves or quarters sliced into sizeable chunks. Add the chickpeas from a jar immediately after adequately washing and draining them if they are canned. When the vegetables are finished, add salt and other ingredients to taste and simmer for 15 minutes. Add more broth if necessary.

While waiting, we prepare the couscous according to the package's instructions, using the casserole's broth instead of water. If the chickpeas are in a can, they are carefully washed and drained before being added. After sprinkling the vegetables with salt and other seasonings, cook them for 15 minutes. If more broth is required, add it. While this is going on, we prepare the couscous according to the directions on the package.

Still, we use the broth from the casserole rather than water.

Couscous with vegetables and raisins

Ingredients for 4 servings

- ✓ 250 gr. couscous
- ✓ 250 ml. chicken broth (or vegetable broth)
- ✓ 1 yellow bell pepper
- ✓ 150 gr. pumpkin
- ✓ 1/2 zucchini
- ✓ 2 cloves of garlic
- ✓ Curry, cinnamon, ginger and ground cumin
- ✓ Fresh coriander
- ✓ 1 tablespoon vegetable margarine
- ✓ Raisins
- ✓ Extra virgin olive oil
- ✓ pepper and salt

Directions:

Before cutting vegetables into tiny cubes, they should be thoroughly washed. To add to the vegetables, finely cut the garlic. Three tablespoons of olive oil should be used to fry the vegetables in a casserole at medium-high heat without overcooking them (it should be a little al dente). When there are a few minutes left, add the raisins, cinnamon, ginger, and cumin. Heat 250 ml of Aztec broth (or any vegetable or meat broth) in a pot.

Remove the pan from the heat once it comes to a rolling boil, stirring in the 250 g of couscous. Three minutes should pass as the couscous soaks in the covered pan. After the three minutes, add a tablespoon of vegetable margarine or olive oil and twirl for a few seconds over the heat to ensure that the couscous doesn't clump and the grain stays loose. The couscous is then blended with fresh coriander and stir-fried vegetables.

Cous Cous al estilo marroquí vegetarian

Ingredients for 4 servings

- ✓ 320 gr cooked chickpeas
- ✓ 1 cup whole grain spelt cous cous
- ✓ 1 eggplant
- ✓ 1/2 red bell pepper cut lengthwise
- ✓ 1/2 green bell pepper cut lengthwise
- ✓ 1 peeled zucchini cut into 1 cm slices
- ✓ 1 large carrot or two medium-sized carrots cut lengthwise
- ✓ 2 onions
- ✓ 2 ripe tomatoes, grated
- ✓ 2 teaspoons of cumin grains
- ✓ 2 teaspoons of Ras El Hanout
- ✓ 1 teaspoon of spices special mixture for cous cous
- ✓ 1.5 l of vegetable stock
- ✓ Pepper
- ✓ Salt
- ✓ a handful of fried or toasted almonds
- ✓ a handful of seedless raisins
- ✓ Extra virgin olive oil
- ✓ 5 mint leaves

Directions: 2hs

Put a little oil in the pot and fry the vegetables, setting aside the zucchini, eggplants, peppers, and carrots after they are finished. If more oil is required, add it after the chopped onion has been fried for 5 minutes. Add the spices while constantly stirring, and then add the shredded tomato. Cook for 7 minutes or until almost no liquid remains in the tomato. Add salt and pepper to taste. Add the reserved vegetables, chickpeas, and vegetable broth to the pot. Increase the heat to its highest setting, and reduce it to its lowest when it starts to boil. Place the steamer on top of the pot containing the cous cous pasta, raisins, and a drizzle of oil. Stir the mixture before putting the lid on. For roughly one hour, cook. The remaining cumin is ground with a little salt in the mortar as we make the dressingr We then add the remaining tomato grated, olive oil, and mint. If the cous cous is still a little firm, place it in a bowl and add a few spoonfuls of the cooking liquid while stirringr Place the chickpeas and vegetables in a bowl after drainingr Serve the cous cous with the strained vegetable broth, or refrigerate for another day.

NOTES: Include the cous cous, veggies, and chickpeas in separate bowls along with the dressingr

Dried fava bean puree

Ingredients for 4 servings

- ✓ 500 gr of peeled dried beans
- ✓ 1 tablespoon cumin
- ✓ 7 cloves of garlic
- ✓ 1 liter of water
- ✓ Olive oil
- ✓ Salt

Directions: 2hs

Before cooking, soak the beans in water for 24 hours. Drain the beans first, then put them in a pot. Add 1 liter of water, 1 teaspoon of salt, and 8 cloves of garlic. Place over medium heat, and after it begins to boil, use a spoon to remove the froth that forms. For one hour, cook it covered. When the time is up, take it off the heat, give it a moment to cool, then grind the beans in a blender. Stir 12 cups of olive oil and 1 tablespoon of cumin once it has reached a creamy smoothness. Place once again over low heat; remove as it begins to boil. Cumin and olive oil should be sprinkled on top before servingr

Traditional Harira

Ingredients for 4 servings

- ✓ 1 cup of meat cut into small pieces
- ✓ 1 cup of chickpeas
- ✓ 2 tomatoes
- ✓ 3 tablespoons of tomato sauce
- ✓ 2 onions
- ✓ 1.5 liters of water
- ✓ 2 tablespoons of noodles
- ✓ 2 tablespoons of flour
- ✓ 2 tablespoons of butter
- ✓ 2 tablespoons of parsley
- ✓ 2 tablespoons of coriander
- ✓ 1 teaspoon black pepper
- ✓ 1 teaspoon salt
- ✓ 1/2 teaspoon saffron (optional)

Directions: 30 min

Cover the chickpeas with water in a large bowl, and let them soak for six or more hours. The onion should be chopped into small pieces and placed in a saucepan. Add the butter, salt, and pepper, and cook the onion over medium heat, occasionally stirring, until it wilts and turns brown. Stir until the color changes, then add the meat and black pepper to the onion. The meat should be cooked with 1 liter of water for 20 minutes or until it is soft. Add the chickpeas to the meat after thoroughly draining them. As soon as the tomatoes have been processed into a sauce-like consistency, add them to the meat mixture and the saffron and thoroughly combine everythingr In a 0.5 liter bowl, combine the flour and tomato sauce. Add this combination to the meat and stir regularly until the mixture thickens. The harira ingredients should be simmered for 5 minutes or until the noodles are cooked before adding the noodles and coriander. With fresh parsley as a garnish, serve the harira hot in bowls and savor!

Harira with chicken

Ingredients for 4 servings

- ✓ 1 chicken breast cut into small pieces.
- ✓ 2 carrots
- ✓ 2 zucchini
- ✓ 2 tomatoes
- ✓ 2 onions
- ✓ 1 chicken stock cube
- ✓ 3 bunches of cilantro
- ✓ 3 tablespoons tomato sauce
- ✓ 3 tablespoons of flour
- ✓ 2 tablespoons of oil

Directions: 1h

Small-sized veggies should be cut and placed in a deep pan over heat. Once the pan is hot, ingredients should be added, including oil, tomato sauce, chicken, seasonings, and enough water. To ensure that the ingredients are fully cooked, we leave them on the fire for 45 minutes. The mixture is well combined in the food processor before being returned to the heat and allowed to boil for five minutes before adding the second bunch of chopped cilantro. We combine the flour with a tiny amount of water, add it to the harira, and stir regularly as it simmers for 10 minutes until it

boils. With some parsley as a garnish, serve the harira. Enjoy!

Spanish First Courses

Cocido Madrileño

Ingredients for 4 servings

- ✓ 250 g Chickpeas
- ✓ 380 g Morcillo
- ✓ 200 g Bacon
- ✓ 3 Bones of salted pork backbone
- ✓ 2 Bone of veal knee
- ✓ 3 fresh Chorizos
- ✓ 3 Cane bone with marrow
- ✓ 150 g Hen
- ✓ 150 g Noodles
- ✓ 3Carrots
- ✓ 3 Potatoes
- ✓ abundant water

Directions: 45 m

On the eve of the stew, we will soak some Castilian chickpeas from the previous eveningr Trick: To prevent them from getting stuck in the cooking the next day, we will add a handful of coarse salt. We will begin by putting to cook, starting from cold water, the meats, the tip of ham, and the indicated bones. Key: Using a skimmer, we will remove the foam that accumulates during the cooking process. To ensure that our stew does not dry, we will add water as it evaporates. We'll have a continuous form, average power fire in the stew. Add the rinsed and drained chickpeas when the water begins to boil. They will take two to three hours to become tender if cooked over a slow fire or around 20 minutes in a quick pot. Put the chickpeas in a net so you can easily remove them once the stew is finished, and serve it in the three classic turnovers. To prevent the chorizo and black pudding from clogging our soup with fat, we cook the cabbage separately and the chorizo and black pudding separately in different pots. The potatoes and peeled carrots are added to the stew pot when it is nearly finished. After the procedure, the meats are removed and placed on a plate with chorizo and black puddingr The chickpeas, potatoes, and carrots are placed in a dish with the sautéed cabbage. When making the soup, strain the stock and add the noodles when it starts to boil. For the thin noodles, this will take two to three minutes.

Valencian Paella

Ingredients for 4 servings

- ✓ 1 kilo and a half of rice for paella
- ✓ 1 chicken
- ✓ 1/2 rabbit
- ✓ 1/2 kilo of "bachoqueta" (flat green bean)
- ✓ 1/2 kilo of "garrofó" (large flat bean)
- ✓ 6 artichokes and 1/2 kilo of snails
- ✓ Salt
- ✓ Oil
- ✓ Paprika
- ✓ Saffron
- ✓ Crushed tomato
- ✓ Few sprigs of rosemary

Directions:

The foundation of every respectable paella is a tasty sofrito. The larger the paella, the better. Fry the chicken, rabbit, beans, artichokes, and snails in plenty of oil (the one in the photo lacks garrofó because it is not in season, and the frozen one is not the same). Finish by seasoning with a bit of salt and paprika. Add the crushed tomato and continue cooking once it has

browned well. Add the water once the sofrito is finished cookingr A good starting ratio is to add three times as much water as rice, though experience will allow you to adjust and perfect these quantities, which you'll end up doing by eye, like my girlfriend's aunt and mother, who were in charge of this paella. The proportions also depend a lot on the fire, the heat, the humidity level, and the paella's size (although tradition dictates that the houseman prepares it). We now add more logs to the fire to increase the fire's power and finish cooking the soup for 25 to 30 minutes. This is an excellent moment to add the saffron or, in its absence, the paella seasoning, which includes salt, garlic, coloring, and a small amount of saffron. Next, add the rice and distribute it throughout the paella in a diagonal motion. While the timer again indicates the fire's power and the rice grain's size, which this point must consume, we cook for 17 to 20 minutes. It must be totally dry and unrestricted. I advise novice cooks to keep a pan of boiling water nearby if you need to add more water. We can also add a few rosemary sprigs halfway through cooking; we will remove them before servingr

Asturian Fabada

Ingredients for 4 people:

- ✓ 480 g of fabes
- ✓ 260 g of onion
- ✓ 2 cloves of garlic
- ✓ 2 Asturian blood sausages
- ✓ 2 Asturian sausages
- ✓ 200 g of bacon
- ✓ 200 g salted pork shoulder
- ✓ 1 bay leaf
- ✓ 5 gr of sweet paprika
- ✓ 45 g extra virgin olive oil
- ✓ salt

Directions:

Because they develop quite a bit, we will start soaking the beans the previous eveningr On the other hand, we will desalinate our lacón in a different bowl. The following day, we put the beans in a pot with a thick bottom, added the garlic, whole peeled onion, olive oil, bay leaf, and paprika, and covered the pot with better mineral water up to two fingers above the beans. We let the beans boil and then stopped the cooking by adding a splash of cold water. This process, known as "asustar les fabes," will be repeated twice more while the food is cookingr This step is completely unnecessary; if you don't mind the excess fat that day, you can add all the meat to the pot where the beans are cooking once we've scared them instead of doing what I usually do, which is to boil the meat separately in a separate small pot. This makes the blood sausage release some of its fat, and we don't have as much at the end of the fabada. Cook it for an additional three hours at a medium-low temperature, scraping as required to prevent dryingr If it does, add small amounts of hot water, either from the pot where we first scalded the meat or on its own. Keep in mind, though, to twice shock the beans with cold water during the cooking process. When the beans are done cooking and the time is up, check the salt and add what is necessary, letting the fabada boil for a few minutes to integrate the salt. Put it in now rather than at the beginningr

Tripe Madrilenian style

Ingredients for 6 people:

- ✓ Veal tripe 1 kg
- ✓ Asturian sausage
- ✓ Black pudding
- ✓ Bay leaf
- ✓ Onion
- ✓ Bacon 180 g
- ✓ Mixed spices for tripe to taste
- ✓ 3 Garlic cloves
- ✓ Chilli pepper to taste
- ✓ 60 ml Tomato sauce

Directions: 1h

Various forms of tripe meat are typically used to make callos a la madrileña. As a result, tripe, leg, and snout from veal are among their constituents. We can specify that we want the weight of the tripe to be divided equally among the three ingredients by asking for one kilogram of tripe. To make the tripe bite-sized after cooking, we thoroughly clean it and cut it into squares

of approximately 2 x 2 cm. Once thoroughly cleaned, we sauté them with a bay leaf, a substantial amount of salt, bacon or ham, and tripe seasoningr Use a regular casserole for cooking the tripe for 4 hours or a quick cooker for 45 minutes. When they are finished cooking, drain them and keep the thick, gelatin-filled cooking water for later use. Add the chorizo and blood sausage, which will have been partially cooked separately, an hour before the typical cooking time has run out. We can prevent the blood sausage from bursting or the recipe from being overly laden with chorizo fat by including them and allowing them to complete cooking with the other components. To give the tripe a spicy flavor, make a sauce by poaching two garlic cloves with finely chopped onion and chile pepper. The cooked tripe, the chopped chorizo, and the black pudding are added, along with a teaspoon of tomato sauce. Additionally, we gradually add the boiling broth. To achieve the ideal texture, we let the mixture boil for 20 minutes until it becomes creamy.

Salmorejo cordobés recipe

Ingredients for 6 people:

- ✓ Loaf bread 200 g
- ✓ Tomato 1 kg
- ✓ Salt to taste
- ✓ Extra virgin olive oil 150 ml
- ✓ Garlic cloves 1

Directions: 1h

To achieve the ideal texture, I prefer to blend the components of salmorejo piece by piece. I begin by washing, chopping off the green stems from the tomatoes, and crushing them. Because I filter the tomato puree through a fine strainer where everything stays, and just the tomato passes, it is not required to peel or remove the seeds. I put the bread in a bowl, covered it with tomato puree, and gave it 10 minutes to soak. I add the garlic clove and blitz it in the Thermomix or a blender to create thick bread and tomato cream. The amount of bread I use is perfect for this texture, but you may change it based on the water in your tomatoes and the crumb's consistency. I follow that by adding extra virgin olive oil. After adding the oil, we return to blending or food processing everything with patience until our salmorejo is homogeneous, a lovely shade of orange, and compact enough to accommodate the traditional garnishes used to embellish each servingr

Easy Black Rice Recipe

Ingredients for 4 people:

- ✓ 3 large cloves of Garlic
- ✓ 3/4 liter of fish stock
- ✓ 1 onion
- ✓ 300 gr of round rice
- ✓ 1 cup of dry white wine
- ✓ 5 tablespoons of crushed tomato
- ✓ 250 gr of squid or cuttlefish
- ✓ 4 pieces squid or cuttlefish ink bags
- ✓ Salt
- ✓ Olive oil

Directions: 1h

Peel the garlic and onion. Make little chunks out of the onion. Crush or chop the garlic into incredibly little bits. Separate each one. Clean the cuttlefish or squid. Cut them into moderate-sized pieces. To crystallize the onions, add a little oil to a sizable frying pan or paella pan. On a medium heat settingr When the onions become transparent, add them and stir them regularly. Add the cuttlefish or squid pieces as well as the garlic. Be careful not to burn them as you gradually increase the heat and stir often (particularly the garlic and onion, which cook more quickly than the meat). Heat the fish stock in a different pot at the same time. Cover to stop it from decreasing and evaporatingr Add a little extra oil if the squid, garlic, and onion mixture begin to dry up. The squid mixture needs to include tomato that has been crushed. Once the squid begins to brown and the liquid in the mixture has slightly subsided, add the rice. Medium-low heat should be used for the next 5 minutes of sautéingr After that, incorporate the white wine and ink. Stir the liquids ferociously to combine. After five minutes, add the fish stock to the preparation. Stir once more, then taste to see whether more salt is necessary. After this, stop stirring altogether. After about five minutes, turn the heat back to medium. About 15 minutes of cooking time should be sufficient to make the rice smooth and broth-free. If the rice still seems to be a little firm after this time (it's

best to test to be sure), it can be left to rest (off the heat) in the pan with a cloth for a few more minutes. Serve with some aioli drizzled on top.

Easy Rice with Chicken Recipe

Ingredients for 4 people:

- ✓ ½ kg of chicken breasts. Also serve fillets of thigh fillets
- ✓ 7 handfuls of rice
- ✓ 2 bell peppers
- ✓ 5 carrots
- ✓ 2 cloves of garlic
- ✓ 2 onions
- ✓ 2 potatoes
- ✓ 1 handful of peas
- ✓ ¼ cup white wine
- ✓ 4 cloves
- ✓ Olive oil
- ✓ 3 bay leaves
- ✓ Pepper
- ✓ Salt

Directions: 45min

Potatoes should be cut into medium-sized wedges, carrots into rounds, and paprika, onion, and garlic should be chopped into small cubes. The chicken is sliced into medium-sized cubes; season with salt and pepper. Cook the chicken chunks in a large skillet with enough olive oil to cover the bottom over high heat. I'll explain why it's acceptable if some fat and meat brown and stick to the pan's bottom during this process. When the chicken is golden brown, remove it from the pan and put it in a big bowl. You may now deglaze, or "clean," anything that has wonderfully stuck to the pot by pouring 1/4 cup of white wine and using a wooden paddle to scrape the bottom and sides. As soon as the stench enters your nostrils at that precise moment, you will go insane. The sauce left over from this deglazing will be saved and served alongside the chicken. In the same saucepan with extra olive oil, sauté the onion, garlic, bell pepper, and carrot for about 5 minutes on medium heat. To taste, deglaze, bay leaves, chicken, and salt and pepper should be added. Add about 7-8 cups of water after turning the heat to high. As soon as it starts to boil, add the potatoes. Ten minutes must pass before servingr The rice will now be added. Omit the measuring cups; instead, use your hands like your grandmother did to add 6 to 7 handfuls of the rice to the broth. This measurement is more "homemade." One more pinch of salt and the peas should be added. Hold off until the rice is done and the liquid has thickened. The objective is to create highly brothy rice that resembles an asopado. If, for some reason, the beverage becomes too dry, add more water. When the rice is finished cooking, take it off the fire and let it cool for five minutes before serving it in a big dish with a lot of bread and olive oil on the side.

Seafood fideua

Ingredients for 4 people:

- ✓ 320 gr of mussels
- ✓ 360 gr of fideua (noodles)
- ✓ 360 gr of cuttlefish or squid
- ✓ 4 or 8 shrimps or prawns of your choice, one or two per person
- ✓ 1/4 kilo of small peeled prawns
- ✓ 250 gr of monkfish or emperor meat
- ✓ Abundant fish fumet
- ✓ 2 white onions
- ✓ 3 cloves of garlic
- ✓ Sweet paprika to taste
- ✓ 3 red tomatoes
- ✓ Saffron
- ✓ Salt to taste
- ✓ Vegetable oil

Directions: 40min

Before making fideuá, the mussels must be well-cleaned. If not, we will have to spend time scraping them to fix any problems we identify with the shell. Ideal mussel preparation involves loading a sizable strainer with the mussels while water runs in the kitchen. They must be carefully cleaned after being scraped. Next, let's take care of the shrimp. I spend time carefully rinsing them and taking the antennae and legs off (although the latter is not mandatory, it will save time and effort for the diners). The heads of little shrimp should already have been removed, as should the shells. If, for whatever reason, they are not yet prepared, peel them now.   But keep in mind that the weight of the peeled shrimp should match the weight specified in the ingredient list.

Additionally, the intestine must be removed (the small black line we will find in the middle of the meat). We can help ourselves by using a toothpick, the fork tip, or a well-bladed knife. Squid or cuttlefish will also be given a thorough wash under fresh water. After that, we'll drain it and make wheels out of it right away. The fish will be taken care of last. Keep only the meat and discard any skin or bones. Next, preheat a saucepan large enough to hold all the mussels. Once it is heated, add the mussels and enough water to cover the solids level. The mussels should all open after ten minutes of cooking under cover (if any do not open, discard them).

We'll take advantage of the time the mussels are cooking in the saucepan to peel the onion and garlic cloves. Both will be divided into tiny pieces, with the first cut into tiny cubes. We'll also use this time to grate and wash the tomatoes. After that, we'll reserve them. We will put out the fire, let the mussels cool, then drain and reserve them after the time has passed. You can immediately mix the rice with the flesh from some or all of the mussels. Nothing needs to be done if you want to keep the mussels in their shells. To continue, we'll need a paella pan (if you do not have one at home, you can replace it with a fairly large non-stick pot or casserole). A small amount of oil will be heated, and the shrimp will be cooked quickly in it after it is hot. Since the primary objective is to seal them, heating them for one minute will typically be adequate (on both sides). We'll remove and reserve the shrimp or prawns to make room for the garlic and onion. We'll sauté these vegetables (I recommend doing this stage at medium-low heat, so they do not overcook). 3 minutes into the cooking process, we'll add the squid or cuttlefish (while tossing the onion and garlic). Two minutes of cooking will be given to this seafood before it is transferred to the edge of the paella. The middle will contain the grated tomato. Cooking the tomato for 8 minutes while stirring frequently is recommended. Before combining it with the remaining components, it should dry out slightly. As it cooks, we will add some salt to taste and the saffron threads (or a touch of coloring). Completely combine everythingr You may have observed that the ingredient list for the fish stock lacked a precise measurement. It's simple to understand: we'll define the metric in terms of the noodles. We will pass them through a cup to determine how many noodles we will need. After that, the fish fumet will be measured twice and then counted.

The noodles will go in the paella's middle, while the tomato will be pushed to the edge (already measured). After that, we'll give them two minutes to brown. The noodles and the rest of the components for the paella will then be combined with a teaspoon of sweet paprika. After mixing everything, we'll take a fish fumet bath (remember that the quantity will be double the measure for the noodles). Ensure that the liquid is above all of the solids. The noodles will now be left to finish cooking while we wait (we will know they are ready because the liquid will have evaporated). After the first five minutes of cooking, the prawns or shrimp will be added. At the eight-minute point, the peeled prawns will be added. The soup should have evaporated normally after an additional two minutes. Add the mussels once they've opened; whether they have shells is up to the cook. After a brief wait, turn off the heat. After resting for at least five minutes to ensure homogeneity, the fideuá is prepared for servingr

Rice with Lobster

Ingredients for 4 people:

- ✓ 1 whole lobster
- ✓ 420 gr of rice for paella
- ✓ 1/4 kilo of peeled shrimp
- ✓ 2 liters of fish fumet
- ✓ 2 red tomatoes
- ✓ 2 onions
- ✓ 2 optional cayenne peppers
- ✓ 1 large spoonful of chorizo bell pepper pulp
- ✓ 1 glass of dry white wine
- ✓ 1/4 teaspoon of cinnamon powder
- ✓ 1/2 teaspoon of nutmeg
- ✓ A few strands of saffron or a touch of food coloring
- ✓ Salt to taste
- ✓ A few sprigs of fresh parsley
- ✓ Olive oil
- ✓ Several stalks of fresh parsley.

Directions: 40min

We'll need a lobster that has been cut in half for this recipe. I suggest going to the fishmonger and having the lobster sliced. The live lobster will be cared for in this manner by the fishmonger. In this manner, the fishmonger will keep the lobster alive and truly fresh (I find it cruel and shocking to do this at home). After that, we'll heat some water in a small pot (half full with liquid will be enough). We'll add the previously washed tomato after it's at a boil and cook it for two minutes, just long enough for the tomato to easily peel with the point of a knife. To proceed, we will cut the tomatoes into cubes after opening them and removing the seeds.

The onion will thereafter be taken care of. It will be peeled before being chopped into strips or julienned. We'll prepare the rice in a paella pan as the next step. If you don't have one, you can also cook our ingredients in a decent pan that is big enough without worrying about running out of room. We'll warm up a thin layer of oil there. The cayenne peppers will go in the oil if we have chosen to use them. The lobster will then be placed and fried for five minutes while being moved around regularly to ensure that every surface is cooked. Remove the lobster and set it aside after this step. The chopped onion should be used in place of the lobster in the paella pan. While stirring constantly, let it cook for 3 minutes. Add the diced tomato after this. Five minutes should pass while stirring constantly. The chorizo bell pepper, nutmeg, cinnamon, and a dash of salt will then be added after this. The saffron will also be added, or a tiny bit of food coloring in the absence. During this time, we will also fish the cayenne peppers out of the preparation (if we have opted to use them). White wine is then added, the mixture is mixed, and it is cooked for 5 minutes so that some alcohol can evaporate. Then, combine the preparation once more after adding the rice. Then we will give it a fish fumet bath.

While we chop up the lobster, let it cook (one or two for each portion). Then we'll include them in the cookingr We will use a spoon to remove the froth that accumulates on the rice as it cooks. Depending on the heating intensity, the pot's thickness, and other variables, cooking rice often takes 20 minutes or a bit less. To avoid overcooking rice, we must take care not to ignore it. If for some reason, we haven't yet peeled our shrimp, we'll do it while the rice cooks. During this time, we will wash, drain, and chop the parsley leaves very finely. For the shrimp to cook with the rice and the leftover liquid, we will add them to the rice halfway through cooking (after 10 minutes). Add the chopped parsley to the rice when it is almost done. When the rice is finished cooking, turn off the heat and let it sit in the pan or pot for 5 minutes to thicken up more before servingr

Vegetable Paella

Ingredients for 4 people:

- ✓ 1 cup paella rice
- ✓ 1 leek
- ✓ 2 onions
- ✓ 4 artichoke hearts
- ✓ ½ red bell pepper
- ✓ 1 garlic clove
- ✓ 2 to mates grated
- ✓ 100 gr fresh green beans
- ✓ 2 cups vegetable broth
- ✓ Salt to taste
- ✓ Pepper to taste
- ✓ A pinch of saffron

Directions: 35min

All the vegetables you plan to use should be cut. Add additional bell pepper strips as a garnish, along with the onion and bell pepper, in small cubes. Also, in tiny pieces is garlic. You can chop the beans, leeks, and artichokes into medium-sized pieces to suit your tastes. If you plan to add another ingredient, cut it into pieces about the same size. Add a good amount of olive oil to a paella pan and cook it to medium-high heat. Begin cooking the bell pepper, onion, and garlic. Watch out that they don't burn. Green beans, artichokes, leeks, and grated tomato should all be included. After a brief period of mixing, add the rice. Add 2 cups of broth, salt, pepper, and saffron to taste. Stir a little before heating up to a boil. Reduce the heat to the minimum when only a few bubbles are left on the surface of the evaporating liquid, then cover. After around 20 minutes, turn off the heat and let the vegetable paella cool before servingr

Migas with chorizo

Ingredients for 4 people:

- ✓ 1 loaf of stale bread from the day before
- ✓ 5 cloves of garlic
- ✓ 1 chorizo sausage
- ✓ 1 red bell pepper
- ✓ 1 teaspoon of paprika
- ✓ Salt
- ✓ Olive oil

Directions: 15min

Place the bread in a basin after cutting it into tiny chunks. Add some salt and moisten it with one glass of water. After thoroughly combining, chill for two hours. The chorizo should be cut into little cubes and cooked in olive oil. Add the six entire, skin-free garlic cloves after it has turned golden. Red bell pepper that has been chopped should be added as well. The chorizo should be taken out of the oil and put aside. The previously moistened crumbs should be added to the same oil and cooked until golden brown over medium heat. Mix in the tablespoon of paprika. Remove from the fire when done, then stir in the chorizo and chorizo bell pepper.

Chickpea Stew with Spinach

Ingredients for 4 people:

- ✓ 400 gr of chickpeas
- ✓ 350 gr of spinach
- ✓ 2 tomatoes
- ✓ 2 onions
- ✓ 2 large cloves of garlic
- ✓ A pinch of cumin
- ✓ 1 egg
- ✓ 2 bay leaves
- ✓ Olive oil
- ✓ 1 teaspoon of paprika
- ✓ Salt
- ✓ Pepper

Directions: 1h30min

Pre-soak the chickpeas the previous eveningr Put them in a big pot with a lot of water and a little salt. The following morning drain the water and give the chickpeas a quick wash. Put them in a big pot and cover them with about three fingers' worth of water. Place the saucepan over high heat, reduce the temperature as soon as it begins to boil, add two bay leaves, and cover. You can make the sofrito in the interim. Cut the tomatoes, onion, and garlic cloves into very small pieces. Garlic, onion, and tomato are cooked in a sizable frying pan with a good amount of olive oil over medium heat. The goal is to cook them for a while at a low temperature to prevent burningr Add a little salt, pepper, cumin, and paprika to this cookingr

Mix thoroughly and continue to cook for a few minutes. The chickpea pot should begin to boil in the interim. When the grain starts to soften, give it a little more than an hour, then stir in the tomato, sauteed onion, and garlic. Give it another 30 minutes to cook. If the chickpeas are still hard, cook them for another 30 minutes; if they are soft or extremely soft, reduce the heat to the lowest settingr Put another saucepan on high heat with water in it. Add the spinach when it begins to boil, stirring for no more than a minute. Discard the heat and strain. All you need to do is blanch the spinach to remove the bitterness from the leaves. Now mix the drained spinach with the chickpeas. Stir well and let everything cook together for about 5 more minutes. After this time, your chickpea and spinach stew is ready.

Beans with chorizo

Ingredients for 4 people:

- ✓ 500 gr of white beans
- ✓ 1 chorizo sausage
- ✓ 1 piece of bacon
- ✓ 2 onions
- ✓ 1/2 bell pepper
- ✓ 2 cloves of garlic
- ✓ 1 bay leaf
- ✓ 1 teaspoon of paprika powder
- ✓ Salt
- ✓ Pepper
- ✓ Olive oil

Directions: 1h30min

Before cooking, soak the beans in water overnight. By doing this, you can be sure that when you prepare them, they will be soft. By doing this, you can be sure that when you prepare them, they will be soft. So with that knowledge, let's move on. Cut the bell pepper, onion, and garlic cloves into small squares before frying them in olive oil over medium heat. While this is frying, lay the beans, the chorizo, chopped into rounds, the bacon, and the bay leaf in a deep pot with about 1 12 liters of water. Increase the temperature and let it boil for a while. Pour the sofrito into the pot when the beans are almost done. Paprika powder, salt, and pepper are all added in one teaspoon's worth. Put a lid on it and cook it slowly. Just keep an eye on it and wait for it to be prepared. How are you going to know when it's done? Very simple, the chorizo-flavored beans will be really soft and flavorful. Serve them hot with a large drizzle of olive oil and some parsley that has been chopped on top.

Lentils with Chorizo Recipe

Ingredients for 4 people:

- ✓ 1/2 kg lentils
- ✓ 200 gr of chorizo for cooking
- ✓ 1 black pudding
- ✓ 2 lts of water
- ✓ 2 onions
- ✓ 3 cloves of garlic
- ✓ 1/2 bell pepper
- ✓ paprika powder to taste
- ✓ cumin to taste
- ✓ oregano to taste
- ✓ salt to taste
- ✓ pepper to taste

Directions: 1h30min

The lentils should first be boiled in a few liters of water. Eliminate the foam that accumulates on the pot's surface. Add the chopped chorizo and the whole blood sausage after about five minutes of cookingr Add the oregano, cumin, paprika powder, salt, and a little pepper. A few more minutes of cooking are required. Prepare a sofrito by chopping the bell pepper, onion, and garlic into small squares and adding them to olive oil. Include in the broth. Add some parsley that has been chopped once the lentils are finished cookingr Remember to use lots of olive oil when serving your lentils with chorizo.

Caldo gallego traditional recipe

Ingredients for 4 people:

- ✓ ½ kilo of potatoes
- ✓ 1 pork backbone
- ✓ 1 spoonful of "unto" if not, pork bacon
- ✓ 1/2 kg of turnip greens
- ✓ 250 gr of bacon with little fat
- ✓ 250 gr of white beans
- ✓ 250 gr of tender veal or a couple of fresh chorizos
- ✓ 250 gr of pork shoulder
- ✓ Sweet paprika powder

Directions: 3hs

We must consider a soaking period like we typically cook with beans. The best scenario is to leave them in a saucepan with water overnight, preferably for at least 12 hours. Desalinating meats are likewise expected, except those that are fresh or tender. Of course, some people don't care for salt and skip this step, but for the most part, soaking the bacon and pork shoulder overnight is standard. The backbone will be treated the same way, or we may even leave it for a few extra nights. It is best to change the soaking water in this situation. We will require a rather sizable saucepan to prepare the Galician broth. We will arrange the soaked and fresh meats, the soaked beans, and the parsley that has been chopped in it. We'll add a sizable amount of water. I estimate that five liters will be needed, so I simmer the ingredients for an hour and a half at medium heat in a covered saucepan. We will return multiple times to remove the layer of foam that will accumulate on the water's surface rather than letting the ingredients cook on their own. We will take advantage of the time to prepare our vegetables while cooking meats and beans. The turnip greens will be thoroughly cleaned and chopped before being placed in a stream of cold water. The choice a cook must make at this point is whether to use the stems or only the leaves. The stems can be used in other recipes if you don't want to include them in this one. Additionally,

we'll prepare the potatoes by peeling and chopping them into cubes or other atypical shapes. To add them to the meat and beans during the final 20 minutes of cooking, we will reserve them. When the meats have been cooking for an hour and a half, we will be ready to take them from the broth. After adding the turnip greens and a teaspoon of sweet bell pepper powder, we will let the remaining ingredients boil for another 30 minutes. Cut the excised meat into small pieces. After the cooking process, we will save it to add to the soup. We will go back to the pot and taste the contents after the extra 30 minutes to see whether the broth's seasoning is appropriate. Since there will always be some salt in the broth, even after the meats have been soaked, the broth should typically be adequately salty. If the opposite is true, we will carefully adjust the seasoning and add extra salt. Since there will always be some salt in the broth, even after the meats have been soaked, the broth should typically be adequately salty. If the contrary is true, we will salt the dish more and carefully adjust the seasoningr

Additionally, this is the time to remove the fat bits from the food. We'll skip this step if you've already used bacon. The meat chunks will then be added to the saucepan, and our caldo gallego recipe will be complete.

Chickpeas with Codfish

Ingredients for 4 people:

- ✓ 1/2 kilo of soaked and drained chickpeas
- ✓ 3 onions
- ✓ 3 cloves of garlic
- ✓ 3 red tomatoes
- ✓ 200 gr of fresh spinach
- ✓ 3 green peppers
- ✓ Olive oil
- ✓ 1 bay leaf
- ✓ 1 tablespoon of sweet paprika
- ✓ Salt to taste
- ✓ Pepper powder to taste
- ✓ 2 eggs

Directions: 3hr

To adequately describe this recipe, we'll assume that you've opted to use raw chickpeas that have previously been soaked and drained following the instructions we provided at the beginning of the post. They must then be placed in a sturdy pan, covered with fresh water, and cooked for a few hours. Ensure the water is at least two fingers higher than the beans and covers them completely. We will add the bay leaf and a little salt to the cooking water. We will utilize the time to take care of other ingredients while we wait. We will peel and slice the onions into little pieces in this scenario. The garlic will also be peeled and chopped highly tiny. We shall thoroughly wash the spinach in this instance. After washing them, I like to soak them for at least five minutes in a dish of water with little vinegar. We'll drain them next and set them aside for this recipe.

The peppers will also be washed. The branches will then be split into little pieces after being removed, opened, and the seeds removed. We'll reserve them after that. If the cod is not already crumbled, we will chop it in this case. The cod ought to be already clean and devoid of any inedible components. For the eggs, we will cook them in a pot with boiling water so that we can get a few hard-boiled eggs. The tomato skin will then be removed and saved in another dish. The remainder will be taken and grated. We shall also hold them for a moment. We'll now heat a saucepan with a generous amount of olive oil. The heat setting for this will be medium. We will sauté the previously peeled and chopped onion and garlic there. The grated tomatoes and the bell pepper pieces will be added after they have cooked for around five minutes. Add the teaspoon of sweet paprika after letting them cook for a couple of minutes. After that, season to taste with salt and pepper and thoroughly combine everythingr This mixture will be transferred to a blender or food processor. After processing it to create a liquid stock, we will add it back to the pot. We'll reheat it once more and incorporate the drained spinach. Before adding the fish, we'll let them two more minutes to simmer. We'll give them another five minutes to fry. When it is time to add the chickpeas to this casserole, we will reheat the sofrito that we just heated if the chickpeas are not quite ready. We'll drain the beans of their cooking water after they're done. As noted before, we will add the cooked and drained chickpeas to the saucepan with

the sofrito that has been heated to medium. We peel and cut into quarters the previously boiled eggs as we wait for the ingredients in the saucepan to finish cookingr Use a ladle to stir the stew, then taste it gently. If necessary, add extra pepper and salt to the dish's flavoring (this can vary greatly, depending on whether desalted or fresh cod has been used). Serve the chickpeas and cod right away, garnishing with hard-boiled egg pieces.

Pisto Manchego

Ingredients for 4 people:

- ✓ 2 zucchini
- ✓ 350 gr of red tomato puree
- ✓ 2 peppers: one green and one red.
- ✓ 2 onions
- ✓ 2 cloves of garlic
- ✓ 1/2 glass of dry white wine
- ✓ olive oil
- ✓ Ground black pepper to taste
- ✓ Salt to taste

Directions: 45min

First, let's get the vegetables ready for subsequent use. The garlic cloves should be peeled and chopped into small bits. After cleaning, slice the zucchini into cubes. Additionally, we will wash the peppers and take off the seeds, stem, and interior white sections. Some people prefer to peel them first to make them softer before being cooked. We cut them into cubes just like the other vegetables. As we've said in the ingredient list, tomatoes must be pureed.

If we haven't already processed them in this manner, now is the ideal time to do it, following a thorough washingr The simplest method is to boil them quickly before mashing them. It is not necessary to remove the skin, however, some people do. The seeds are the same way; many people prefer to filter the puree to get rid of them, however, it is not required. The garlic should next be fried in a hot frying pan with a generous amount of olive oil. Although another vegetable oil can be used, olive oil gives the ratatouille a distinct (and delicious) flavor. At this time, we'll also begin pan-frying the onion-shaped pieces. Add the peppers and simmer for a few minutes while the onion becomes somewhat translucent. We think the zucchini will be added once the paprika has thoroughly softened. The tomato puree will be added next as we continue to add the components in a sequence of softness. The wine will also be added to the pan. The food will be cooked for 15 minutes. After this, season the dish with salt and pepper, stir it up, then taste it to see if the seasoning needs to be changed. You can simmer the ratatouille a little longer if you prefer a less soupy dish.

Fish Stew

Ingredients for 4 people:

- ✓ 4 large wheels of white fish hake, sea bass, or grouper
- ✓ 8 clams
- ✓ 8 large prawns
- ✓ 8 mussels
- ✓ 3 potatoes
- ✓ 1 medium paprika
- ✓ 2 onions
- ✓ 2 fresh crushed gourds
- ✓ ½ glass of white wine
- ✓ 2 garlic cloves
- ✓ 1 bay leaf
- ✓ 1 glass of fish stock or water
- ✓ Fresh parsley to taste
- ✓ Salt to taste
- ✓ Pepper to taste

Directions: 40min

Peel the potatoes and slice them into medium-sized pieces. Additionally, mince the garlic cloves and cut the onion and paprika into thin strips. Place aside. Crush the tomatoes after removing the skin. Thoroughly clean the fish and seafood. Depending on your preference, you can leave the skin on the prawns or remove it.

Once you have prepared everything, we may begin cookingr You will require a sizable pot or deep frying pan. It should be heated to medium-low, then the onion should be fried until transparent before, followed by the paprika and garlic. Please take care not to burn them. After adding the potatoes and stirring briefly, add the smashed tomato. The bay leaf should now be added

as well. To the cooking, add salt and pepper. Let everything cook for a couple of minutes.

Boiling the mixture will cause the white wine to evaporate. Add the mussels and clams now. You can now add one glass of water or fish stock. Reduce the heat after waiting until it begins to boil. Ten minutes of gentle boiling with the addition of the fish. If extra salt is required, check the level first. Add the prawns after this. Simply wait until the potatoes are done cooking before turning off the heat. The parsley should be added only before servingr

Soup with fish and seafood

Ingredients for 6 people:

- ✓ 1 kilogram of monkfish and hake
- ✓ 24 clams
- ✓ 1 leek
- ✓ 26 shrimps
- ✓ Flour
- ✓ ½ red bell pepper
- ✓ 2 onions
- ✓ 2 cloves of garlic
- ✓ 2 carrots
- ✓ 2 tomatos
- ✓ 2 tablespoons brandy
- ✓ Almonds
- ✓ Parsley
- ✓ Salt
- ✓ Stale bread
- ✓ Extra virgin olive oil

Directions: 90 min

Place the skins, heads, and scrapes in a pot with 2 liters of salted water after washing them. Reserve the meat. Clean the leek after scraping the carrot. Add them chopped along with half of a peeled onion. Cook for 30 minutes while skimming the surface. Leave the clams in the salted water to soak. Shrimp heads and shells should be fried in oil after being peeled. Brandy, then allow it to evaporate. Mash, add some broth, filter, and combine with fumet. The pepper should be scrubbed and washed. Combine it in a bowl with the remaining onion half, and sauté for 5 minutes. For 5 more minutes, add the rinsed and grated tomato. Stir in 1 teaspoon of flour as you toast. It should be moved to the blender, blended, and then added to the broth. 2 stale bread slices should be crushed in a mortar along with 50 g of almonds, 1 clove of peeled garlic, and 1 sprig of cleaned and chopped parsley to create a paste. To dissolve it, combine it with a little broth before adding it to the remaining fumet. When the clams open and the fish is thoroughly cooked, add the cleaned, diced fish meat, the rinsed, drained shrimp, and the clams.

Picadillo soup

Ingredients for 4 people:

- ✓ 1/2 chicken (500 gr. with carcasses)
- ✓ 2 eggs
- ✓ 3 carrots
- ✓ 1 salted bone (preferably knee bone)
- ✓ 1 leek
- ✓ 100 gr. of serrano ham
- ✓ 120 gr. of soup noodles. The same amount of rice would also work (optional).
- ✓ Fresh mint leaves

Directions: 40min

The leek should also be washed, peeled, and sliced into two substantial pieces. We combined everything in a pot, the chicken cut, and the salted bone. Although a piece of veal bone would also be excellent, we have chosen a piece of backbone. As an illustration, consider the kneecap. Together, we cook it for at least an hour; if using a rapid cooker, 20 minutes will do. The process of cooking the eggs and the soup's final presentation. We simultaneously cook the two eggs in lots of water. After the chicken and veggies have finished cooking, drain the liquid and keep it. We let the chicken and bone cool before deboning it to prevent burns. Chop the mint leaves and the ham (if we haven't purchased it in strips). The egg should be peeled and sliced or chopped into small pieces. We lit a pot on fire. After adding the strained broth, add the beef, ham, egg, and mint. Over medium heat, combine everything and cook for the designated amount while adding the noodles. Put food in bowls. A few spoonfuls of the broth are added first, followed by a significant amount of noodles and the remaining ingredients.

Garlic soups

Ingredients for 6 people:

- ✓ 10 cloves of garlic
- ✓ 6 eggs (1 per person)
- ✓ 180 g of Serrano ham
- ✓ 12 slices of stale bread
- ✓ 3 liters of meat broth or water
- ✓ Salt
- ✓ Pepper
- ✓ 50 ml of extra virgin olive oil
- ✓ 2 tablespoons of sweet paprika de la Vera

Directions: 40min

Garlic can be peeled and cut into fillets of any thickness. For the soup to be outstanding, the garlic must contribute flavor and the emulsion between the water and the oil. Keep aside in a basin. Select a sizable saucepan, warm the bottom oil, and add the garlic. Sauté until they turn golden (but be careful not to snatch them). Include the sliced ham as well. Stir thoroughly, using an enveloping motion with a wooden spoon, until the tastes are well blended. Six pieces of stale bread should be added and rotated twice once the garlic has taken on a toasted honey color. Add the sweet paprika after turning off the heat in the pan.

Although many people make it with fiery paprika, I prefer it this way. The paprika serves two purposes: it gives the bread its red color and adds flavor. To avoid the paprika burning, do this with the heat turned off. Additionally, the soup would be ruined by the awful harsh taste of everythingr We thoroughly mix everything so that the oil combines with the garlic, ham, hard bread, and paprika. Reheat the casserole while adding the stock or water. Depending on the size of the casserole, 3 liters should be plenty. Always keep the broth on the low side because the secret to making this soup is that the water or broth never boils during the cooking process. After another two to three minutes of sautéing, we add the meat broth while stirringr You may also use water to prepare it if you don't have any broth. It will be pretty similar, less potent, but still delicious. It is not required to stir the soup during the first 20 minutes of cooking over moderate heat. The last six slices of bread we had earlier toasted with some extra virgin olive oil are added after 20 minutes. We set them down and let them float till they soften. Salt and freshly ground black pepper should be added. Before adding salt, taste the broth because it might not be necessary depending on the amount of ham and how salty it already is. Add the cracked eggs to the soup. Normally, I add one egg per person, but it depends on each one whether they want two or three, according to their preferences. Give it two to three minutes to set. Separating the whites from the yolks and adding only the whites to the soup is an additional alternative.

Then, with the help of the soup's heat, the yolk is added to each dish. The wonderful yolk blends with the soup when we pour it into the bowl. The egg will either be a spinning egg or little bits poached. We serve extremely hot food in bowls or, where available, ceramic casseroles (it is the proper thing to do). Enjoy! They can be built quickly, and they are easy to elaborate. You can adjust this full soup however you desire. Depending on each person's preferences, you might add ham, chorizo, fried bacon, bonito, etc.

Andalusian Gazpacho

Ingredients for 4 people:

- ✓ 1/2 green bell pepper
- ✓ 1 dl olive oil
- ✓ 1/2 kilo of ripe tomato
- ✓ 1 clove of garlic
- ✓ 1/2 cucumber
- ✓ 1 slice of white bread
- ✓ 4 tablespoons of wine vinegar
- ✓ fine salt

Directions: 1h30min

Cucumber, bell pepper, garlic, and bread that has been soaked in water are also added to the blender along with the blanched, skinned, and diced tomatoes.

After a brief blending period, add the salt, vinegar, and oil. Taste to see if any adjustments are required. Put through a chinois into a tureen, then set aside for an hour to cool. Individual glasses of Andalusian gazpacho should be garnished with bread cubes, cucumber, onion, tomato, and hard-boiled eggs.

Watermelon Gazpacho

Ingredients for 4 servings:

- ✓ Watermelon, seedless and skinless, 500 g
- ✓ 500 g tomatoes
- ✓ 1 tablespoon vinegar
- ✓ 2 cloves garlic
- ✓ 3 tablespoons extra virgin olive oil
- ✓ Salt, to taste

Directions: 10 min

Chop the tomatoes and melons. We can use a basic blender to a multipurpose food processor like the Thermomix to purée our watermelon soup. Blend the tomatoes, watermelon, peeled garlic cloves (without the germ), oil, vinegar, and salt in a blender. Blend the mixture until it is uniform and emulsified. If required, taste and adjust the salt and vinegar. Store in the refrigerator until you're ready to serve after straining until the consistency is fine. Individual bowls of the chilled watermelon soup should be served, and the garnishes should be black olive rings, a small amount of shredded feta cheese, and some chopped basil.

Green Gazpacho

Ingredients for 4 servings:

- ✓ 2 peeled cucumbers
- ✓ 1 slice of bread without crust
- ✓ 3 tablespoons of sherry vinegar
- ✓ 1 clove of garlic
- ✓ 1 teaspoon sugar
- ✓ 100 gr of spinach
- ✓ 1 green bell pepper
- ✓ 1 stick of celery
- ✓ 100 gr of walnuts
- ✓ 1 little parsley
- ✓ 1 handful of fresh basil, about 10-12 leaves
- ✓ 2 tablespoons of yogurt
- ✓ 150 ml olive oil
- ✓ Salt to taste
- ✓ Pepper

Directions: 10 min

In a blender jar, combine all the peeled ingredients. To make an excellent green gazpacho, blend everything very thoroughly. We now put it through a chinois or strainer to eliminate skin or other impurities. Serve with carrot sticks on the side and season to taste with salt and pepper.

Chapter 3 Main Courses

Italian Main Courses

Zucchini Parmigiana

Ingredients for 4 servings:

- ✓ 1 kg of zucchini
- ✓ 190 gr cooked ham
- ✓ 180 gr of provola cheese
- ✓ 280 ml of béchamel sauce
- ✓ extra virgin olive oil
- ✓ 60 gr of parmesan cheese
- ✓ salt

Directions: 1h

After being washed and trimmed, the zucchini should be immediately grilled on a baking sheet. Provola should be cut into small pieces. Add a little oil to a baking dish. A thin coating of béchamel sauce should be placed on top of the first layer of zucchini. After layering slices of provola and cooked ham, béchamel sauce, Parmesan cheese, and yet another layer of zucchini should be added. Up until all the ingredients have been utilized, proceed in this manner. The remaining grated Parmesan cheese should be sprinkled over everything, leaving only the béchamel and provola cheese on top of the last layer of zucchini. Bake the zucchini parmigiana at 180 degrees for 30 minutes.

Zucchini fritters

Ingredients for 4 servings:

- ✓ 650 gr of zucchini
- ✓ 1 egg
- ✓ 1 tablespoon chopped parsley
- ✓ 30 gr of flour 00
- ✓ 30 gr of grated Parmesan cheese
- ✓ extra virgin olive oil
- ✓ salt
- ✓ pepper

Directions: 30m

After being washed and dried, the zucchini should be grated using a grater with a large hole. Salt them and let them drain in a colander for approximately 10 minutes before moving them to a clean dish towel and thoroughly wringing them out to remove all of their water.

In a bowl, combine them with the egg, flour, cheese, parsley, salt, and pepper. The fritters are made by adding a large spoonful of the mixture to a heated non-stick frying pan and crushing it there. Using the same method, cook the additional pieces for 5 minutes on each side over medium-low heat. They must be cooked inside and golden brown. When ready, spread them out on a paper towel and season them with salt. Sour cream should be served alongside warm zucchini fritters.

Zucchini meatballs

Ingredients for 4 servings:

- ✓ 6 zucchini
- ✓ 2 eggs
- ✓ 5 slices of bacon
- ✓ milk
- ✓ 4 tablespoons grated Parmesan cheese
- ✓ 1 l peanut oil for frying
- ✓ breadcrumbs
- ✓ salt

Directions: 30m

After washing and drying the zucchini, grind it with a large-hole grater while cutting the ends. Salt and let them drain in a colander for approximately ten minutes before moving them to a clean dish towel and thoroughly wringing them out to remove all of their water. The meatball mixture will become very floppy and sagging if the excess moisture is not entirely drained. Pancarrè slices need to be soaked in milk, thoroughly pressed, and then cut into little pieces. Add it to the zucchini along with the eggs and Parmesan cheese. After completely blending the ingredients with your hands, shape the mixture into meatballs by breaking off tiny pieces. Cook the meatballs in a ton of hot peanut oil after covering them in breadcrumbs. Fry the meatballs in hot peanut oil. Allow them to fully brown before draining the excess oil with a slotted spoon and setting them on absorbent paper to dry. Serve the heated zucchini meatballs with salt.

Zucchinis au gratin

Ingredients for 4 servings:

- ✓ 3 tbsp breadcrumbs
- ✓ 6 zucchini
- ✓ 3 tomatoes for sauce
- ✓ 2 tablespoons grated Parmesan cheese
- ✓ thyme
- ✓ salt
- ✓ parsley
- ✓ basil
- ✓ marjoram

Directions: 40m

It is necessary to wash, trim, and cut the zucchini in half lengthwise. After that, use a spoon to remove the inside seeds. If you use Romanesque zucchini, you may skip this step because they are less watery. On a baking sheet lined with parchment paper, arrange the zucchini and sprinkle with 3 tablespoons of breadcrumbs, 2 tablespoons of grated Parmesan cheese, a bunch of chopped basil and parsley, a bunch of thyme, marjoram, and salt.

The zucchini should be topped with sliced, thoroughly drained, and tomato-seed-free tomatoes, and some oil should be sprinkled on top. Cover with aluminum foil if the zucchini's surface darkens significantly while being baked for 35 to 40 minutes at 180 °C in a stationary oven. After removing the zucchini gratin from the oven, serve it. Although they can be eaten warm, they are also delicious cold.

Rice Stuffed Tomatoes

Ingredients for 4 servings:

- ✓ 8 ripe rice tomatoes
- ✓ 160 gr of parboiled or Ribe rice
- ✓ 1 tablespoon chopped parsley
- ✓ 6 potatoes
- ✓ extra virgin olive oil
- ✓ oregano
- ✓ pepper
- ✓ basil
- ✓ salt

Directions: 3h

After washing the tomatoes, cut off the top and set it aside to serve as the "hat" of the stuffed tomato. Put the tomato pulp through a vegetable grinder after removing it. To season, mix some basil leaves, dried oregano that has been diced, chopped parsley, salt, and pepper. After combining the rice and tomato pulp, they must macerate for at least 1.5 hours. To cook rice for longer without losing its consistency or turning into unpleasant "gruel," choose ripe (or parboiled) rice when making your selection.

When the allotted time has passed, fill the tomatoes with the rice that has been flavored and soaked in the pulp after the tomatoes have been sliced. Finally, cover each tomato with the upper cap. In an oil-greased baking dish, put the potato wedges and the tomatoes with the rice within. Salt and extra virgin olive oil should be added to the potatoes before roasting for about an hour at 200 °C. After taking the tomatoes and rice out of the oven, you can eat them hot or cold.

Spinach Omelette

Ingredients for 4 servings:

- ✓ 4 eggs
- ✓ 240 gr of spinach already cleaned and washed
- ✓ 240 gr of finely sliced provola cheese
- ✓ 2 spoons of parmesan cheese
- ✓ 200 gr cooked ham
- ✓ extra virgin olive oil
- ✓ pepper

- ✓ salt

Directions: 75min

Making the spinach omelet is not difficult and doesn't take much time, except for the "rest" that the roll needs before it can be cut. First, the spinach must be blanched in a lot of boiling, moderately salted water. Drain the extra water from them, then firmly crush them between your palms.

Then, chop them roughly with a knife. Shell the eggs and then divide them into yolks and whites. Whip the egg whites until stiff using a hand whisk or an electric mixer. The egg whites have properly absorbed air if they do not slide when the bowl is tipped upside down.

The chopped spinach, grated Parmesan, salt, and pepper should all be thoroughly incorporated with the egg yolks. While being mindful not to disturb the mixture, add the egg whites and thoroughly stir with a spatula. As a result, your spinach omelet will be lighter and creamier. In the meantime, preheat the oven to 180 °C, and line a 25 x 35 cm rectangular mold with baking paper. At this stage, lightly oil the mixture and then pour it into the baking paper. Make it even and level using a spatula. It takes 15 minutes to bake and cook the omelet. Keep the baking paper and cooked spinach omelet together as you transfer them to a work surface.

After flipping it over, place a brand-new parchment paper layer on top, and then remove the cooking sheet. Place the sliced ham and cheese on top of the omelet. Utilizing the baking paper, tightly roll the omelet. It should be wrapped in a kitchen towel and placed in the refrigerator to cool and set up for at least two hours. Slice the spinach omelet roll when the required time has gone, and serve it as an appetizer or a main course with a fresh salad.

Zucchini flan

Ingredients for 4 servings:

- ✓ 250 gr of zucchinis
- ✓ 4 eggs
- ✓ 45 gr of flour 00
- ✓ 290 gr of milk
- ✓ 1 small shallot
- ✓ 1 medium carrot
- ✓ 30 gr of grated Parmesan cheese
- ✓ 1 tablespoon chopped parsley
- ✓ 140 gr fresh cream
- ✓ 140 gr cooked ham
- ✓ extra virgin olive oil
- ✓ salt
- ✓ pepper

Directions: 30 min

After being sliced in half lengthwise, the zucchini should be skinned before being cut into thin rounds. Simmer the finely diced shallot and zucchini in a bit of oil in a skillet for about 10 minutes. Add some salt. The sifted flour should be well mixed with the whisked eggs in the bowl to avoid lumps.

Grated Parmesan, diced ham, parsley, grated carrot, fresh cream, milk, cooked zucchini, and Parmesan should all be added.

Mix well, then season with salt and pepper as required. Put everything in an ovenproof dish about 20 by 10 centimeters with parchment paper lined and lightly oiled. Approximately 30 minutes of oven baking at 180 degrees. Allow the zucchini flan to cool for about 10 minutes at room temperature once it has finished cooking before cutting it into generous squares and presenting it to guests.

Smoked salmon meatballs

Ingredients for 4 servings:

FOR THE MEATBALLS

- ✓ 520 gr of potatoes
- ✓ 220 gr of smoked salmon
- ✓ 2 eggs
- ✓ chopped parsley
- ✓ salt
- ✓ pepper
- ✓ breadcrumbs

FOR THE SAUCE

- ✓ 100 gr of greek yogurt
- ✓ 100 ml fresh cream

- ✓ lemon
- ✓ salt

Directions: 2h

After peeling and boiling in salted water, mash the potatoes using a potato masher. The smoked salmon should be roughly chopped and added to the potatoes. Add the parsley and the beaten eggs after that. Add salt and pepper to taste, then mix well. The balls can either be formed into small balls with your hands, covered in breadcrumbs, and fried in hot oil, or they can be placed on a baking sheet covered with parchment paper, sprayed with oil, and baked for 20 to 30 minutes at 200°C (until golden brown).

To prepare the sour cream, combine the cream and yogurt, add a few drops of lemon juice, and season with salt. After letting the salmon balls sit in the refrigerator for at least an hour, serve alongside.

Asparagus pie

Ingredients for 4 servings:

- ✓ 2 rolls of ready-made puff pastry
- ✓ 4 pumpkin flowers
- ✓ 1 small leek
- ✓ 1 kg of asparagus
- ✓ 500 ml béchamel sauce
- ✓ extra virgin olive oil
- ✓ salt

Directions: 1h

The leek must be carefully cleaned and thinly sliced. Two tablespoons of oil are heated and fried in a frying pan. Trim off the white and woody sections of the stems. If necessary, add a few teaspoons of water. After that, follow them around. To the fried leeks, add the asparagus. Cook for about 20 minutes after saltingr Pick up a 20 cm diameter baking pan, and line the inside with baking paper.

One of the two puff pastry rolls that have already been made should be used to line the pan's bottom and sides. Add the béchamel sauce after adding the asparagus to the pie. Cover with open zucchini flowers that have been cut into leaves. Top it off with the second disk of puff pastry, carefully sealing the borders

and cutting any excess pastry. After lightly brushing the top of the rustic pie with milk, bake it in a preheated oven for 15 minutes at 350 degrees.

Meatballs with sauce

Ingredients for 4 servings:

- ✓ 400 gr of minced veal or beef
- ✓ 500 gr of tomato pulp
- ✓ 2 eggs
- ✓ 50 g grated Parmesan cheese
- ✓ 110 ml milk
- ✓ 4 slices of bacon
- ✓ 1 bunch of parsley
- ✓ 1 small onion
- ✓ pepper
- ✓ salt
- ✓ 3 tablespoons extra virgin olive oil

Directions: 45min

Trim the edges of the bacon, then soak it in milk. Give it at least 10 minutes to soak. After thoroughly pressing it out, place it in a bowl and add the minced meat. With your hands, combine the two eggs, the grated Parmesan cheese, the parsley that has been finely chopped, salt, and pepper. Your meatballs with sauce should have a particular consistency; it shouldn't be too hard, as that would cause the meatballs to rupture while cookingr To check if the consistency is right, take the dough in one hand and hold it down vertically for a few seconds.

If it crumbles gradually and does not separate, it is done; if not, add more Parmesan cheese or breadcrumbs. To avoid the meatballs becoming too tough, be careful not to add too much. Make little balls the size of 4 cm using your hands, though you can make them smaller if you choose. In a skillet, add a few teaspoons of extra virgin olive oil, a small onion that has been thinly sliced, enough water to prevent scorching, and a dash of salt. Before adding the meatballs and capping the pot, add the tomato pulp, season with salt and pepper, and cook for a few minutes. The mixture should be simmered a little longer until it turns translucent. Over low heat, let it simmer for about twenty minutes. After cooking, if the sauce is still too liquid, simmer it uncovered for a few minutes to let the excess liquid evaporate and thicken the sauce. Serve the meatballs in the sauce with some chopped parsley on top.

Artichoke stew

Ingredients for 4 servings:

- ✓ 6 artichokes
- ✓ 800 gr veal meat (stew)
- ✓ 200 ml white wine
- ✓ 1 onion
- ✓ 1 lemon
- ✓ 30 gr pine nuts
- ✓ extra virgin olive oil
- ✓ sale
- ✓ pepper

Directions: 110min

Cut the artichokes into pieces, clean them by removing the tougher outer leaves, and then soak them for about 30 minutes in a dish of water, lemon juice, and a little salt. The artichokes should be rinsed, drained, and cooked for about 15 minutes or until soft while covered in a skillet with three tablespoons of oil, a glass of water, and a pinch of salt. In a tiny frying pan, toast the pine nuts for a few minutes, careful not to burn them. The onion should be finely chopped and then added to a skillet with a tablespoon of oil, a knob of butter, and a little water. Add the previously floured veal stew, and let it cook through in the pan. When the wine has completely evaporated, add a pinch of salt and half a glass of boiling water or broth. When the stew is tender, let it simmer for approximately an hour and a half with the cover on the pan. If extra hot water is required, add it. Add the artichokes and pine nuts at the end of cooking, and season everything for a few minutes. Remind yourself to adjust the salt and pepper before serving the artichoke stew.

Meatloaf stuffed with cooked ham and sottiletta

Ingredients for 6 servings:

- ✓ 600 gr of beef or veal meat
- ✓ 1 egg
- ✓ 3 spoons of milk
- ✓ 3 slices of bacon
- ✓ 1 tablespoon of breadcrumbs
- ✓ 2 tablespoons grated Parmesan cheese
- ✓ 1 bunch of fresh parsley
- ✓ 4 slices of cooked ham
- ✓ 10 sottilette
- ✓ 120 gr of speck
- ✓ extra virgin olive oil
- ✓ pepper
- ✓ thyme
- ✓ salt

Directions: 115min

Combine the veal or beef, egg, parsley that has been finely chopped, bacon that has been melted in a bit of milk and squeezed well, grated Parmesan cheese, breadcrumbs, a touch of salt, and a pinch of pepper in a bowl. With your hands, thoroughly combine everythingr Make a rectangle of the mixture by flattening it on greaseproof paper or foil. The sottilette should be placed on top of the cooked ham slices. Gently roll the meatloaf using baking paper or film, compacting it thoroughly at the sides.

Slices of speck should be placed over the meatloaf, slightly overlapping each one as you go, after removing the paper. To construct a huge candy, wrap the meatloaf in plastic and tightly seal it. For it to take shape, let it rest in the refrigerator for at least 30 minutes. Oven temperature is set to 200 °C. After removing the foil, center the meatloaf on a baking sheet lined with parchment paper. Place the vegetables around the meatloaf after peeling, dicing, and slicing the potatoes, carrots, and onions.

Add oil and thyme sprigs to the meatloaf, then bake them in a hot oven. The meatloaf has to cook for at least 50 minutes. Wait at least five minutes after it is prepared before slicing and serving it with the cooked vegetables.

Baked sea bass with vegetables

Ingredients for 2 servings:

- ✓ 2 sea bass without scales and entrails
- ✓ 4 yellow potatoes
- ✓ 1 bell pepper
- ✓ 3 zucchini
- ✓ 2 red onions
- ✓ 2 tbsp olives
- ✓ 180 gr of cherry tomatoes
- ✓ 4 cloves of garlic
- ✓ aromatic herbs
- ✓ black pepper
- ✓ salt
- ✓ extra virgin olive oil

Directions: 1h

At 180°C, turn on the oven. The potatoes should be peeled before being sliced into half-inch-thick rounds. Slice the peppers into strips after cleaning them. Slice the zucchini into rounds. Slice the red onions into four pieces. Put all the freshly prepared veggies, the cherry tomatoes that have been rinsed, two garlic cloves, salt, and pepper in a bowl. Add three tablespoons of oil. Combine all the ingredients. The sea bass should be rinsed and dried with paper towels. Each fish should have a garlic clove inside, along with salt and pepper on the interior of the belly. Put the vegetables around the sea bass in a baking dish lined with paper. Add the olives, flavorful herbs, and oil after salting and peppering the fish outside. The fish is placed in the oven with aluminum foil covering it. After 15 minutes of baking, remove the foil and bake for 25 to 30 minutes.

Fillet steak with balsamic vinegar

Ingredients for 1 serving:

- ✓ 250 gr beef fillet
- ✓ 120 ml balsamic vinegar
- ✓ flour

- ✓ salt
- ✓ butter

Directions: 15h

Melt a knob of butter in a pan on a high heat settingr Cook the tenderloin over medium-high heat after flouring both sides. The fillet should be cooked for 3 minutes on each side before being put on a platter to keep warm. Put the balsamic vinegar into the pan with the cooking fluids, let it decrease, then add the fillet back to the pan and cook it over low heat for one minute to flavor it.

Roast Stuffed Chicken

Ingredients for 6 servings:

- ✓ 1 boneless chicken with skin
- ✓ 200 gr of sausage without skin
- ✓ 2 fennels
- ✓ 1 small carrot
- ✓ 1 small zucchini
- ✓ 1 small bell pepper
- ✓ half a glass of vegetable stock
- ✓ 1 garlic clove
- ✓ salt
- ✓ pepper
- ✓ rosemary
- ✓ sage
- ✓ extra virgin olive oil

Directions: 140min

Purchase a boneless, skin-on chicken from your butcher, preferably one that has already been split open. You simply need to stuff it with the fillingr On the work surface, place it. Sprinkle salt and pepper within. Over the core region, apply the sausage paste. Place the sticks of carrot, pepper, and zucchini on top of the sausage. The chicken should be rolled and tied with kitchen stringr Place the chicken in the middle of a baking dish that has been lightly oiled. Place the fennel around the chicken after thinly slicing it. Add salt and pepper to taste. Over the baking dish, distribute the herbs and garlic. Add some oil and then the broth. Bake the roast in an oven, preheated to 180 ° C. After an hour of cooking, ensure there is still liquid in the pot. When it's done, slice it and serve it hot with roasted fennel and gravy.

Stew casserole

Ingredients for 6 servings:

- ✓ 1 kg of beef cheeks
- ✓ 2 onions
- ✓ 2 carrots
- ✓ celery leg
- ✓ 1 tin of peeled tomatoes
- ✓ sage
- ✓ rosemary
- ✓ 1 garlic clove
- ✓ 1 glass of red wine
- ✓ olive oil
- ✓ salt
- ✓ pepper

Directions: 2h30min

Peeled and chopped onion, carrot, celery, and garlic are sautéed in a medium pot with a bit of olive oil. Add the cubed beef cheeks once thoroughly cooked, brown them on all sides, and season with salt and pepper. Allow drying after adding the red wine. Then, add the peeled tomatoes, tied-up sage, and rosemary, and simmer for two hours while stirring occasionally. Serve soft polenta beside the stew while it is still hot.

Spring veal

Ingredients for 6 servings:

- ✓ 1 kg of veal swivel
- ✓ 500 gr of green beans
- ✓ 4 carrots
- ✓ 60 gr butter
- ✓ 3 tablespoons of Olive oil
- ✓ 1 glass of white wine
- ✓ carrot
- ✓ celery
- ✓ pepper
- ✓ salt

Directions: 120min

Clean and wash carrots and green beans. Carrots should be julienne-cut and boiled for 10 minutes in salted water. After draining, add 20 gr of butter and 2 teaspoons of oil to a skillet and sauté. Take the veal and quickly brown it in a skillet with oil and 40 g of butter on all sides. Add the well-cleaned and washed celery and carrot after the meat has been thoroughly browned. Over low heat, cook with the lid on for about an hour. After the roast has finished cooking, move it to a dish and use a blender to puree the cooking juices. Slice the meat thinly after it has cooled. Serve the rump with the vegetables and a layer of cooking juices.

Pizzaiola Meat

Ingredients for 4 servings:

- ✓ 400 gr of thin veal slices
- ✓ 250 ml of tomato sauce
- ✓ 1 garlic clove
- ✓ 2 tablespoons of extra virgin olive oil
- ✓ 1 teaspoon of oregano
- ✓ pepper
- ✓ salt

Directions: 40min

In a pan with oil, brown the garlic. Remove it once it has begun to brown, then stir in the tomato puree. 15 minutes of high-heat cooking followed by seasoning with salt, pepper, and a dash of oregano Place the meat pieces on top of the sauce, then spread it out around the edges. Cook them on both sides and then completely slather them in tomato sauce. Slices of pizzaiola should be served hot. You can make a nice sauce for spaghetti by adding more tomato.

Salmon in salt crust

Ingredients for 4 servings:

- ✓ 2 kg of salmon
- ✓ 3 kg coarse salt

Directions: 1h

Set the oven to 220 °C and turn it on. On a baking sheet, sprinkle some coarse salt, set the salmon on it, and completely cover it with salt. Bake for 40 minutes. When serving, remove the crust, rinse the meat to remove any salt traces, and top the salmon with mayonnaise.

Saltimbocca Roman style

Ingredients for 4 servings:

- ✓ 500 gr of veal (slices)
- ✓ 200 gr of raw ham
- ✓ Sage to taste
- ✓ 50 gr of butter
- ✓ 100 ml dry white wine
- ✓ flour 00
- ✓ salt
- ✓ pepper

Directions: 30 min

Sage leaves should be washed and dried. The veal slices should be free of visible fat before being flattened and evenly distributed with a meat tenderizer. Put a prosciutto slice and a sage leaf on each piece of meat. Use a toothpick to hold everything together. Quickly coat both sides of the saltimbocca in flour. Place the saltimbocca in the hot butter in the frying pan, starting with the ham side, and brown for a few minutes. Then, add the wine and let it evaporate over high heat while turning the saltimbocca to brown them on both sides. Once the saltimbocca is cooked, season with salt and pepper while considering the prosciutto's flavor. Add a small quantity of water to create a creamy sauce to serve with the dish.

Gilthead bream in almond crust

Ingredients for 4 servings:

- ✓ 4 gilthead bream fillets
- ✓ 2 tablespoons shelled almonds
- ✓ ½ clove of garlic
- ✓ a small bunch of parsley
- ✓ 30 gr of peeled almonds
- ✓ 3 slices of pancarrè or bread in cassette
- ✓ 1 tablespoon of breadcrumbs

- ✓ extra virgin olive oil
- ✓ a handful of caper flowers
- ✓ salt
- ✓ pepper

Directions: 35 min

Cut the fillets from the gilthead bream after removing the scales. You might request that your fishmonger perform this procedure. Remove any bones using tweezers. The fillets should be placed in an oiled baking pan. Add salt and pepper to taste. The oven temperature is set to 180 °C. Blend the breadcrumbs, diced bacon, parsley, and almonds in a blender. Add a dash of salt and pepper and one tablespoon of extra virgin olive oil. Blending in short bursts will keep the mixture gritty and prevent the almonds from becoming powdered. The sea bream fillets are covered with almond paste. Add a few capers as decoration and bake for 15 minutes. To gratinate, turn the grill up for the final five minutes of cookingr Serve the sea bream fillets as soon as they are well cooked.

Ginger chicken with potatoes

Ingredients for 4 servings:

- ✓ 8 large chicken wings
- ✓ 700 gr of potatoes
- ✓ 150 gr of breadcrumbs
- ✓ 1 sprig of rosemary
- ✓ curry powder
- ✓ Ginger powder
- ✓ 1 tablespoon chopped parsley
- ✓ 100 ml white wine
- ✓ extra virgin olive oil
- ✓ salt
- ✓ pepper

Directions: 2h

Cut the chicken wings in half at the joint using a large, sturdy knife. Pour the wine and two tablespoons of oil over the wings in a bowl. Mix in the salt, pepper, and chopped rosemary needles before coveringr Refrigerate everything for at least 30 minutes to let it marinate. The potatoes should be peeled, sliced into wedges or cubes that aren't too small, blanched, or boiled for three minutes in barely salted water. Drain, then set apart. Use a strong knife to cut the chicken wings at the joint. Over the wings in a bowl, add the wine and two tablespoons of oil.

Before covering, combine the salt, pepper, and chopped rosemary needles. Allow everything to marinate in the refrigerator for at least 30 minutes. Peeling, slicing, and boiling the potatoes for three minutes in barely salted water is the proper preparation method. Drain and put aside. Combine the breadcrumbs, chopped parsley, 1 teaspoon curry powder, and 1 teaspoon ginger powder in a large dish. Add salt and pepper to taste. Covering the wings from the marinate thoroughly with the seasoned breadcrumbs, pressing them firmly onto the chicken wings. Use parchment paper to line 2 baking sheets. Place the potatoes in one and the wings in the other. Drizzle a little oil over the potatoes and season them with salt and oil. For 40 to 45 minutes, bake both preparations at 190 °C in a ventilated oven or until they are both crispy. Serve the potatoes at the table with the ginger chicken.

Lemon escalopes

Ingredients for 4 servings:

- ✓ 600 gr of veal (thin slices)
- ✓ flour
- ✓ 1 lemon
- ✓ salt
- ✓ extra virgin olive oil

Directions: 20min

The veal slices are floured before being browned in a skillet with a small amount of extra virgin olive oil. Add the lemon juice diluted with a drop of water when the escalopes turn golden. Once the lemon has completely evaporated, continue to simmer at medium heat. At the very end of cooking, add salt. Put some decoration on the meat by grating some lemon zest over it.

Deviled chicken

Ingredients for 4 servings:

- ✓ 1 free-range chicken 1 kg - 1.5 kg

- ✓ 1 garlic clove
- ✓ 2 teaspoons of salt
- ✓ 1 sprig of peeled rosemary
- ✓ 1 teaspoon of sweet paprika
- ✓ 4 tablespoons of seed oil
- ✓ 2 sage leaves
- ✓ 1 sprig of peeled thyme
- ✓ fresh or powdered chili pepper
- ✓ 1 teaspoon dried oregano
- ✓ a few drops of lemon juice

Directions: 1h 10min

Purchase a medium-sized chicken, preferably free-range, weighing between 1 kg and 1 kg and a half. Ask your butcher to divide it into four pieces. Dry it thoroughly after rinsing it with water. Any residual feathers can be removed by setting the chicken's skin on fire on a burner. In a blender, combine the salt with all the other spices and herbs. Blend in the garlic, which has been carefully diced.

Add a few drops of lemon juice and the seed oil to the mixture in a bowl. Apply the mixture to the chicken and give it a good massage. For the meat to absorb all the flavors fully, let it sit at room temperature for at least an hour. The deviled chicken can be cooked on the grill or the griddle while generously brushing with the spice oil you set aside. Alternatively, you can bake it for about an hour at 160° C in a hot oven while frequently flipping it and spraying it with spice oil. The deviled chicken should be served hot.

Sicilian-style chicken breast

Ingredients for 4 servings:

- ✓ 6 slices of chicken breast
- ✓ 1 glass of marsala wine
- ✓ flour to taste
- ✓ olive oil to taste
- ✓ 1 garlic clove
- ✓ 3 bay leaves
- ✓ salt and pepper to taste

Directions: 40min

The chicken breast slices should be well-washed and dried before being cut into strips. Roll them on a flour-filled plate and shake vigorously to ensure they retain very little flour. Cook the bay leaf and smashed garlic in a bit of oil in a frying pan. Transfer the chicken there once it's hot, then brown it for five minutes while turning it over. Following the Marsala deglaze, cover the pan and simmer for five minutes. When the chicken is finished cooking, taste and adjust the seasonings before placing it in a serving dish with the cooking liquids and adding fresh bay leaves as a garnish (remember to remove the cooked ones). Serve the chicken hot off the grill.

Milanese cutlet

Ingredients for 4 servings:

- ✓ 4 veal chops (loin)
- ✓ 2 ounces of butter
- ✓ 2 eggs
- ✓ very fine breadcrumbs
- ✓ salt to taste

Directions: 30min

Trim the fat from the margins of the veal steaks before making incisions along the edge to keep them from curling while they cook. To make them thinner, use a beef tenderizer. Break the eggs into a dish, lightly beat them, then dip the steaks before drenching them in breadcrumbs and pressing firmly. Cook them on each side for 5 to 6 minutes after melting the clarified butter in a frying pan and allowing it to bubble. Place the steaks on kitchen paper to absorb any extra grease, then serve them hot and fresh immediately.

Fried codfish Roman style

Ingredients for 6 servings:

- ✓ 600 gr of wet and dried codfish
- ✓ 400 gr of cold water
- ✓ 10 gr of brewer's yeast powder
- ✓ 360 gr of flour
- ✓ 1 liter of peanut oil for frying
- ✓ 3 gr of fine salt

Directions: 15min

Dissolve the yeast in the water, add the previously sifted flour, and whisk the mixture until it has a smooth, creamy consistency. The container should be wrapped in plastic and left to rise for two hours at room temperature. When the oil has risen, heat it to 165 degrees. Cod should be cut into chunks weighing 100 and 150 gr each, bones removed. Codfish pieces should be dipped in the batter one at a time and fried till golden brown in heated oil. The fried cod should be drained and dried on absorbent paper. The cod can be served without adding salt.

Arrosticini

Ingredients for 6 servings:

- ✓ 2 kg of sliced sheep or lamb meat
- ✓ 35 cm wooden skewers
- ✓ cube

Directions: 10min

Make sure the meat is thoroughly deboned and clear of any bones or cartilage before preparing the arrosticini. A specific tool called a cube, wooden sticks, and a razor-sharp knife with a thin blade are necessities. Slices of leaner beef should be placed between chunks of fatter flesh until the cube reaches the appropriate height. Compact the layers of flesh with your hands before cutting along all the slits in the tool, starting on one side and moving to the other.

The profile of the arrosticino will look better (aesthetically) the sharper and more decisive the cut. The arrosticini should be grilled for 4-5 minutes, flipping them halfway through. In Abruzzo, people utilize electric roasters, convenient devices that automatically turn roasts and cook them to perfection.

Mixed fried fish romagnola style
with vegetables

Ingredients for 4 servings:

- ✓ 400 gr of shrimp tails size 36/40
- ✓ 1 kilo of squid to clean

- ✓ 400 gr of sardines
- ✓ 1 light zucchini
- ✓ 1 long eggplant
- ✓ plenty of flour
- ✓ 1 liter and a half of peanut oil

Directions: 35 min

Leave the shrimp's tail on when removing the carapace. Empty the squid's insides, peel off the skin, and remove the beak from the head. Cut them in half if they are huge. Remove the entrails from the sardines, wash, and dry them. Sliced zucchini and eggplant are placed in a colander with a flat plate on top to function as a weight, and the veggies are allowed to drain for an hour. The peanut oil should be heated to 170 degrees just before fryingr Separately flour the fish from the veggies, then begin frying a serving of vegetables for each person before adding a fish. The mixed fried cooks fairly quickly; as the shrimp turn pink and the squid begins to swell, the dish is finished. After draining on straw paper, the mixed fried fish should be seasoned and served with lemon slices.

Chicken with sauce

Ingredients for 4 servings:

- ✓ 1 free-range chicken cut into pieces
- ✓ 2-3 slices of thick-cut raw ham
- ✓ 400 g of peeled tomatoes
- ✓ 1/2 glass of dry white wine
- ✓ 1 garlic clove
- ✓ 1 teaspoon of chopped marjoram leaves
- ✓ 1 tablespoon of extra virgin olive oil
- ✓ Salt
- ✓ pepper

Directions: 60min

This chicken with sauce is simple to prepare. Heat the oil in a big skillet, then brown one of the three slices of thinly sliced ham. Add the cut-up chicken, allow it to cook evenly, and then season with salt and pepper. Garlic and marjoram should be added at this point. Stir in the wine and let it evaporate. Include the chopped, peeled tomatoes. For 30 to 40 minutes, cook. The chicken in the pan should now be ready to be removed from the heat. It should be served with its sauce, which will still be quite liquid but somewhat thickened after cookingr

Curried Cauliflower Meatballs

Ingredients for 4 servings:

- ✓ 500 g of cauliflower
- ✓ 2 potatoes already boiled (about 300 g)
- ✓ 1 yolk
- ✓ 40 g of grated Parmesan cheese
- ✓ 1 teaspoon of curry powder
- ✓ chopped parsley and mint
- ✓ 2-3 tablespoons of breadcrumbs (+ more for the breadcrumbs)
- ✓ extra virgin olive oil
- ✓ salt
- ✓ pepper

Directions: 45min

This chicken with sauce is simple to prepare. Heat the oil in a big skillet, then brown one of the three slices of thinly sliced ham. Add the cut-up chicken, allow it to cook evenly, and then season with salt and pepper. Garlic and marjoram should be added at this point. Stir in the wine and let it evaporate. Include the chopped, peeled tomatoes. For 30 to 40 minutes, cook. The chicken in the pan should now be ready to be removed from the heat. It should be served with its sauce, which will still be quite liquid but somewhat thickened after cookingr With your hands, combine the pepper and salt to taste until the mixture is smooth. Form into balls about the size of a mandarin orange using barely damp hands. Place them in a dish, and spread them evenly with breadcrumbs. Bake them at 200° for 25 minutes after placing them on a baking sheet covered with parchment paper. Warm the curried cauliflower balls after removing them from the oven.

Rabbit with Peppers

Ingredients for 4 servings:

- ✓ 1 rabbit already cut into pieces

- ✓ 40 g of stale bread crumbs
- ✓ about 1/2 liter of red wine
- ✓ 2 peppers
- ✓ 1 garlic clove
- ✓ 2 onions
- ✓ 1 bunch of parsley
- ✓ 1 sprig of rosemary
- ✓ 1 tablespoon of sugar
- ✓ 1 hot pepper
- ✓ extra virgin olive oil
- ✓ salt

Directions: 1h 35min

The rabbit is browned in a frying pan with two teaspoons of hot oil for a few minutes. A tablespoon of oil and water is heated in a pot. After stewing the chopped onion and full garlic clove for 10 minutes, add the peppers and bread crumbs. Finally, season with some chopped rosemary and parsley and cook for another 20 minutes. The wine should be heated along with the sugar, salt, and chili pepper. Add the hot wine to the pan with the peppers and the stew; simmer for about an hour. After cooking, take the garlic clove out. Place the stew and its sauce on a hot serving plate and garnish with a few handfuls of parsley that has been chopped. The pepper-stuffed rabbit is prepared.

Pan-Fried Trout

Ingredients for 4 servings:

- ✓ 800 g of trout fillets
- ✓ 60 g of raisins
- ✓ 1 yolk
- ✓ 2 onions
- ✓ 3 sage leaves
- ✓ 1 celery stalk
- ✓ 1 sprig of rosemary
- ✓ a glass of broth
- ✓ flour
- ✓ lemon peel
- ✓ white wine vinegar or apple vinegar
- ✓ salt
- ✓ extra virgin olive oil

Directions: 40min

On a cutting board, first, divide the fish fillets in half. Flour them lightly, taking off any extra if necessary. In a skillet, heat three tablespoons of oil. Add the finely chopped onion, celery, rosemary, and sage. After 10 minutes, add the breaded fish fillets. Add five tablespoons of vinegar, raisins, and some finely shredded lemon peel. Stir. A little glass of broth should be added after a few minutes; cover and simmer for about 10 minutes. Leaving the cooking liquid in the pan, remove the fillets and place them on a serving platter. Mix the egg yolk diluted with a tablespoon of broth into the cooking liquids over low heat. Then, season with salt and let the mixture decrease. Serve the sauce alongside the pan-fried fish fillets.

Shrimp and mango salad

Ingredients for 4 servings:

- ✓ 200 g of songino
- ✓ 16 cherry tomatoes
- ✓ 100 g of rocket
- ✓ 12 shrimps
- ✓ 1 carrot
- ✓ 1 mango
- ✓ a few olives
- ✓ 1 lemon
- ✓ pepper
- ✓ extra virgin olive oil
- ✓ salt

Directions: 15 min

Cooking the shrimp in salted water is the first step in making the shrimp and mango salad. Cook for around 4 minutes (the exact time depends on the size of the crustaceans). Let them cool after draining them. Start by placing the thoroughly dry and washed songino in a bowl in the interim. The cherry tomatoes should be rinsed and sliced in half before being added to the arugula. The carrot should be peeled, cut into ribbons with a potato peeler and added to the salad dish. Peel the mango, cut the pulp into cubes about 1 cm on each side and combine it with the other ingredients. Add the shrimp from which you have removed the head, carapace, and olives. Create an emulsion separately using lemon juice, oil, salt, and pepper. Before serving, add the prepared citronette to the shrimp and mango salad.

Grilled squid

Ingredients for 2 servings:

- ✓ 2 big squids
- ✓ 8 olives
- ✓ 5 capers
- ✓ 2 anchovies
- ✓ 1 garlic clove
- ✓ 100 ml of extra virgin olive oil
- ✓ 1 bunch of parsley
- ✓ ½ lemon
- ✓ pepper
- ✓ salt

Directions: 20 min

If you did not purchase the shellfish already cleaned, the first step in preparing the grilled squid is to clean them. To get the sack with the entrails out, gently peel off the head. Peel off the skin after removing the cartilage pen. Remove the beak, then separate the entrails and eyeballs from the tentacles before giving everything a thorough wash under running water. Incise the sac with horizontal cuts.

Give the sauce preparation your full attention. Grate the lemon zest, and slice the parsley into small pieces. The desalted capers, peeled garlic, olives, and anchovies should all be combined in a bowl. After that, use an immersion blender to combine everythingr To the capers and anchovies combination, add the lemon zest and parsley. Mix in the oil and lemon juice after seasoning with salt and pepper. In a bowl, place the squid and drizzle with the prepared sauce. A cast-iron griddle should be heated, and then the squid should be placed on it and cooked for 5 minutes, flipping once halfway through. A heated grill can be used for the same procedure. The grilled squid is ready for consumption.

Pan-fried salmon

Ingredients for 4 servings:

- ✓ 4 salmon fillets of about 200 g each
- ✓ 350 g of cherry tomatoes
- ✓ 50 g of green olives
- ✓ 40 g of capers in brine
- ✓ 1 garlic clove
- ✓ extra virgin olive oil
- ✓ 200 ml of dry white wine
- ✓ pepper
- ✓ salt

Directions: 35 min

This pan-fried salmon is quick and simple to make. The salmon fillets should be washed and, if required, deboned. Dry them, then add a little oil and a garlic clove to a pan. Set the heat to medium and add the salmon slices skin side down as soon as the oil is hot. The salmon should be browned for about 5 minutes before being turned over and browning for a few minutes on the other side. Gently flip them over once more. Add the capers, green olives, and half-cut cherry tomatoes at this time. Add salt, stir, then white wine. Cook for another 10 to 15 minutes or until the wine and water that the tomatoes released have evaporated. Pepper should be ground to finish. The salmon is ready to be pan-fried.

Monkfish with tomato sauce

Ingredients for 4 servings:

- ✓ 1 kg of monkfish in slices
- ✓ 300 g of tomato pulp
- ✓ 1 dl of dry white wine
- ✓ 1 garlic clove
- ✓ 1 sprig of rosemary
- ✓ a few sprigs of marjoram
- ✓ 1 small piece of hot pepper
- ✓ 1 tablespoon chopped parsley
- ✓ vegetable stock
- ✓ extra virgin olive oil
- ✓ salt
- ✓ pepper

Directions: 45 min

It's simple to prepare monkfish with tomato sauce. To start, thoroughly clean and dry the monkfish slices. Finely cut the garlic clove with the rosemary, marjoram, and chili pepper. A piece of fish should be well covered after being dipped in the mince. Repeat the procedure with the remaining slices, placing them on a plate one at a time. Slices are placed in a large skillet that has been heated with three to four teaspoons of oil and are gently turned to brown evenly. Wine should be sprinkled on and allowed to evaporate. Add the tomato pulp and simmer for ten to fifteen minutes over medium heat, if required, adding a little hot stock. The sauce should be moderately thick at the end of the cooking process—not too liquid, but also not too thin. Monkfish should be served with tomato sauce and salt and pepper seasonings to taste.

Savory pie with artichokes and potatoes

Ingredients for 6 servings:

- ✓ 1 round puff pastry roll
- ✓ 4 artichokes
- ✓ 3 potatoes
- ✓ 1 small onion
- ✓ 2 eggs plus 1 yolk (for brushing)
- ✓ 2 generous tablespoons of grated Parmesan cheese
- ✓ 100 g of smoked scamorza cheese
- ✓ chopped fresh parsley
- ✓ extra virgin olive oil
- ✓ 1 lemon
- ✓ black pepper
- ✓ salt

Directions: 1h 15 min

The artichoke and potato pie recipe is fairly straightforward. The artichokes should first be cleaned by peeling the harder outer leaves and filleting the stalks with a potato peeler. Remove the tips with a clean cut, then cut them into quarters. Remove the internal hay, then add it to a bowl with water and lemon juice. Chop the onion, cook it in a skillet with a few tablespoons of oil, and then stir in the chunked

potatoes. Add the chopped artichokes after cooking for a few minutes. Add fresh parsley that has been chopped, season with salt and pepper, and boil the veggies until they are tender but not mushy. After being cooked, remove it from the heat and allow it cool in a big basin. In the meantime, whisk the eggs in a bowl with the cheese that has been grated and a little salt. Add the eggs and the diced scamorza to the veggies once warmed to room temperature. Gently stir to combine. Puff pastry and its paper are used to line a round baking pan with a diameter of approximately 23 cm. The filling is then added, leveled off, and the bottom of the pastry is punctured with a fork. Brush the pastry with egg yolk and fold the edges in. For around 35 minutes, bake at 180°C in a preheated oven. The artichoke and potato pie should be served warm or lukewarm after coming out of the oven and cooling for 5 to 10 minutes.

Salmon trout baked in foil

Ingredients for 4 servings:

- ✓ 4 salmon trout fillets
- ✓ 4 artichokes
- ✓ fresh parsley
- ✓ 30 g of fresh ginger
- ✓ 4 garlic cloves
- ✓ pink pepper
- ✓ Worcester sauce
- ✓ 1 lemon
- ✓ extra virgin olive oil
- ✓ salt

Directions: 45 min

Artichokes should first be cleaned by removing the harder leaves, trimming the tips, and filleting the stems. They should be divided in half, the inner hay removed, and then thinly sliced before being placed in a basin of water acidified with lemon. Sliced artichoke and chopped stalks are cooked in a pan with two tablespoons of hot oil. Salt and chopped parsley should be added last. Because they will be cooked in the oven, remember that the artichokes should have just begun to soften. Four pieces of aluminum foil should be cut and placed on the work surface one at a time. Put two drops of Worcester sauce, two grated ginger pieces, two pink peppercorns, one garlic clove with its peel, and a small amount of chopped artichoke in the center of each piece. Add a trout fillet to the top, season with salt, oil, and additional pink pepper to taste, and then seal the foil. Cartocci should be baked for 15–20 minutes at 200° in a preheated oven after being placed on a baking sheet. Salmon and trout fillets are served in foil with a sprinkle of raw oil after being taken out of the oven.

Turkey breasts bolognese style

Ingredients for 6 servings:

- ✓ 6 slices of turkey breast
- ✓ 6 slices of raw ham
- ✓ a few black truffle shavings
- ✓ parmesan cheese in flakes
- ✓ butter
- ✓ Marsala wine
- ✓ flour
- ✓ extra virgin olive oil
- ✓ salt
- ✓ black pepper

Directions: 30 min

A knob of butter and two tablespoons of oil should be heated in a skillet before preparing the turkey breasts alla Bolognese. Slices of turkey should not overlap as they are placed in the pan after lightly floured. Salt and pepper on both sides while searing over high heat. A few teaspoons of marsala should be sprinkled over the meat, and allowed to evaporate, and then the cooking liquid should be removed with a few tablespoons of warm water. The fillets should then be thoroughly covered in the sauce. Place a slice of prosciutto crudo, lots of Parmesan flakes, and a few very thin slices of truffle on each piece before removing it from the pan. With the lid on, reheat the pan over medium heat while allowing the cheese to melt without browning it. Serve the Bolognese-style turkey breasts hot.

Mullet Livornese style

Ingredients for 4 servings:

- ✓ 1 kg of red mullets

- ✓ 350/400 g of tomato pulp
- ✓ parsley
- ✓ 1 garlic clove
- ✓ extra virgin olive oil
- ✓ salt
- ✓ pepper

Directions: 35 min

Clean and eviscerate the red mullet before preparing it Livornese style. In a skillet big enough to hold all the mullet, heat 4 tablespoons of oil, then sauté the chopped parsley and garlic. Add the tomato pulp, salt, and pepper once they've begun to turn color, and then simmer for about five minutes. The red mullet is then added. Cook them for around twenty minutes over low heat, with a lid on and then without. Turning the fish has the risk of shattering them; therefore, try to avoid doing so to prevent sticking the sauce. After cooking, allow the dish to cool and rest for 5 to 10 minutes while keeping it warm. Then, serve the red mullet alla livornese and top it with additional chopped parsley, if you like.

Swordfish with honey and chips

Ingredients for 4 servings:

- ✓ 4 slices of swordfish of about 200 g each
- ✓ 20 new potatoes
- ✓ 1 garlic clove
- ✓ 1 bunch of cherry tomatoes
- ✓ 1 glass of wine vinegar
- ✓ 2 tablespoons of toasted pine nuts
- ✓ 4-5 teaspoons of wildflower honey
- ✓ chives
- ✓ myrtle leaves
- ✓ parsley
- ✓ pepper
- ✓ extra virgin olive oil
- ✓ salt

Directions: 1h

Slices of swordfish should be marinated before being cooked with wildflower honey, cherry tomatoes, and new potatoes. Put them on a platter, top them with some sliced garlic, myrtle leaves, and a drizzle of oil, and let them sit for 10 minutes. Slices of swordfish should be cooked for about two minutes on each side or until a crust forms in a pan with three tablespoons of hot oil. Place them on a baking pan and bake at 200° for approximately 5 minutes. After removing them from the oven, let them 10 minutes to rest somewhere warm. In the interim, chop the chives and parsley finely, add a little salt, a pinch of pepper, and cube the tomatoes. The vinegar should be heated in a skillet, reduced by half, then wildflower honey should be added to create the honey sauce. Taste the mixture to check the flavor; add more honey if it's too sour. Let cool. Incorporate everything into the tomatoes, combine well, then add the oil, pine nuts, and salt before letting them stand. The chips should be boiled in salted water, dried, and seasoned in a skillet with oil. Place the chips and honey sauce on the swordfish slices as you arrange them on the serving dish.

Roast rabbit

Ingredients for 8 servings:

- ✓ 1 kg and 300 g of rabbit in pieces
- ✓ a glass of dry white wine
- ✓ 100 g of bacon or lard
- ✓ 30 g of butter
- ✓ 4 leaves of sage
- ✓ 1 garlic clove
- ✓ 2 sprigs of rosemary
- ✓ pepper
- ✓ extra virgin olive oil
- ✓ salt

Directions: 1h 30 min

The roast rabbit recipe is fairly straightforward. The bacon should first be cut into cubes and chopped sage and rosemary. Add the garlic clove, half of the bacon, and half of the seasonings to the melted butter in a large pan. Include the cleaned and dried rabbit pieces, the leftover bacon and herbs, and two tablespoons of oil, salt, and pepper. Over high heat, it will take about 4-5 minutes to thoroughly brown the meat on all sides. Wine should be drizzled over the meat, evaporated, and then cooked for 30 to 40 minutes at a low temperature in a covered skillet with frequent stirringr

Once done, move the roast rabbit to a warm serving dish and proceed with dishingr

Chicken nuggets with radicchio and gorgonzola cheese

Ingredients for 4 servings:

- ✓ 500 g of thinly sliced chicken breast
- ✓ 160 g of spicy gorgonzola cheese
- ✓ 1 head of red radicchio from Treviso
- ✓ 20 g of pine nuts
- ✓ 00 flour
- ✓ 1 glass of dry white wine
- ✓ white pepper
- ✓ salt
- ✓ butter
- ✓ nutmeg

Directions: 1h

Starting toasting the pine nuts until golden brown on the bottom of a non-stick skillet, being careful not to burn them, is the first step in making the chicken bites with radicchio and gorgonzola recipe. Switch off the heat and leave the area. Remove the leaves and stalks from the radicchio before rinsing it under running water to clean it. Then, using a small knife, cut away the thickest portion of each leaf's central rib. Place aside. Gorgonzola should remove its rind before cutting it into thin, slender sticks. Arrange the chicken slices and a radicchio leaf lengthwise on a cutting board. Then set a gorgonzola stick at the base. Wrap the individual morsels beginning with the Gorgonzola stick, after sealing the side edges of each slice to stop the filling from escapingr They are secured with a toothpick. Pass the snacks in a floured dish, so they stay covered, shaking off any extra. Then, brown the morsels by flipping them around in a non-stick pan heated with a liberal knob of butter. Use half of the white wine to deglaze. Add 12 glasses of water, nutmeg that has been grated, salt, and pepper. Lower the flame, cover with a lid and cook for about ten minutes. Then reveal and allow to dry (but not dry out). While the remaining wine deglazes the cooking liquid and reduces, remove the morsels from the pan and keep them warm, preferably in aluminum foil. Place the chicken nuggets with radicchio, gorgonzola, and sauce in a serving dish along with the toasted pine nuts, then serve.

Pumpkin cutlets

Ingredients for 4 servings:

- ✓ 700 g of cleaned pumpkin
- ✓ flour
- ✓ breadcrumbs
- ✓ 3 eggs
- ✓ marjoram
- ✓ thyme
- ✓ mint
- ✓ peanut seed oil
- ✓ salt
- ✓ pepper

Directions: 35min

The recipe for these pumpkin cutlets is simple. Cut the squash into wedges, then remove the skin after removing the seeds and filaments. Slice the flesh into equal, 1/2 cm thick pieces. Several marjorams and thyme sprigs should be free of leaves. After that, add a few mint leaves and finely slice everythingr Set aside after combining the herbs with around 250 g of breadcrumbs. Each slice should be thoroughly coated on all sides with flour before being dipped in softly beaten eggs with salt and pepper, then in flour once more, eggs once more, and then breadcrumbs (to prevent them from falling apart during frying). The breaded slices should be dipped in hot oil and cooked for a few minutes, rotating them halfway through. In a tray covered in paper towels, drain them as you go. After that, place them in a serving dish, sprinkle them with salt, and add some fresh mint leaves between them. Serve.

Veal with tuna sauce

Ingredients for 6 servings:

For The Veal

- ✓ 800 g of veal swivel
- ✓ 1 onion
- ✓ 2 carrots
- ✓ 1 celery rib
- ✓ 2 bay leaves
- ✓ 6-7 black peppercorns
- ✓ 5 cloves
- ✓ 1 garlic clove
- ✓ 1 liter of water
- ✓ 500 ml of dry white wine
- ✓ salt

For The Tuna Sauce

- ✓ 4 hard-boiled eggs
- ✓ 150 g of tuna in oil (drained weight)
- ✓ 1 tablespoon of salted capers
- ✓ 6 anchovy fillets in oil
- ✓ salt
- ✓ pepper
- ✓ veal stock to dilute

To Serve

- ✓ a few desalted capers
- ✓ parsley or celery leaves to taste

Directions: 4h 30min

To prepare the meat for vitello tonnato, tie it up firmly with kitchen string if the butcher hasn't already done so. Put it in a big pot with the peeled, chopped carrots, the onion, which has been cut into segments, and the celery stalk, which has been sliced into two to three pieces. Bay leaves, garlic cloves, peppercorns, and salt should be added. Add the wine and water to the entire area. Once it starts to boil, turn the heat to medium-low and let it cook for about an hour. Once done, drain the meat, reserving some of the broth (part of it will go into the tuna sauce), and let it cool. The meat should rest in the refrigerator for two hours after being wrapped in plastic wrap. Spend some time making the sauce by gathering the boiled eggs cut into slices and placing them in a container with high edges. Add the anchovy fillets, desalted capers, and drained tuna. Using an immersion blender, combine all the ingredients and a little cooking stock for the meat until you get a smooth sauce with the right consistency and not too runny. Use a long knife with a smooth blade to slice the meat into thin pieces. Place them on a serving plate with as little overlap as possible, then top them with tuna sauce. Refrigerate for a minimum of one hour. When serving, garnish the veal with a few chopped celery or parsley leaves, desalted capers, and some freshly ground pepper.

Mozzarella in carrozza

Ingredients for 4 servings:

- ✓ 8 slices of bread carrè
- ✓ 2 spoons of milk
- ✓ 3 eggs
- ✓ provola or mozzarella or fior di latte (preferably not fresh dairy products of the day)
- ✓ salt, pepper, flour.

Directions: 15min

In a dish, beat 3 whole eggs. Add a touch of salt, pepper, and 2 tablespoons of milk. Stir to combine. Separately, start making the mozzarella in carrozza by sandwiching two pieces of bread with a slice of mozzarella (ideally cut into slices a few hours in advance and allowed to dry in the refrigerator, covered by a plate). You can split the slices in half to create smaller triangles when you're done. Before dipping in the beaten egg and pressing down firmly on the sides to ensure that the mozzarella sticks are on the inside, sprinkle the breadcrumbs in flour, being sure to coat the edges as well (some people avoid this step, but I prefer it because the breadcrumbs are crispier). Put some oil in a frying pan, and when the oil is very hot (try dropping a drop of a beaten egg; if it fries immediately, it is ready), add the mozzarella in carrozza. Fry a few pieces at a time; if you fry them all at once, the oil will cool down too much and the fry will become dripping with oil. However, with very hot oil, the fry will immediately form an exterior crust that does not absorb too much oil. Place on a plate with paper towels after browning both sides. Hot mozzarella with carrozza should be served. If you'd like, you can prepare it a few hours ahead of time and bake it briefly right before servingr

Caged Eggs

Ingredients for 4 servings:

- ✓ 4 eggs
- ✓ 2 slices of pancarré
- ✓ 50 gr of grated Emmental cheese

- ✓ 8 slices of bacon
- ✓ Enough salt
- ✓ Enough black pepper
- ✓ Enough fresh chives

Directions: 20 min

Use a silicone muffin mold to make the preparation of this dish easier because it will make it simple to remove the cooked eggs. A real cage protecting the components without allowing them to escape should be formed by the sausage adhering to the edges of the two slices of bacon used to line each mold. Four discs the size of the molds should be cut from the two slices of bacon and placed into the molds to form the base of the bacon's edges. Put a good amount of pressure with your hands while inserting the diced Emmental cheese into each mold. You should lightly salt the eggs before cracking them into the cages you've made. Depending on the level of cooking that would please your taste, bake for 5 to 12 minutes in a 220 °C oven. When your caged eggs have through cooking, remove them from the oven, let them cool for a moment, then remove them from the molds. Finally, season them with pepper and chives. Here are your caged eggs, ready for consumption.

Eggs bull's eye

Ingredients for 2 servings:

- ✓ 4 medium eggs
- ✓ Extra virgin olive oil to taste
- ✓ Salt to taste
- ✓ Pepper to taste

Directions: 5 min

Four eggs are cracked into a pan with EVOO drizzled on top. Add some freshly ground black pepper and a dash of salt. Cook until the yolks are liquid and covered with a glossy film and the egg whites are set (about 2 minutes). To produce a semi-liquid or firm yolk, you can cook the egg longer if you'd like. You can now serve your eggs. Enjoy!

Baked Spinach Omelette

Ingredients for 4 servings:

- ✓ 1 kilo of Spinach
- ✓ 200 gr of Mozzarella
- ✓ 6 Eggs
- ✓ 2 tablespoons of Extra Virgin Olive Oil
- ✓ 1 clove of Garlic
- ✓ Enough Salt
- ✓ Enough pepper
- ✓ Enough nutmeg
- ✓ 50 gr of grated Parmesan cheese

Directions: 40 min

Clean the spinach by separating the plants into leaves, typically more damaged, and wash them well in lots of cold water to get rid of all the soil. When the spinach is still wet, place it in a deep pan with the extra virgin olive oil and begin to cook it over low heat. Then, cover the pan with a lid and let the spinach cook with the crushed garlic clove. When cleaning spinach, separate the plants into their more damaged leaves and thoroughly wash them in a lot of cold water to remove all the soil. Place the spinach in a deep skillet, add the extra virgin olive oil, and simmer over low heat while the spinach is still moist. After that, seal the pan with a lid and allow the spinach and crushed garlic to cook together. A few minutes before turning off the heat, season the spinach with salt and allow it to cool. Beat the eggs in a basin with a dash of nutmeg, salt, and pepper. Add the chopped, ice-cold spinach to the egg mixture first, followed by the diced mozzarella and grated Parmesan cheese. Combine the ingredients, then preheat the oven in static mode to 200 °C. Heat a nonstick pan, add the omelet mixture as it reaches the proper temperature, and let it cook until it is all set. Take it out of the oven at that moment and serve it hot.

Eggs In Purgatory

Ingredients for 4 servings:

- ✓ 1/2 onion
- ✓ Extra virgin olive oil to taste
- ✓ 500 g Tomatoes (pureed or peeled)
- ✓ Salt to taste
- ✓ Pepper to taste
- ✓ 6 Medium eggs
- ✓ Water to taste
- ✓ Basil or parsley to taste

Directions: 40 min

The modernized version of eggs in purgatory is made by browning the sliced onion in a frying pan with a lot of oil. Cook the tomatoes for 10 minutes on low heat after adding them and seasoning them with salt and pepper. Cook for another 10 minutes after adding the water and stirringr The original recipe specifies a somewhat liquid rather than a thick, final product. When the sauce is finished, taste it, then crack one egg at a time into the pan while being careful not to break it. It will take around 10 minutes to cook with the lid on low heat until the egg white solidifies. Cook for a short while longer before adding basil or parsley. Immediately serve the eggs in purgatory hot and accompanied by a tasty prepared loaf of bread.

Asparagus Bismarck style

Ingredients for 6 servings:

- ✓ 1 Kg asparagus
- ✓ 120 g butter
- ✓ 50 g grated parmesan cheese
- ✓ 6 eggs
- ✓ lemon
- ✓ salt

Directions: 40 min

For the Bismarck-style asparagus recipe, clean the asparagus by cutting off the stringy end of the stalks. Next, tie the asparagus stalks into bunches and boil them in a pot of salted, lemon-acidified water. Divide evenly amongst six individual heated plates after thorough drainingr Cook the eggs and melt a tablespoon of butter in a separate frying pan. Next to the 6 sections of boiling asparagus, put them. Melt the butter in the same frying pan. Serve the asparagus immediately after seasoning it with Parmesan cheese and melted butter.

Eggs flamenco style

Ingredients for 4 people:

- ✓ 250 gr potatoes cut into small cubes
- ✓ small chorizo (or calabrian spicy salami) 1
- ✓ serrano prosciutto (or mountain prosciutto) 100 gr
- ✓ peas (fresh or frozen) 100 gr
- ✓ tomato sauce 250 ml
- ✓ eggs 1 for each diner
- ✓ oil for frying to taste

Directions: 20 min

Set the oven to 200 degrees. The first step is to cut the potatoes into cubes and boil them for a few minutes, depending on the size of the potatoes. With a fork, test them; they don't need to be overcooked because the cooking will continue in the pan and the oven. The chorizo is placed in the hot, non-stick frying pan with a tablespoon of oil. It is not essential to add any additional fat; the chorizo's inherent fat content will suffice. Peas and tomato sauce are next, followed by the chopped serrano ham. Stir thoroughly, then simmer it for 10 minutes or so. Stir for two to three minutes after adding the finished potatoes. Transfer everything to a baking pan with a non-stick liningr Place an egg in each of the little "holes" you've created between the ingredients, which should correspond to the number of diners. Bake for 5 to 10 minutes in the oven or until the eggs are set.

Baked Stuffed Squid

Ingredients for 4 people:

- ✓ 4 medium squid
- ✓ 1 garlic clove, optional
- ✓ 100 gr of breadcrumbs
- ✓ 1 sprig of parsley
- ✓ 100 gr of pine nuts or almonds
- ✓ white vinegar or white wine to taste
- ✓ extra virgin olive oil to taste
- ✓ 50 gr of parmesan or pecorino cheese
- ✓ salt to taste
- ✓ pepper to taste

Directions: 40 min

Start cleaning the squid by removing its head, fins, tentacles, outer skin, and internal organs. Since this final procedure is a little tricky, I advise using scissors to trim off the squid's tip and release any leftover gunk. Under cold water, this procedure should be carried out. The squid's fins and tentacles should now be coarsely chopped and placed aside for the fillingr Get the stuffing ready. Put the chopped tentacles and fins, lots of chopped parsley, minced garlic, breadcrumbs, grated Parmesan or pecorino cheese, chopped pine nuts or almonds, salt, and pepper in a bowl. The mixture should become compact and moist after being drizzled with a small amount of extra-virgin olive oil and a lot of vinegar or white wine while stirringr Fill the pouches with a spoon, but don't fill them up; this will stop the contents from pouring out when cookingr A toothpick is used to seal the squid. The squids should be evenly spaced out in a baking dish lined with baking paper, which has been moistened with a little white wine. The stuffed squids should be baked for 20 minutes at 180°C. Add some bread crumbs and a few drops of oil to the squids halfway through cookingr When the time for the gratin coating has passed, remove the squid from the oven and serve it on a plate with a seasonal fresh salad.

Swordfish in crust

Ingredients for 4 people:

- ✓ 1 800 g slice of swordfish
- ✓ 2 garlic cloves
- ✓ 400 g of flour
- ✓ 1 sprig of basil
- ✓ 1 sprig of rosemary
- ✓ Salt to taste
- ✓ pepper to taste
- ✓ For the sauce
- ✓ 6 shrimps
- ✓ 1 sole bone
- ✓ 70 g of butter
- ✓ 2 yolks
- ✓ 1/2 glass of white wine
- ✓ 25 g of flour
- ✓ to taste salt
- ✓ pepper to taste

Directions: 40 min

Prepare the sauce by shelling the shrimp, boiling the shells in a pot with a half-liter of water and the sole bones for 20 minutes, and then filtering the broth. Chop the crustacean pulp A, combine it with 40 g of butter, and refrigerate. Melt the remaining butter, stir in the sifted flour, and then add two ladles of fish stock when it turns a rich color. Cook the mixture for 5 minutes, add the wine and cook for 5 minutes. Finally, add the butter and cook for an additional 5 minutes to thicken. Add the salt, pepper, and egg yolks while the heat is off. Roll out the dough after making it compact and homogeneous by combining the flour, a good pinch of salt, and just enough water. Place the swordfish slice in the center. Garlic, basil, and rosemary are chopped, and the fish is seasoned with salt and pepper. The C pastry is then sealed over the fish and baked for 40 minutes at 180 degrees. Sliced swordfish is served with the sauce once the crust has been opened.

Baked sea bass

Ingredients for 2 people:

- ✓ 1 Sea Bass
- ✓ 1 clove of Garlic
- ✓ 1 Lemon
- ✓ Enough Extra Virgin Olive Oil
- ✓ Enough Parsley
- ✓ Enough Salt

Directions: 40 min

Cleaning the sea bass is the first step in preparing the baked sea bass. Make a cut in the belly with scissors, remove everything inside under running water, and then thoroughly wash the outside. Open the inside of the baking dish, add a bit of salt, and sprinkle some parsley before placing the fish inside. After that, slice the lemon and insert it into the fish's belly. A garlic clove should be divided in half, the core removed, and inserted into the fish. Finally, bake after sprinkling extra virgin olive oil. The sea bass can be served after 20 minutes of baking at 180 degrees.

Prawns with leeks and ginger

Ingredients for 4 people:

- ✓ 500 gr of prawns
- ✓ 1 Leek
- ✓ 30 gr of fresh ginger
- ✓ Soy Sauce
- ✓ Extra virgin olive oil

Directions: 35 min

Cut the leek into small pieces before adding it to the shrimp and ginger. The ginger should then be peeled and chopped into strips. Take the shrimp, peel off the shell, and thoroughly wash them in running water. Leeks are added to a frying pan with extra virgin olive oil. Add the ginger and soy sauce after about 10 minutes of sautéingr Cook over high heat for a further 10 minutes after adding the shrimp. You are prepared to serve your shrimp with leeks and ginger once the cooking time is over.

Fillets of sea bass with lemon

Ingredients for 4 people:

- ✓ 8 seabass fillets
- ✓ 2 lemons
- ✓ 4 tablespoons of extra virgin olive oil
- ✓ 1 glass of white wine
- ✓ Enough flour
- ✓ Enough parsley
- ✓ Enough salt

Directions: 20 min

Clean the fish and separate it into eight fillets if you have not already had your go-to fishmonger handle this. The sea bass fillets in flour. Oil and garlic are fried in a pan. Place the sea bass fillets in a single layer and brown both sides for a few minutes. Put salt in. After adding the two lemons' juice, simmer for 10 minutes. Take the sea bass fillets out of the pan and mix the cooking juices with the wine. Allow the alcohol to decrease and evaporate for five minutes. Add some lemon sauce to the fish. The lemon-sauced bass fillets are ready for consumption.

Coconut shrimp tails

Ingredients for 4 people:

- ✓ 350 gr of fresh shrimp
- ✓ 2 tablespoons of breadcrumbs
- ✓ 3 tablespoons grated coconut
- ✓ 1 pinch of Indian curry
- ✓ 1 egg
- ✓ 50 milliliters of water
- ✓ 1 pinch of black pepper
- ✓ 1 pinch of sweet paprika
- ✓ 3 tablespoons of rice flour
- ✓ salt
- ✓ 400 milliliters of peanut seed oil

Directions: 45 min

After buying the shrimp, thoroughly wash them under running water and then remove the heads, legs, and carapace, leaving the tiny portion that makes up the end of the tails attached. Pour the egg into a bowl and then start preparing the batter. Add the Indian curry powder, powdered black pepper, and rice flour to the egg, then season with salt. Start whisking and continue until a thick batter is created. Till the batter is soft and smooth, gradually add water. Place the breadcrumbs and grated coconut in a separate container and combine them. Once the shrimp tails are finished, put them in the refrigerator for 30 minutes so the batter hardens and the breadcrumbs stick to the shrimp well. Dip the shrimp tails one at a time, leaving the tail in the batter before frying them in the coconut mixture when the shrimp tails have had a chance to rest for 30 minutes, fry them in hot peanut oil, a couple at a time, until they are golden and crispy. To remove the extra frying oil, drain the potatoes and spread out a couple of sheets of paper towels over them. The warm and fragrant coconut shrimp tails are ready for consumption.

Gilthead bream fillets au gratin with lemon

Ingredients for 6 people:

- ✓ 3 sea bream fillets
- ✓ 1 lemon
- ✓ 1 garlic clove
- ✓ 3 tablespoons of breadcrumbs
- ✓ 6 tablespoons of extra virgin olive oil
- ✓ aromatic herbs
- ✓ salt

Directions: 35 min

Start by preparing the fish's breadcrumbs. After chopping the herbs and garlic, combine them with the breadcrumbs in a bowl. The breadcrumbs should be mixed with three tablespoons of extra virgin olive oil. Recipe for fillets of gilthead bream. When the breadcrumbs resemble wet sand, add the grated lemon zest and stir well. Put the fillets of gilthead bream on a baking sheet that has been greased. Preparation of Gilthead bream fillets. Cover the fillets with the freshly made breadcrumbs after seasoning them with the remaining oil and a dash of salt. Bake for 25 minutes at 180 degrees. Finish cooking the fish by placing it on the grill for 5 minutes. The gilthead seabream fillets are extremely wonderful when served au gratin with lemon after being taken out of the oven.

Sea bass baked in foil

Ingredients for 2 people:

- ✓ 2 Fresh sea bass
- ✓ 10 Cherry tomatoes
- ✓ 10 Olives
- ✓ 1 untreated lemon
- ✓ Parsley
- ✓ Salt
- ✓ Extra Virgin Olive Oil

Directions: 35 min

First, prepare the ingredients that will flavor your sea bass, slice the lemon, drain the olives from the brine, and cut the cherry tomatoes into small pieces after washing them. Then, with the help of a pair of scissors, take the sea basses, cut into the underside and, under tap water, clean them of all their internal contents. At the end of the operation, the fish should be completely clear and clean. Then you can start filling them. Arrange them on two sheets of baking paper, salt them inside, and put in the cherry tomatoes, olives and finally, the lemon. In addition to the inside, you can also put some cherry tomatoes and olives on the outside. Before closing your foil, add some parsley and extra virgin olive oil. Then wrap them in parchment paper and place them in a baking dish you will put in the oven. After about 25 minutes of cooking in a static oven at 180 degrees, your delicious sea bass baked in foil is ready.

Codfish meatballs

Ingredients for 4 people:

- ✓ 500 gr of codfish
- ✓ 300 gr of stale bread
- ✓ 1 handful of Parsley
- ✓ 1 clove of Garlic
- ✓ 60 gr of grated Parmesan cheese
- ✓ Salt
- ✓ 1 teaspoon of Mustard
- ✓ seed oil
- ✓ breadcrumbs
- ✓ flour

Directions: 20 min

Cook the fish for 20 minutes, or until the meat starts to flake, in boiling water. Drain and allow coolingr Crush the parsley and garlic. Remove the cod's skin, if it is there, press off the extra water, and then slice it up. Soak the crusty bread in water while you wait. Bread should be squeezed out and put in a bowl. Add a dash of parsley, garlic, mustard, Parmesan cheese, and salt to the dish. Put the fish in. All components should be combined thoroughly to create a homogenous composition. Make 8 meatballs, then coat them in flour before dredging them in breadcrumbs. The meatballs should be fried for 5 to 6 minutes or until golden brown on the outside. Drain, then salt the surface with a paper towel. The fish meatballs can now be served.

Pan-fried swordfish

Ingredients for 4 people:

- ✓ 2 slices of Swordfish
- ✓ 1 clove of Garlic
- ✓ 1 handful of Cherry Tomatoes
- ✓ 1 handful of Parsley
- ✓ Salt
- ✓ Pepper
- ✓ Extra Virgin Olive Oil
- ✓ 50 milliliters of white wine

Directions: 20 min

Slices of swordfish should first be cleaned. Rinse them under running water, dry them thoroughly, and gently cut off the outer skin. At this point, warm up some oil and a half-cut garlic clove in a pan. Swordfish should be cooked for two minutes in a pan with oil, salt, and pepper. Add the parsley cut on the other side of the slices. Add the cherry tomatoes sliced in half at this step and deglaze with wine. Serve the food hot and make sure the meat is cooked to the proper doneness.

Baked salmon with potatoes and tomatoes

Ingredients for 4 people:

- ✓ 4 Slices of Salmon
- ✓ 2 Potatoes
- ✓ 1 Onion
- ✓ 2 Tomatoes
- ✓ 1 teaspoon of Black Pepper grains
- ✓ Enough Salt
- ✓ 50 milliliters of White Wine
- ✓ Extra Virgin Olive Oil

Directions: 40 min

The potatoes should be peeled and chopped. After the water begins to boil, put them in a pot with water and simmer them for 10 to 15 minutes. Slice the onion thinly after cutting it in half. The tomatoes should be washed and sliced into large pieces. The black peppercorns should be crushed roughly in a mortar. Add the potatoes, tomatoes, onion, and two tablespoons of extra virgin olive oil to a baking dish. Season with salt and stir. Slices of salmon should be added, followed by mild salting and white wine. On top of the salmon slices, add the black peppercorns and lightly smash them. Bake for 20 to 25 minutes at 220 °C. After the fish has finished cooking, remove it from the oven and give it a few minutes to rest before servingr

Veal rolls with zucchini, ham and plums

Ingredients for 4 people:

- ✓ 400 g slices of veal rump
- ✓ 8 slices cooked ham
- ✓ extra virgin olive oil
- ✓ 1 zucchini
- ✓ 10 prunes
- ✓ 1/2 glass white wine vinegar
- ✓ 1 garlic clove
- ✓ pepper
- ✓ salt

Directions: 1h 10min

The veal slices should be placed on a spotless cutting board. Put cooked ham slices and zucchini ribbons inside. Roll the pieces up, then fasten them with a toothpick. Heat up a sizable frying pan. Let the garlic clove sizzle in the extra virgin olive oil. While cooking, add the prunes and let them flake. Water should be added. Put the rolls in the oven to cook after getting the cream, sealing them on all sides. Add white wine to the deglaze, then finish cookingr Serve the buns; two should be enough for each person. Put the plum sauce in and sprinkle fresh thyme on top.

Roast Beef

Ingredients for 6 People

- ✓ 800 gr of veal loin
- ✓ 2 Carrots
- ✓ 2 Celery stalks
- ✓ Olive Oil
- ✓ 1 Onion
- ✓ Red Wine
- ✓ Salt to taste
- ✓ Pepper to taste

Directions: 1 hour and 20 min

The fattiest section of the roast beef should be placed face down in a saucepan with 2-3 teaspoons of olive oil, heat it over medium heat, and brown for 5 minutes on each side over high heat. Prepare the chopped vegetables in the meantime. The carrots, celery, and onion should be cleaned, dried, and chopped finely before being placed in an oven dish with oil, salt, and pepper to taste, a coffee cup of water, and half a cup of red wine. Once the meat has finished browning, transfer it to the baking dish with the vegetables, and bake everything for 40 minutes at 180 degrees, rotating the meat and adding water as necessary. After 40 minutes, place the meat on a cutting board and slice it thinly while the vegetable combination is processed in a mixer to create a creamy sauce. The cream should still be somewhat liquid, so we put it on the stovetop over low heat to thicken it. Simply add the slices to the cream once it has cooled if the meat has already reached the ideal cooking temperature. In contrast, if the meat is still too rare for our tastes, we can simply submerge the slices of meat in the liquid vegetable mixture to finish cooking the meat and the cream at the same time, which will enhance the flavor of the dish. This is the roast beef recipe; all left to do is follow it and enjoy this superb second dish.

Meat Pie with Mushrooms and Speck

Ingredients for 4 People

- ✓ 600 g of minced beef
- ✓ 2 eggs
- ✓ 200 g of stale bread crumbs
- ✓ 2 cloves of garlic
- ✓ milk
- ✓ chopped parsley to taste
- ✓ 50 g of grated parmesan cheese or spicy pecorino cheese
- ✓ breadcrumbs to taste
- ✓ 120 g of speck in slices
- ✓ 400 g of champignon mushrooms
- ✓ extra virgin olive oil
- ✓ salt

Directions: 1 hour

Breadcrumbs should be broken up into little pieces and soaked in milk. Drain and squeeze the breadcrumbs once they have softened. Add the bread that has been squeezed dry, the eggs, the grated Parmesan and spicy pecorino, the parsley, the salt, and the minced meat to a bowl. After combining the ingredients with your hands, set the mixture aside. Utilizing a moist towel, gently clean the mushrooms. Cut them lengthwise into small pieces. An entire garlic clove should be browned in a small amount of oil. Add the mushrooms and chopped parsley, and cook for 5 minutes on high heat, stirring occasionally. Reduce the heat after removing the garlic clove and adding salt. Cook for ten more minutes on low heat, drizzle in hot water as necessary. Increase the heat when the food is about done, then dry the cooking liquid. Add breadcrumbs and oil to a baking pan to grease. Spread the remaining mixture over the bottom of the baking pan by flattening half of the mixture into the pan. Distribute a layer of mushrooms and then a layer of speck throughout the surface. Use the remaining dough to cover, level, and sprinkle some bread crumbs on top. To ensure there are no gaps, lightly press the pie's top. The oven to 180 degrees Celsius. For around 30-35 minutes, bake the meat pie with the mushrooms and speck in the preheated oven. After baking, remove the pie from the oven and allow it to cool before removing the mold. Serve the meat pie with speck, mushrooms, and a seasonal salad.

Roast lamb with potatoes

Ingredients for 4 People

- ✓ 1 kg of lamb in pieces (leg or shoulder)
- ✓ 1 red onion
- ✓ 1 kg of potatoes
- ✓ 4 tablespoons of extra virgin olive oil
- ✓ Bolognese brine
- ✓ 2 sprigs of rosemary
- ✓ 4 cloves of garlic
- ✓ Sardinian pecorino cheese

Directions: 2 hours

A 180°C oven is to be used. Oil a baking pan, then add the coarsely grated onion. The potatoes should be washed, peeled, and cut into wedges. To remove splinters, wipe the lamb with kitchen paper, paying specific attention to the areas where the bone cuts were made. After cleaning the rosemary, pick out the leaves, and use a crescent-shaped knife on a chopping board to slice them finely. In the oven dish, combine the lamb, potatoes, garlic cloves that have been peeled, and rosemary. After fully blending the ingredients, top the dish with a generous amount of grated Pecorino cheese and a dash of Bolognese sauce. The actual cooking time will vary depending on the size of the meat; bake for around 45 minutes. If required, preheat the grill near the end of the cooking to brown the meat and potatoes on the outside. To avoid the meat drying out and losing its juiciness, take care not to overcook it.

Chicken and Potato Doughnut

Ingredients for 4 People

- ✓ 1 kgr of potatoes
- ✓ 200 grs. of thinly sliced bacon
- ✓ 40 grs. of grated grana cheese
- ✓ 500 gr. of chicken breast slices
- ✓ salt
- ✓ pepper
- ✓ fresh thyme

Directions: 1 h 20 min

Peel and cut the potatoes into thin slices. The bacon should overflow the edges of a 24 cm doughnut-shaped mold as it is lined with it. Potatoes should be sliced very thinly. Potatoes should be spread out and then lightly seasoned with salt, pepper, and fresh thyme. (Pay heed to the salt; during cooking, the bacon will melt and season the potatoes, enhancing their flavor.) Chicken, grated Parmesan cheese, and potatoes should be layered, always seasoning between layers. Fold the bacon inward and close. For about an hour, bake at 180° in a preheated oven. Turn the doughnut onto an oven-safe pan, drain off all the accumulated fat, and then put it back in the oven for a few minutes to brown. This chicken and potato donut is prepared for consumption. Don't miss the collections below the image if you like potatoes and cooking beefy major dishes! You can choose from a variety of potato recipes and those from my chicken recipe library.

Bites of Meat

Ingredients for 4 People

- ✓ 700 gr. of sliced rump steak
- ✓ 1/ glass of oil
- ✓ 80 grs. of parmesan cheese
- ✓ black pepper to taste
- ✓ salt to taste
- ✓ 100 grs. of breadcrumbs
- ✓ 2 garlic cloves

Directions: 40 hours

Slice the rump steak into strips that are 2-3 cm broad. Place the meat to be marinated in a bowl filled with oil, salt, pepper, and thinly sliced garlic. Prepare the breadcrumbs with the grated Parmesan cheese and arrange them in a tray (or a large serving dish). One at a time, coat the pork strips in the breadcrumbs and Parmesan. The beef strips should be rolled up and pierced with a skewer stick. Place the skewers on top of the baking paper-lined bottom of a baking sheet. Crispy baking takes 15-20 minutes at 220 degrees.

Fillet Wellington Style

Ingredients for 8 People

- ✓ 1 kg veal tenderloin
- ✓ 100 g of prosciutto
- ✓ 400 g of champignon mushrooms
- ✓ 1 roll of puff pastry
- ✓ 1 yolk
- ✓ salt
- ✓ mustard to taste
- ✓ pepper
- ✓ extra virgin olive oil

Directions: 1h 30min

After giving the meat a salt and pepper seasoning, brown the meat in a pan with a few tablespoons of hot oil. Because you only need to prepare the edges rather than cook them. The fillet should be taken off the fire, brushed with mustard, and left to rest. Clean, slice, and mix the mushrooms with salt and pepper. When the mixture is uniform, cook the mushroom mousse in a skillet over very high heat until it dries.

Distribute the prosciutto pieces on a sheet of foil, season them, and then top them with the mushroom mousse. Placing the fillet on top will enable you to seal the entire area, creating a cylinder. Make sure to tightly seal the whole container to ensure that the components come into touch and form a candy. For 15 minutes, allow to rest in the refrigerator. The puff pastry is next; stretch it a little with a rolling pin, after which you should remove the fillet from the refrigerator, take off the foil, and lay it in the middle of the dough. Remove any extra dough before wrapping and sealing the edges of the sheet. For an additional five minutes, refrigerate with a foil cover. After taking off the foil, cut some ear-shaped slits in the puff pastry, brush with beaten egg yolk, and bake at 200°C for about 20 minutes. Your Wellington fillet will be done when golden brown; remove it from the oven, let it rest for a few minutes, then slice and serve it hot.

Fillet steak in mushroom crust

Ingredients for 6 People

- ✓ 800 g Mixed Mushrooms
- ✓ 200 g Pancetta
- ✓ 150 g Eggs
- ✓ 6 Slices of Bread
- ✓ Pepper
- ✓ 1 Salt
- ✓ Garlic One Clove
- ✓ 1 Tablespoon of Breadcrumbs

Directions: 40 min

Slice the mushroom heads after cleaning them and removing the lowest portion of the stem. After browning a garlic clove in a skillet, add the mushrooms and cook for 10 minutes, seasoning with salt and pepper halfway through. Cut the heat and let it cool. Take a beef tenderloin and carefully put salt, pepper, and olive oil on it with your hands. For 15 minutes, brown it in a casserole with a sprinkle of Olive Oil, rotating it frequently to ensure even cookingr Once the mushrooms have cooled, place them in a blender along with the breadcrumbs, bacon that has been diced, an egg, salt, and pepper. Blend until the mixture is uniform and smooth. Give it 30 minutes to rest in the refrigerator. Once the required amount of time has passed, roll the dough into a one-centimeter-thick sheet. After placing the fillet on top of the pastry and covering it with bacon slices, fold the pastry up tightly around the meat to seal the edges. Bake the fillet at 200 degrees for 20 minutes after placing it in a crust on a baking sheet lined with parchment paper. Turn off the oven as soon as the crust is golden, and allow the fillet to cool slightly before servingr

Meatballs with eggplant and caciocavallo cheese

Ingredients for 4 People

- ✓ 200 g of minced beef meat
- ✓ 150 g of minced pork meat
- ✓ 1/2 eggplant
- ✓ 2 slices of bacon
- ✓ 1 egg
- ✓ 3 spoons of grated caciocavallo cheese
- ✓ 50 ml of milk
- ✓ 4 tablespoons of breadcrumbs
- ✓ 1 garlic clove
- ✓ pepper
- ✓ salt

Directions: 35min

The process of making meatballs with caciocavallo cheese and eggplant is really quick and easy. The eggplant should first be gently washed and cubed. Place the tablespoons of extra virgin olive oil and the crushed garlic clove in a sizable frying pan. Put the skillet over medium heat, add the garlic, and when it turns golden, add the cubes of eggplant and mix, tossing occasionally. Add a pinch of salt to the cooked eggplant cubes after cooking them for about 10 minutes at medium heat. Break up the bacon slices, add them to a cup with the milk, and wait for it to soften while you let the eggplant cool. Put the combined minced meat, egg, warm eggplant, grated caciocavallo cheese, soaked and well-squeezed bread, and a pinch of salt and pepper in a large bowl. After thoroughly mixing everything to create a dense yet soft mixture, add the breadcrumbs and thoroughly combine. Take a small amount of the mixture and, using damp hands, shape it into a meatball about the size of a walnut. Repeat the process until all

of the dough has been used. You may start preparing the rest of the meal when the meatballs are done.

Take a large frying pan and fill it with a lot of sunflower oil. The meatballs should cook for 5 to 10 minutes in a heated pan over a medium-high flame, flipping them occasionally to ensure even cookingr The fire must not be too strong, or the meatballs will burn, and their interiors will stay raw. After the meatballs have finished cooking, place them on paper towels and season them with salt. Eat the food while it is still hot. It is nevertheless suggested to reheat this second beef dish in the pan (or the microwave) for a few minutes right before serving, even though it can be prepared in advance.

Chicken pizzaiola

Ingredients for 4 People

- ✓ 4 chicken breasts
- ✓ 100 g of mozzarella
- ✓ 500 ml of tomato puree
- ✓ 1/2 teaspoon of oregano
- ✓ 1 clove of garlic
- ✓ extra virgin olive oil
- ✓ salt
- ✓ pepper
- ✓ basil

Directions: 40 min

Start trimming the chicken breasts of excess fat and gristle before making the chicken pizzaiola. Once this is finished, thoroughly dry the breasts and salt and pepper them. Next, put the chicken breasts in a frying pan that has been preheated with 2 to 3 tablespoons of olive oil. Cook them till golden brown on both sides. Cooking completed, cover and set away. At this point, add a few basil leaves and one or two cloves of finely minced garlic to the same pan after adding the tomato puree. Add the salt, pepper, and dry oregano last. Over low heat, whisk the sauce every few minutes for approximately five minutes. After this, add the previously browned chicken breasts and simmer for 10 minutes at a moderate temperature. Add the mozzarella slices to the chicken breasts as a finishing touch. Cook the dish over low heat for about 5 minutes with the cover on. Serving the chicken hot with a sprinkle of freshly ground pepper and a few basil leaves for garnish. The pizzaiola with chicken is now ready for consumption.

Pork chops with balsamic vinegar

Ingredients for 4 People

- ✓ 1 yellow bell pepper
- ✓ 200 g pork meat
- ✓ 1 onion
- ✓ 2 tablespoons of 00 flour
- ✓ 1 garlic clove
- ✓ 2 tablespoons of tomato paste
- ✓ salt
- ✓ 20 ml of balsamic vinegar
- ✓ extra virgin olive oil

Directions: 1h 10 min

Cut the meat into bite-sized pieces before assembling the balsamic vinegar-glazed pork bites. After that, clean and treat the garlic. Put the meat cubes, minced garlic, and balsamic vinegar in a bowl. Stir while coveringr For around 30 minutes, let stand. Take a yellow bell pepper, clean it, and take the seeds out. Set it aside after cutting it into little cubes. Pick a white onion rather than a red one, clean it, and cut it into cubes. The onion can be diced, depending on desire. After the pork has rested for 30 minutes, add two tablespoons of flour and incorporate it into the balsamic vinegar pork pieces. The previously chopped onion is cooked in extra virgin olive oil in a deep pan. The diced peppers should then be added and let for two minutes to simmer. Balsamic vinegar and pork bites should be added. Cook for 5 minutes on low heat, stirring occasionally. Add the tomato paste, a dash of salt, and a ladle of water after the pork chunks have browned. Without a lid, stir and simmer for 10 minutes at low heat. Serve the hot pork bits with balsamic vinegar when they are finished cookingr

Chicken rolls with beer and speck

Ingredients for 3 People

- ✓ 6 slices of chicken breast
- ✓ 3 carrots
- ✓ 18 green beans
- ✓ 1 glass of beer
- ✓ 6 slices of speck
- ✓ 2 tablespoons of extra virgin olive oil
- ✓ 1 teaspoon of sugar
- ✓ 30 g of butter
- ✓ pepper
- ✓ salt

Directions: 1h10 min

Trim the green beans first, scrape the carrots, and wash the produce. Salt the boiling water, add the carrots and cook for 15 minutes. After adding the green beans, simmer for a further 10 minutes. After that, drain the vegetables and put them in a bowl with ice and cold water. Numerous sticks of carrots should be cut lengthwise. After lightly beating the chicken breast pieces, place them in the work area and sprinkle them with a little salt and pepper. Speck should be placed on each piece of chicken breast, and carrots and green beans should be equally distributed. The rolls should be rolled up and secured with a few toothpicks. The rolls are browned on all sides over high heat in a pan with heated oil and butter. Add sugar and simmer for an additional two to three minutes. Finally, add the beer, reduce the heat, and cover the pan to continue cooking the roulades for 30 minutes. Finally, take the top off, increase the heat, and let the sauce thicken until it slowly takes on a creamy consistency. With their sauce on the side, serve the chicken roulades with beer and bacon hot.

Chicken escalopes with mushrooms

Ingredients for 4 People

- ✓ 400 g of champignon mushrooms
- ✓ 400 g of chicken

- ✓ 40 g of butter
- ✓ vegetable broth
- ✓ extra virgin olive oil
- ✓ 1 garlic clove
- ✓ flour 00
- ✓ salt
- ✓ pepper

Directions: 45 min

You must first start with the foundation, which is the chicken, to prepare the chicken escalopes with mushrooms. If you have enough thin chicken pieces on hand, you can start flouring them immediately; otherwise, you must prepare the chicken first.

If you start with the breasts, you will need to trim the extra fat before slicing the pieces into thin enough pieces to cook quickly. After doing this, as previously said, coat the chicken slices thoroughly with 00 flour by dipping them in it. But get rid of the extra flour. Heat the butter in a sizable frying pan now. Add the chicken slices to the heated butter and cook for 3 to 4 minutes on each side or until golden. The time required for cooking will depend on how thick your slices are. The chicken is now prepared; save it for a minute. Spend your time on the mushrooms, which need to be thoroughly cleaned to eliminate the soil from their surface. It is preferable to rub them with a damp towel rather than wash them under running water unless doing so is very rapid. In actuality, they won't absorb water in this way. After slicing them, add the mushrooms to the frying pan where you cooked the chicken. Add a browned garlic clove to the oil before adding the thinly sliced mushrooms. Use salt, pepper, and optional parsley when seasoningr After removing the mushrooms, stir in a few tablespoons of warm vegetable stock. Your mushroom escalope will be covered in this creamy sauce. Add the mushrooms after the sauce thickens, then add the chicken breast slices. After a few more minutes of cooking, serve your chicken and mushrooms to your visitors.

Chicken chunks with arugula

Ingredients for 4 People

- ✓ 4 tablespoons of extra virgin olive oil

- ✓ 4 spring onions
- ✓ 800 g of chicken breast
- ✓ pepper
- ✓ salt
- ✓ flour 00
- ✓ 1/2 glass of white wine
- ✓ 2 spoons of balsamic vinegar
- ✓ 200 g of rocket

Directions: 45 min

Start with the spring onions, which need to be washed and sliced to make the chicken bits with arugula. Additionally, prepare the chicken breast by cutting it into 3 cm-wide cubes. Spring onions should be diced, added to hot oil in a nonstick skillet, and cooked for a few minutes. Add the flour-coated chicken cubes and cook them over high heat until they are evenly browned. Add turmeric or mustard powder to the flour to flavor the sauce. Sprinkle the chicken with salt and pepper before adding the white wine. After letting it go, add the balsamic vinegar. Over low heat, continue to cook for another 15 minutes. To prevent the chicken from sticking to the pan bottom, keep an eye on the cooking and stir it occasionally. After taking the pan off the heat, the dried and rinsed arugula leaves should also be added. Stir and set aside for a few minutes before serving, being sure to cover the skillet with a lid so that the heat from the chicken causes the arugula to wilt slightly. The arugula chicken bits should be served hot.

Chicken meatballs and fried potatoes

Ingredients for 4 People

- ✓ 400 g of chicken breast
- ✓ 4 potatoes
- ✓ 1 egg
- ✓ breadcrumbs
- ✓ extra virgin olive oil
- ✓ pepper
- ✓ salt

Directions: 1h15min

The chicken breasts must first be prepared to make the chicken and potato meatballs. Before being chopped into little pieces, these must first be stripped of any remaining surface fat and cartilage. The potatoes should then be thoroughly salted and boiled for 30 minutes. Potato cooking times can change depending on their size. You may heat them in the microwave if you want to hasten the cooking process. After that, the chicken pieces will be placed in the mixer and finely minced to create very fine ground meat. Remove the outer skin from the potatoes when finished cooking and purée them using the particular equipment. If you don't have access to this gear, mash the potatoes with a fork's tines, careful not to leave any lumps in the puree. Mix in the mashed potatoes after adding the chicken to the ground meat. Add the egg, salt, and pepper to taste, followed by the shredded cheese and a teaspoon or two of breadcrumbs. To prepare your meatballs, you must first create a mixture that is quite dense and not sticky. Take a tiny amount of dough and roll it between your hands to form the traditional meatball shape. After that, carefully brush the meatballs with extra virgin olive oil before dipping them in the breadcrumbs. Once you've completed this operation, keep going in this manner. Transfer to a nonstick frying pan with plenty of seed oil already heated. Your meatballs can be added after the oil is hot, and they should be cooked for about 4-5 minutes on each side so that they brown evenly. When the meatballs are ideally golden and ready, they are placed on paper towels to absorb any remaining oil. Simply serve them to your guests while they are still warm.

Arrosticini

Ingredients for 4 People

- ✓ 600 g of sheep meat
- ✓ 40 ml of extra virgin olive oil
- ✓ chilli pepper
- ✓ Rosemary
- ✓ salt

Directions: 20 min

You must start with the essential component, sheep meat, while making arrosticini. In actuality, you must eliminate any remaining fat from this. Although it's crucial to trim the meat of any excess fat, a bit should be left on for a smooth finish. In actuality, you will soften the flesh in this manner. Only after thoroughly cleaning the meat will you be able to slice it into pieces with a width of about 1 cm on each side. To preserve the unique appearance of this classic dish, the pieces of meat mustn't be too huge. Depending on your preference, when you have received your meat cubes, you will skewer them on either wooden or aluminum skewers. Add about 10 pieces of meat to each skewer as you create as many arrosticini as possible. If you do this at home, prepare the grill to cook them on in the interim. Rosemary sprigs, salt, and pepper should all be sprinkled over the meat before cookingr After this is finished, the meat must be cooked over hot coals for a few minutes. Depending on the size of the meat pieces you have cut, cooking times will vary. The meat should have a light outer crust and be perfectly done. Once prepared, serve them hot to your visitors so they may savor them at their best. You might serve them with a green salad or cherry tomatoes. Rolls made in the Sicilian fashion are a great alternative.

Veal escalope with trifle zucchini

Ingredients for 2 People

- ✓ 6 slices of veal
- ✓ 2 zucchini
- ✓ 3 spoons of flour
- ✓ 20 ml of red wine
- ✓ 1 garlic clove
- ✓ parsley
- ✓ salt

Directions: 35min

Wash the zucchini and slice them into tiny circles to make veal escalopes. The crushed garlic clove and the extra virgin olive oil tablespoons should be placed in a medium-sized frying pan. The heat should be set to a moderate flame. Add the zucchini slices and sauté for a few minutes over high heat when the garlic is browned. Then, reduce the heat and let the zucchini slices cook until they are soft. Transfer the zucchini to a platter, then top with freshly chopped parsley. The veal escalopes should then be made while the zucchini is kept warm and set aside. Cut the veal slices in half or into triangles; flour the veal slices; and re-heat the pan in which the zucchini was cooked. When the pan is heated, add a drizzle of extra virgin olive oil and cook the beef slices, flipping them to ensure equal cookingr Red wine should be used to coat the meat, then allowed to evaporate. The meat should cook for at least 5 minutes after you add the zucchini halfway through, arranging them evenly over the meat. Once cooked, taste the meat for salt and keep it warm until you're ready to eat. Baked potatoes can be served as a side dish with this entrée.

Spanish Main Courses

Baked Chicken Thighs with Potatoes

Ingredients for 4 people

- ✓ 4 chicken thighs, with their thighs and drumsticks
- ✓ 4 potatoes
- ✓ 1 onion
- ✓ 2 carrots
- ✓ 2 tomatoes
- ✓ 4 cloves of garlic
- ✓ 1 red bell pepper
- ✓ Dried thyme
- ✓ Dried rosemary
- ✓ salt and pepper
- ✓ olive oil

Directions: 1h 20Min

The potatoes and onion must be peeled. Slice the potatoes, carrots, and onion into thin strips. Julienne the onion. We also sliced the bell pepper and tomato into large chunks. Place the whole, unpeeled garlic cloves and other ingredients in the bottom of a baking dish and distribute them equally. Add the chicken thighs to the vegetables after salting and peppering them thoroughly. A little glass of water should be poured over them. The addition of some dried thyme and rosemary will give the thighs a special touch. Season the thighs with salt and pepper. We add the baking sheet when the oven has been preheated to 200°C. The chicken thighs are left here for 20 to 25 minutes or until this side is well-browned. At this point, take the baking sheet out of the oven and flip each chicken thigh over. Add a little extra oil, dried rosemary, thyme, salt, and pepper to the other side. Add a bit more water if the tray's bottom is drying out. If not, there is no need for it. Re-bake for approximately another 25 minutes in the oven. Until the vegetables are soft and the chicken is well-browned and cooked throughout.

Chicken Meatballs in Spanish Sauce

Ingredients for 4 people

- ✓ 1kg chicken minced meat
- ✓ 2 eggs
- ✓ crumbs of bread (or 1 slice of sliced bread)
- ✓ 1 dash of milk
- ✓ 3 cloves of garlic
- ✓ 2 onions
- ✓ 1 liter of chicken broth
- ✓ 1 tablespoon of flour
- ✓ 1/2 teaspoon cumin
- ✓ 1/2 glass of white wine

- ✓ A handful of chopped parsley
- ✓ 25g of breadcrumbs
- ✓ flour
- ✓ salt and pepper
- ✓ oil

Directions: 80 min

We add the baking sheet when the oven has been preheated to 200°C. The chicken thighs are left here for 20 to 25 minutes or until this side is well-browned. At this point, take the baking sheet out of the oven and flip each chicken thigh over. Add a little extra oil, dried rosemary, thyme, salt, and pepper to the other side. Add a bit of additional water if the tray's bottom appears to be drying out. If not, it is not necessary. Rebake in the oven for about another 25 minutes. Until the chicken is thoroughly cooked and the vegetables are tender. So that the outside of them is thoroughly coated in flour; after all the meatballs have been formed, we cook them in lots of oil. To prevent them from drying out too much, the aim is to seal them on the exterior while leaving the interior raw. On absorbent paper, set aside. Now pour a thin layer of the oil we used to sear the meatballs into a large frying pan. Add the final, finely chopped clove of garlic after heating on low. Allow it to cook for a few minutes so it doesn't brown. Add the onion, diced. It is stirred often, adding salt and pepper as needed, and cooked for about 15 minutes at medium heat. Increase the heat after adding the white wine once it is soft.

Decrease the alcohol's evaporation. It should only take a few minutes. After adding the chicken broth, we combine everything in a blender or mixer at home. The sauce will be thoroughly ground until it is smooth. Lacking any bumps. We go back to the pan and, if required, add more chicken broth. We require a sauce that is quite liquid but still has substance. The meatballs are also added, and we ensure that each one has absorbed the sauce well. Allow everything to cook for a further 10 minutes at a low temperature so that the meatballs can finish cooking inside and the flavors can meld.

Eggplants Stuffed with Minced Meat

Ingredients for 4 people

- ✓ 4 eggplants
- ✓ 1 onion
- ✓ 2 cloves of garlic
- ✓ 1 red bell pepper
- ✓ 300g pork minced meat
- ✓ 500g of crushed tomato
- ✓ 300g veal minced meat
- ✓ 1 teaspoon dried thyme
- ✓ 1 teaspoon dried rosemary
- ✓ 70g flour
- ✓ 70g butter
- ✓ 1 teaspoon nutmeg
- ✓ 100g grated cheese
- ✓ 1l of whole milk
- ✓ pepper
- ✓ olive oil
- ✓ salt

Directions: 105 minutes

Cut off the eggplant's stem. Then use a knife to cut each piece in half lengthwise without getting to the skin's surface. To achieve cuts "in the form of a grid," we make some cuts, first lengthwise and then widthwise. Once this is finished, place the eggplants on a baking sheet, drizzle the flesh with a bit of oil (the eggplant will quickly absorb it), and bake for 30 minutes at 180°C. We wait about 20 minutes before moving on. After that, take them out and give them a moment to warm up. After that, scoop out the pulp while leaving the peel intact. It will separate extremely readily because it has only half-baked. Olive oil is heated in a big frying pan over low heat. Add the finely chopped red bell pepper, onion, and garlic once it is hot. Add salt and pepper to taste, then simmer for 15 minutes while stirringr Add the previously sliced eggplant flesh after 15 minutes. Add the minced pork and beef, along with the remaining vegetables. The meat is crumbled with a wooden spoon so that it is not in very large pieces and combined with the other ingredients. Cook for two to three minutes or until the raw color disappears. The crushed tomato and teaspoons of thyme and rosemary can now be added. Although oregano can be used in place of these two spices, I prefer the combo's flavor. After thoroughly combining all the ingredients, we let them simmer over low heat for around 30 minutes. Until the tomato and minced meat have completely lost all their released water, make the béchamel sauce as it evaporates. You can also use olive oil in place of the butter in another high saucepan. Once the butter has melted, add the floor for about three minutes, mix and toast. "Roux" is the name of this blend. Following this, we gradually add the milk. 200 ml should be added, and 200 ml should be mixed into the roux. Once this is finished, add 200 ml more and stir once more.

Continue doing this until all the milk has been utilized, at which point a thin béchamel sauce will be produced. After which, stir in a teaspoon of nutmegr The only task remaining is to stuff the eggplants after everything else has been completed. Take the shells and generously stuff them with the prepared fillingr Each shell may have as much filler as desired. The most crucial thing is to complete everythingr After that, we drizzle béchamel sauce over each stuffed eggplant. Finally, we top them with cheese and grated cheese before reintroducing them to the oven and setting the grill to 200°C. We keep them here for ten minutes long enough for the cheese to grate.

Zucchini Meatballs

Ingredients for 4 people

- ✓ 5 zucchini
- ✓ 2 eggs
- ✓ 2 cloves of garlic
- ✓ 1/2 onion
- ✓ 30g bread crumbs
- ✓ chopped parsley
- ✓ 1/2 teaspoon ground cumin
- ✓ Flour
- ✓ Oil

Directions: 30 min

Grate the zucchini, including the peel. Grate some zucchini and place it inside a fresh towel. We tightly encapsulate and squeeze it within the same one. We want them to lose as much water as they can. Place the zucchini in a basin without any water. Add the finely diced onion, garlic cloves, and parsley. Use your hands to thoroughly combine the ingredients, then add the eggs, breadcrumbs, and cumin to create a homogeneous dough. You can add a few more breadcrumbs if you notice that it is too "liquid" to shape afterward. Create ping-pong ball-sized balls out of the dough. They should be dredged in flour and fried in lots of oil. The goal is to fry it just long enough to allow the outside to brown without overheating the within. In other words, it will be fried quickly at a high temperature. Remove and set on paper that is absorbent.

Baked Lamb Shoulder with Potatoes

Ingredients for 4 people

- ✓ 2 lamb shoulders of about 500g each
- ✓ 3 potatoes
- ✓ 1 onion
- ✓ 2 cloves of garlic
- ✓ salt and pepper
- ✓ olive oil

Directions: 45 min

The lamb shoulder should be placed in an oven tray first. Then we give it a drink of water. We sprinkle it with salt and pepper, then drizzle oil to finish. White wine is sometimes added, but I prefer the flavor of this roast just the way it is. An excellent suckling lamb, please. If any powerful ingredients do not diminish its taste, you may include them. Afterward, we roast it for about 35 minutes at 230 C in the oven. Peel the potato and do that while it bakes. After that, we divided it into slices that were one centimeter thick. Fillet and peel the garlic cloves. We also cut it into thin slices, in other words. The onion is treated in the same way. It is peeled and then sliced into strips. The garnish is all set aside. Remove the lamb shoulder from the oven when it has cooked for 35 minutes. Place all of the garnish on it after removing it from the tray. Place it there, and then add the salt. Reposition the lamb shoulder and add another glass of water to the top. Add some salt and pepper and another dab of oil before servingr After that, put it back in the oven for about half an hour.

Potato Omelette

Ingredients for 4 people

- ✓ Ingredients
- ✓ 500 gr of unpeeled potatoes
- ✓ 5 eggs
- ✓ 1 medium onion
- ✓ Salt to taste
- ✓ Olive oil

Directions: 50 min

Peel the potatoes, then cut them into not-too-thin slices or wedges. Julienne-strip the onion after chopping it. With lots of olive oil, heat a sizable non-stick frying pan that can accommodate all components. Add the potatoes and simmer for 5 minutes at medium heat. Onions are then added. Put the lid on and slightly reduce the heat. Stirring occasionally, cook the mixture for 30 minutes or until the potato is tender and gently browned. The onion shouldn't be brown, but it should be transparent and almost golden. Place the potato and onion mixture in a sizable plastic container after removing them. You will now add salt, to taste, and mix to distribute it evenly. Beat the eggs thoroughly after chopping them in a smaller plastic container. Next, combine the potatoes, onion, and eggs with the other ingredients.

You will now complete preparing the omelet. Look at the photographs to see what you need: the mixture must curdle and assume the appropriate appearance. Put a little olive oil in the pan you used to sauté the items before adding the mixture. Cook it for one minute. Then turn the tortilla over. Simply flip the pan over its lid with the aid of a large plate or the pan's lid, then carefully press the tortilla back into the pan to finish cooking on the other side. Give the tortilla another minute to set. Simply turn off the heat at this point, then carefully take the tortilla out of the pan. It may be set down on a big dish, a platter, or a wooden board.

How To Make Garlic Shrimp

Ingredients for 2 people

- ✓ 450 gr of peeled shrimp
- ✓ 5 large garlic
- ✓ 1 chili pepper
- ✓ 100 ml of olive oil
- ✓ 50 ml of white wine.
- ✓ Fresh parsley
- ✓ Salt

Directions: 20 min

What kind of shrimp do you have first, though? If they are still whole and fresh, you must cut off the head, tail, and legs before peeling them and removing the intestines, which are a thin black thread. Finally, quickly wash them in some water. If you have peeled shrimp instead, all you need to do is wash them. Prepare the garlic and let them drain in a strainer. Slice the garlic, but don't make them too thin or tiny. Cook them in extremely hot oil until they get a light brown color. Be careful not to burn the slices; doing so would impart an unwelcome bitter flavor to this lovely dish. Oh, and if you want spicy food, you can choose to sauté the garlic and medium-sized chopped chili pepper. Take it as a cue to add the shrimp when you notice the first hints of browning in the garlic. With enthusiasm, brown them in this oil. Since it should only last five minutes, savor every last bit of this heavenly aroma. I'm done. Overcooking will result in the soft shrimp meat becoming rough. Garlic-dyed prawns should be quickly covered in the wine after adding a pinch of salt and stirringr For a few more minutes, cook it on high heat to allow the alcohol to evaporate. Sprinkle some fresh parsley over the shrimp to finish it off. You can also include a dash of pepper if you like. Stir well, then pour them into an earthenware casserole while they're still hot, if possible boilingr However, it doesn't matter if you don't have an earthenware casserole; the key is to serve the food hot.

Biscayne Codfish

Ingredients for 4 people

- ✓ 1 kg of cod cut in thick loins

- ✓ 4 skinless bell peppers
- ✓ Pulp of 2 choricero peppers
- ✓ 1 small tomato
- ✓ 1 medium onion
- ✓ 2 cloves of garlic
- ✓ A couple of tablespoons of flour for sealing the fish
- ✓ Olive oil
- ✓ Salt

Directions: 1h

In a deep container, desalt the cod 24 hours beforehand. Water should permanently be changed. In a big pot, coat the fish with flour and seal it with oil. Place aside. Grind the bell peppers, choricero peppers and tomato in a blender. Sauté the onion and garlic, sliced into small cubes, in the same pan where you seared the salmon. Add the previously ground sauce and a dash of salt to the pan, and cook for 30 minutes on low heat. Cover the pan and simmer the cod pieces for 15 to 20 minutes. Serve after removing from heat. You can add chopped parsley leaves and more olive oil.

Chorizo in Cider

Ingredients for 6 people

- ✓ 1 and 1/2 liters of natural Asturian cider without gas
- ✓ 3 bay leaves
- ✓ 10 Asturian chorizo sausages
- ✓ 5 cloves of garlic optional

Directions: 55 min

If you've opted to utilize garlic, we'll start by getting it ready. Simply peel them, and then slice them into extremely thin pieces. Then, to begin cooking, we will choose a decent pot or a (very) large frying pan. At first, we'll allow it to warm up a little bit before adding the chorizos to seal them partially. On each side, let them fry for a few minutes at medium heat. To ensure better internal cooking, we can shape certain bites with the tines of a fork. As we go, we retrieve the chorizos and add the small pieces of garlic to the same frying pan. With the leftover fat, we will sauté them for a minute. Skip this step if you choose not to use the garlic. We will now add the cider and bay leaves to the same panThe

fire will be fueled more vigorously to begin to boil the liquid. Add the chorizos once the cider has begun to boil. Half the heat is used for cooking them for 30 minutes. The reduction of the cider will also be visible. We can set up a chopping board while our meal cooks. This is so that we may remove the chorizos from the cooking process and cut them into slices a few centimeters thick. When removing the chorizos, there is no need to shut off the pot. We can continue to use modest heat. We will slice the chorizo and add it to the cider sauce. We will also include any remaining oil in the cooking if there is some on the cutting board. Give the chorizo some time to rehydrate. Next, switch the heat off.

Cod in Pil Pil Sauce

Ingredients for 4 people

- ✓ 4 pieces of fresh cod with skin (not too thick, preferably)
- ✓ 400 milliliters of olive oil
- ✓ 6 cloves of garlic
- ✓ 1 chili pepper
- ✓ Salt optional

Directions: 45 min

We will start by peeling the garlic and slicing it into skinny slices using a sharp knife. The chili pepper will also be cleaned and cut into fillets with a knife. The slices of garlic and chili should then be cooked in olive oil in a saucepan or frying pan until they are brown but not roasted or crispy. Once they have reached this stage, turn off the heat and drain the vegetables using a strainer. Taking the pan off the heat source is preferable to allow the oil to cool slightly. It makes no difference if the heat is off because there is always a lingering heat. We will accomplish this because, while reusing the oil, we intend to emulsify it with the fish juices rather than heat it to the point where it fries the fish instead of having the intended result. If the cod isn't previously cleaned, we'll do that next. We need to confirm that it is dry and bone-free. If the fish is not desalted cod, we will sprinkle a little salt on each piece before turning the oil back on over low heat. After that, fry each piece of fish with the skin facing up.

There shouldn't be any overlap between the fish sections. The fish will release its juices as it cooks. With the aid of a spoon, we will lightly coat the upper portion, which includes the skin, in oil from the pan to cook it. While we work on this endeavor, the oil will combine with the cod's gelatin to create the pil pil "sauce." You'll observe that it starts to thicken and somewhat curdle. While the fish is cooking, we may also move the case around a little and swirl the oil with a spatula. If the cod fillets are thin, it can only take a few minutes of cooking on one side for the fish to be done.

On the other hand, if they are thick chunks, you might need to flip them over toward the end of cooking to ensure that all sides are cooked through you choose the latter, be sure to cook the skin side of the meat quickly. Make sure the fish doesn't disintegrate above anything else. You can choose to remove the cod when it's done cooking and keep blending the fluids so that the pil pil thickens even more, depending on the consistency you desire for the sauce. If you'd like, you can also add a little extra oil. In any case, make sure to whisk everything thoroughly. If required, taste the pil pil and adjust the seasoningr Return the garlic, chile, and cod, if you removed it, to the cooking once the sauce has reached the required consistency. Serve the meal right away after they have cooled to the pil pil's temperature. The point is that it reaches the diners with the oil still very hot.

Baked Suckling Pig

Ingredients for 8 people

- ✓ 1 whole suckling pig or suckling pig of maximum 5 kilos.
- ✓ 4 cloves of garlic
- ✓ A sprig of fresh parsley
- ✓ 2 tablespoons of pork lard
- ✓ 2 bay leaves
- ✓ Coarse salt to taste
- ✓ Peppercorns to taste
- ✓ Water
- ✓ 150 milliliters of optional wine
- ✓ Several sprigs of rosemary optional

Directions: 3hs 20min

The suckling pig must be entire but thoroughly washed before beginning this dish. To avoid doing all this labor at home, ask your supplier or butcher to give it to you completely cleaned. This entails taking the animal's offal or entrails out and only cutting it longitudinally underneath. From this point on, we will use the fork tip to pierce the suckling pig's meat. We shall accomplish this in a broad way across its surface. To enable heat to escape while cooking is the goal. If not, it would become entrapped and cause bubbles in the pig's skin. You can also use the point of a sharp knife to make a few small cuts in the skin as an alternative.

Afterward, we'll set the meat aside while preparing the seasoningr But first, we'll turn the oven's temperature up to 180 degrees. According to tradition, a mortar is required if you truly want to prepare the suckling pigr The garlic cloves will be placed there after being peeled and the tips removed. In addition, 4 or 5 gr of pepper and a dash of coarse salt will be added to taste (preferably fresh, which will give more flavor to the seasoning). Finally, thoroughly rinse the parsley, drain it, and separate the leaves before adding them to the mortar. The entire combination will next be ground until it forms a more or less uniform paste. After that, add the lard to the mortar and stir everythingr This spice will coat the suckling pig's entire surface and an ovenproof dish. The suckling pig should then be placed in the serving dish. We have a few possibilities because, traditionally, the animal is never placed directly on the dish's bottom. The first is to obtain several rosemary sprigs and cover the dish's bottom before putting the piglet on top. The meat will also acquire a delightful fragrance as a result. The weight of the suckling pig can be spread over two moistened wooden spoons placed at the bottom of the dish as an alternative, more primitive solution. The final and most contemporary solution is swapping the dish for an oven rack. However, it is best to set a baking tray lower so that you may catch any liquids the suckling pig may discharge while bakingr I typically bake the suckling pig with a small amount of liquid, which should be put at the bottom of the baking dish or on the tray underneath the rack to prevent it from drying out while cookingr I combine 200 milliliters of water with 150 milliliters of red wine (white wine may also be used). Some chefs favor using nothing but water. Keeping the piglet hydrated is the final goal, but the wine will also impart flavor. The bay leaves will then be added to the wine and water mixture. Then, after placing the suckling pig inside the oven, we will reduce the temperature to 150 degrees. Place the dish so that it is directly in the center of the oven and that heat is emitted from above and below. Cook the suckling pig for one and a half hours. We'll check the oven often to ensure the liquid hydrating the meat hasn't run out. Some chefs favor using nothing but water. Keeping the piglet hydrated is the final goal, but the wine will also impart flavor. The bay leaves will then be added to the wine and water mixture. Then, after placing the suckling pig inside the oven, we will reduce the temperature to 150 degrees. Place the dish so that it is directly in the center of the oven and that heat is emitted from above and below. Cook the suckling pig for one and a half hours. We'll check the oven often to ensure the liquid hydrating the meat hasn't run out. Before putting the suckling pig back in the range, you might choose to brush it with a bit of additional butter. When we increase the oven temperature, the suckling pig will bake for one and a half hours at 180 degrees. As before, we will check the suckling pig periodically to ensure that the liquid does not run out, and if it does, we will bathe the meat in the additional liquid before it settles to the bottom of the dish. We'll shock the suckling pig with heat when this period is up. This is what will toast and crisp up the skin. The suckling pig will simply cook for the final 15 minutes at 200 degrees once we raise the temperature. The portion of the piglet we want to toast should be left facing up for this process step. The suckling pig will then need to be turned one more. I'm done now. The suckling pig will be ready to eat once this cooking period is over. Enjoy!

Baked Lamb

Ingredients for 2 people

- ✓ 1 shoulder of lamb from one to one and a half kilos
- ✓ Salt to taste
- ✓ 4 cloves of garlic
- ✓ Provencal herbs
- ✓ Ground pepper to taste
- ✓ 2 small white onions

- ✓ Vegetable oil
- ✓ 1 glass of dry white wine

Directions: 1h 20 min

To use the tray as a base for the lamb, we will first remove it from the oven. We'll then turn the oven's temperature up to 180 degrees Celsius. Peel the garlic cloves, crush them, or, if necessary, finely chop them before beginning to work on the meat. We'll use this to peel and cut the onions into rings. Before placing the lamb on the oven tray, I advise greasing the surface. After that, arrange the lamb shoulder that has been washed and season with salt and pepper to taste. The meat should next have oil drizzled over it. Massage the meat to evenly distribute the oil, combined with the salt and pepper you've already used, over the entire surface. After that, evenly scatter the garlic over the entire lamb. Lightly massage it one more to help it adhere to the surface and absorb the previously applied oil.

Along with the onion rings and a teaspoon of Provencal herbs, crown the lamb. The wine will be used to wash the lamb, and we'll ensure the onions are well covered. After that, we'll transfer the tray to the preheated oven and cook the lamb for either 60 or 90 minutes, depending on how much meat is on it. We will return to the oven halfway through the cooking period to turn the meat and cover it with the cooking liquid (the wine plus the juice given off by the meat). We can include a little water if additional liquid is required. Increase the oven's temperature to 220 degrees when the cooking period has ended. The lamb will also be turned once more, and the juice or broth on the tray will be used to hydrate it. Once more, if there is not enough liquid, some water can be added. To allow the skin to brown and become slightly crispy, we will continue to cook the lamb for an additional 20 minutes (if you wish, you can return halfway through this additional time to return and baste the meat again). I'm done now. The lamb is now prepared for cutting and servingr

Octopus À La Gallega

Ingredients for 4 people

- ✓ 1 medium octopus

- ✓ 3 potatoes chopped in pieces
- ✓ 1 tablespoon of paprika powder
- ✓ 1 medium onion
- ✓ 2 bay leaves
- ✓ Sea salt to taste
- ✓ Olive oil to taste

Directions: 40 minutes

The previous evening, thaw the octopus in a medium pot in the fridge. When it is time to cook it, add a medium onion, bay leaves, and a sprinkle of salt to a large pot of water once it has thawed. To prevent the octopus from losing its skin while cooking, you will "scare the octopus" when boiling the water. With care to avoid burning your fingers, hold the octopus by the head and dip its tentacles into the water for a few seconds. Remove it, then repeat the procedure twice more (three in total). Depending on its size, allow it to cook in the pot after being "scared" for about 30 to 40 minutes. In the meantime, boil the peeled and chopped potatoes in a smaller saucepan. Take them off the heat when they are finished cookingr Take the cooked octopus out of the water, give it some time to rest, and then cut it into pieces using a knife or pair of kitchen shears. Finally, arrange the chopped potatoes and octopus on a plate or wooden board and top with a generous amount of olive oil, sea salt, and paprika. Enjoy fantastic Galician cuisine by thoroughly combining all the ingredients.

Cod Shells in Green Sauce

Ingredients for 4 people

- ✓ ½ kg of fresh or desalted cod shells
- ✓ 2 large garlic cloves
- ✓ 1 tablespoon of wheat flour
- ✓ 1 white onion
- ✓ 1 cup of dry white wine
- ✓ 1 and 1/2 cup fish stock
- ✓ 1 chili pepper
- ✓ A bunch of fresh parsley
- ✓ Olive oil
- ✓ Salt to taste optional

Directions: 30 minutes

The cod shells must be clean before you begin this recipe. Recall that we stated at the beginning of this note that if they are salted cod shells, we must first conduct the desalination technique. We'll need to remove the skin and beard from this portion of the cod (although some cooks prefer not to remove the latter). We'll put the cod shells aside for the time being and focus on the garlic cloves instead. After peeling them, we'll slice them into really tiny bits. The onion will also be similarly chopped into small pieces. We'll also thoroughly wash the parsley (I also soak it in water with a dash of vinegar for at least five minutes). We will next drain it and finely slice the leaves. After that, we'll reserve it. The chili pepper will next be washed and cut into ribbons. We will warm a generous amount of olive oil in a conventional saucepan, casserole, or nonstick frying pan. The garlic, onion, and chili pepper will all be cooked there. We will do this over medium-low heat to prevent the garlic from browningr We will only cook it for a short time. To continue, we will thoroughly combine the flour with the preparation. The previously cleaned cod shells will be added after that. We'll let them simmer in the oil for a few minutes over low heat. We'll achieve this by frequently (and very delicately) stirring the ingredients in the pan with a cooking spoon or by hand. The parsley and wine will then be added. Again, carefully combine everything, then wait a few minutes for the alcohol to evaporate completely. Pour in the fish stock after that. Combine thoroughly with the remaining ingredients, then cook for five minutes. We will now taste the sauce and, if necessary, add a little salt to adjust the seasoningr We must pay attention to this stage if we utilize fresh cod shells instead of salted ones. That's it. The cod shells are currently prepared for servingr

Cod Ajoarriero

Ingredients for 2 people

- ✓ 400 gr of desalted codfish
- ✓ 3 ripe tomatoes
- ✓ 1 bell pepper
- ✓ 1 green bell pepper
- ✓ 3 cloves of garlic
- ✓ 1 spring onion
- ✓ Salt to taste

- ✓ Olive oil
- ✓ Fresh parsley leaves for garnish

Directions: 40 minutes

The cod must first be desalinated the day before. Set aside after finely chopping the green bell pepper and spring onion. The red bell pepper can be chopped into strips or cubes, depending on your preference. Make thin slices of garlic. To make a paste, grate the tomato or pulse it in a food processor. Avoid going overboard; making a sauce is not necessary. Sauté the garlic in a generous amount of olive oil in a heated frying pan or casserole. Add the spring onion and green bell pepper, and simmer for a few minutes. Ensure that it doesn't burn. Add the fish, either crumbled or diced, and simmer for a few minutes. Add the smashed tomatoes and the bell pepper. Let each ingredient simmer in its own sauce. Add a little water if needed. Reduce the heat, season it with salt, and let it simmer for 15 to 20 minutes. Your cod ajoarriero is ready at this point. Add some parsley leaves to it before servingr

Hake in Green Sauce

Ingredients for 2 people

- ✓ 1 cup of dry white wine
- ✓ 1 medium white onion
- ✓ A couple of cloves of garlic
- ✓ 3 cups of fish fumet
- ✓ Olive or vegetable oil
- ✓ Several sprigs of fresh parsley
- ✓ 4 hake wheels a couple of centimeters thick
- ✓ 2 tablespoons of wheat flour
- ✓ Salt

Directions: 40 minutes

We'll start by taking care of the parsley and getting it ready. It will be thoroughly washed, dried, and the leaves will be carefully chopped. To get the equivalent of two-thirds of a cup of chopped leaves. We shall save this element for the time beingr Let's deal with the garlic next. Crush or finely cut the cloves after peeling them. Next, add a little oil to a big frying pan or saucepan and heat it over medium heat. The pieces of garlic will be added there and briefly cooked. We'll sauté them for a few minutes, tossing them constantly to keep them from burning until they turn golden. The flour is then added, and the garlic and oil are combined. Add the wine once these components have been thoroughly combined. After that, add the broth and mix one more. Add the parsley after the sauce has been cooking for a few minutes. It's time to place each hake slice properly on the casserole or pan's bottom. To perform this task, it is advised to use a wooden spatula while attempting to cause the fish as little harm as possible. Before turning each wheel to cook on the other side, wait three to four minutes. They should only be cooked for a short time, similar to the first side. It's crucial to carefully monitor the cooking time because if we rush things, the wheels can start to come off. The hake pieces will be taken out of the saucepan. We will taste the remaining sauce to make sure it is properly seasoned before drizzling it over them. If extra salt is required, add it and stir well.

Rabbit In Salmorejo

Ingredients for 8 people

- ✓ 2 kilos of rabbit cleaned and cut into pieces
- ✓ 8 cloves of garlic
- ✓ 1 hot pepper
- ✓ 1 spoonful of paprika of La Vera
- ✓ Cumin powder to taste
- ✓ Coarse salt to taste
- ✓ 350 milliliters of white wine
- ✓ 200 milliliters of wine vinegar
- ✓ Olive oil
- ✓ Thyme to taste
- ✓ Oregano powder to taste

Directions: 1 hour 20 minutes

To start, we'll presume that the rabbit has already been washed and prepped for use in this dish. If so, we will put it on hold for the time beingr Continue by keeping in mind that if you want to make this dish the truly traditional method, you will need a sizable mortar. After peeling the garlic cloves, we will set them there. We'll also wash the hot pepper, cut off the remaining branch, flake it up, and put it in the mortar. A teaspoon of coarse salt and one more spoonful of paprika will also be added. Then, we'll blend everything till it's homogeneous. Once we get to this stage, we will add the vinegar and combine it with the paste. A teaspoon of cumin, a spoonful of olive oil, and a dash of salt will be diluted in the marinade once the vinegar and wine have been combined (then we will taste and add more, if necessary). When the marinade is prepared, we'll pour it into a big bowl and add the rabbit pieces. Then, sprinkle them with a teaspoon of thyme and oregano powder. Finally, we'll make sure the mixture has adequately covered them. We'll cover the container and put it in the fridge after that. Although the rabbit should marinade for at least 4 hours, you can leave it overnight. Remove the container from the refrigerator, open it, remove the rabbit pieces, and drain them after the marinating period (preferably the day after the salmorejo is prepared). Reserve the remainder of the marinade at this time.

Next, heat a small amount of oil in a sizable saucepan or frying pan. We'll use it when it's hot to brown the rabbit parts. We'll move them around so that their entire surface will cook. Only the amount of time required to brown the rabbit's surface will be delayed (about 10 minutes in total). The remaining salmorejo will next be used to bathe it. We'll leave the pot or pan uncovered and cook it for 10 minutes. After this period of time is over, we'll flip the rabbit pieces over, cover the pan, and reduce the heat to the lowest setting to finish cooking the meal for another 30 minutes or so, or until the rabbit is soft. Our salmorejo-style rabbit will be ready to eat when the cooking process is finished. Have a nice supper.

Galician Empanada

Ingredients for 6 people

- ✓ 500 gr of strong flour
- ✓ 1 tablespoon of salt
- ✓ 1 egg yolk to glaze the dough.
- ✓ 150 ml of olive oil
- ✓ 2 cups of water
- ✓ 30 gr of baker's yeast

Directions: 1 hour 50 minutes

Pour the yeast and water into a basin, and whisk until the yeast is completely dissolved. Allow standing for a while. In the meantime, combine the flour and salt in a separate basin. Create a hole in the center of the flour, then fill it with the yeast-infused water. The next step is to continue mixing with your hands until you have a homogeneous paste. (Using a bowl for this step is optional.) To make things easier, use an electric mixer (or, for technology enthusiasts, move the flour directly to a table or work area). This uniformly textured dough will need to have oil added to it.

Once more, you must continue knitting the dough until the fat is thoroughly incorporated and it no longer sticks to your hands. We will now set up this dough for a period of restingr It must be placed on a greased surface, covered with a cloth, and left for an hour. Due to the yeast's effect, the empanada dough should have significantly expanded after that hour of rest. Just divide it into two equal portions and use one for the top layer and the other for the bottom of the empanada. Place the dough on a work surface or table from one of the portions. To achieve a consistent thickness, roll out with a rolling pin. We now require the baking pan for the empanada. Place the dough flattened with the rolling pin on the greased and floured surface. Make holes in the dough with a fork to stop air pockets from forming due to the heat. You must distribute the stew over that layer of dough once it is prepared (I'll explain below). The rolling-pin spreading process will be repeated for the second half of the dough. After the stuffing stew is set, it will be placed over the first portion. To create the appearance of a huge pie, fold the ends of the bottom layer to seal the openingr This time, poke holes in the top layer of dough with a fork. The egg is the only component we still need to use. We're going to "paint the dough" with a kitchen brush before putting the empanada in the oven. Place the empanada in an oven to 180 degrees Celsius for 40 minutes.

Tuna Marmitako Recipe

Ingredients for 3 people

- ✓ 1/2 kg fresh tuna
- ✓ 1/2 kg of potatoes

- ✓ 1 large onion
- ✓ 2 cloves of garlic
- ✓ 1/2 green bell pepper
- ✓ 2 peeled tomatoes
- ✓ 1 tablespoon of chorizo bell pepper
- ✓ Salt to taste
- ✓ A handful of green peas (optional)

Directions: 45 minutes

Cut the tuna, potatoes (that have been skinned), onion, bell pepper, and potatoes into medium-sized cubes. Very finely chop the tomato and garlic. The onion and garlic should be sautéed in a deep pot with a substantial amount of olive oil until golden brown. The potatoes are then added, and you mix for about 3 minutes. Then stir three times before adding enough water to thoroughly cover the potatoes, the tomato, chopped green and red peppers, and a touch of salt. The potato will be ready after around 15 minutes of boilingr If required, season this broth with extra salt. Add the tuna slices and peas after this. Turn down the heat and give it another 10 minutes to cook. After the allotted time has passed, let the food sit for three minutes, and then serve it in a large dish with a generous drizzle of extra virgin olive oil.

Potatoes to the Importance

Ingredients for 6 people

- ✓ 3/4 kilo of potatoes
- ✓ 3 eggs
- ✓ Vegetable oil
- ✓ Salt to taste
- ✓ Wheat flour
- ✓ 2 sprigs of parsley
- ✓ Some optional saffron strands
- ✓ 2 cloves of garlic
- ✓ 1 small white onion
- ✓ 1 small glass of dry white wine
- ✓ 2 cups of vegetable stock

Directions: 45 minutes

Peeling potatoes is the first step. We will next calculate a thickness for each circle slightly less than a finger. We'll then take a flat dish and spread flour on it; we'll use this later to coat the potatoes. We'll also receive a tiny bowl. We'll break the eggs and use a hand mixer to beat them. We can also leave them prepared to coat the potatoes if we do it in this manner. We will now heat a jet of oil in a large frying pan or saucepan. Before frying each potato in the oil, we will coat it thoroughly with flour and then dip it in the beaten eggr Each potato wheel should be fried on all sides. When ready, take them out of the oil and put them on a dish with a piece of absorbent paper below to soak up any extra fat. The potatoes will now receive a light salting, and we'll set them aside for the time beingr Then we'll make a special seasoning called mojo. Peel the garlic first, then put it in a mortar. After thoroughly draining the parsley, wash it. The leaves should then be separated and added to the garlic in the mortar. Add a little salt and, saffron is optional. The ingredients will be processed in the mortar until a paste is produced. The onion should next be peeled and sliced into extremely tiny cubes. Once more, warm a little oil over a medium-low flame. We'll use it to fry the onion once it's heated. After one minute of sautéing, we will add the mortar-and-pestle paste. Add the wine after cooking the paste for an additional minute. After mixing, wait another minute until the alcohol evaporates.

After that, bring the potatoes and arrange them in the frying pan while attempting to maintain even spacing between them. For leisurely cook, we shall reduce the fire's intensity. After that, we'll add the stock and boil the mixture for 20 minutes. The intention is for practically all of the liquid to have evaporated by the conclusion of this period. Keep an eye on the cooking, and add a little water to the potatoes if you notice they are becoming too dry. Taste the potatoes to check the seasoning after the cooking period is complete. If required, add a bit extra salt to fix it. You can also include a small amount of freshly ground black pepper. All there is to it is that. Now that the potatoes are ready, serve them.

Fabes with Clams

Ingredients for 4 people

- ✓ 500 gr of fabes
- ✓ 500 gr of clams
- ✓ 2 white onions

- ✓ 2 bay leaves
- ✓ 2 liters of fish broth
- ✓ 4 cloves of garlic
- ✓ A few strands of saffron
- ✓ 100 milliliters of dry white wine
- ✓ 1 sprig of fresh parsley
- ✓ Salt to taste
- ✓ Water
- ✓ Ground black pepper to taste
- ✓ Vegetable oil

Directions: 3hs 15min

The beans need to be soaked the previous night, as we instructed at the beginning of this paragraph. Drain and rinse them overnight. The fabes should then be placed in a big saucepan and covered with fish stock. Depending on the size of the pot, different amounts of fumet will be produced. The liquid level must be higher than the level of the beans; this is crucial. We will now get the vegetables ready, so we can use them in the dishPeel the onion, cut them into cubes, and add them to the pot. We will use a sharp knife to peel and finely chop the garlic (this portion of the recipe only calls for three cloves). They will also be included in the mix. Lastly, add the bay leaves to the saucepan and a little salt and pepper powder to taste. Before lighting the fire, we will thoroughly combine everythingr After that, put a lid on the saucepan and cook them for three hours. We will return to the preparation to add a tiny glass of cold water every half-hour while the fabes are cookingr This process, known as "scaring the fabes," aims to maintain the beans' consistency and stop them from crumbling or shatteringr We'll take advantage of the opportunity to take care of the clams while the fabes are cookingr We will first place them in a sizable pot or container and cover them with water and salt. They will be left there for 30 minutes.

Peel the other onion and cut it into pieces as you wait. The final garlic clove will also be peeled, chopped, or, if possible, crushed. Remove the clams once they have completed soaking, clean them, and then store them. Then, we'll heat a little oil (or a non-stick pan) in a large frying pan. Once it's heated, we'll sauté the freshly chopped onion and garlic. Stirring often, simmer it for 5 minutes over medium-low heat. When the onion becomes transparent, we'll add the wine to the mixture. Toss in a sprinkle of pepper and salt to taste, combine everything, and then soak in wine. Clams are next added, and the pan or pot is covered. The goal is to give them a few minutes to cook so they will open. Once the clams have opened, turn off the heat and set them aside until the fabes are almost done cookingr After this step, wash, drain, and chop the small parsley. We'll save it for the very end of the recipe. We will taste the fabes to check the seasoning after about 15 minutes of cookingr We will season it with a bit of salt and pepper if necessary.

Additionally, we shall blend in saffron or coloringr The clams, their sauce, and wine will then be added. As we wait for the beans to finish cooking, we will once more take cover. The beans must be cooked and prepared for serving when the cooking time is up. The only thing left is to choose whether to add the parsley while they are still in the pot or after each dish is served.

Potatoes Rioja style recipe

Ingredients for 4 people

- ✓ 1 kg of potatoes
- ✓ 1 medium onion
- ✓ 250 gr of chorizo
- ✓ 2 chorizo peppers
- ✓ 1 green bell pepper
- ✓ ½ teaspoon of sweet paprika
- ✓ 1 chili pepper (optional if you want a spicy touch)
- ✓ 1 bay leaf
- ✓ Salt to taste
- ✓ Olive oil

Directions: 45 minutes

Potatoes should be peeled and cut into medium-sized bite-sized pieces. Cut the onion, green bell pepper, and choricero bell pepper into pieces about the same size as potatoes. Add a small amount of olive oil to a big saucepan large enough for everything to fit comfortably, and cook the onion and bell pepper for a few minutes over medium heat. After frying for a few more minutes, add the chorizo, which you had earlier cut into slices about the same size as the potatoes. Cover all the ingredients with water. Add the bay leaf, a teaspoon of sweet paprika, and the bell pepper with chorizo. Include the chile pepper if you choose to use it. Simmer this stew at a low temperature until the potato is tender. Salt to taste, but remember that the chorizo can already include some salt. Simply adjust the amount of water in the recipe, adding more if necessary, to get the desired level of brothiness. Your potatoes prepared in the Rioja way are now ready.

How to Make Porrusalda with Codfish

Ingredients for 4 people

- ✓ ½ Kg of salted cod
- ✓ 2 large leeks
- ✓ 3 medium potatoes
- ✓ 3 cloves of garlic
- ✓ Olive oil
- ✓ Salt to taste

Directions: 40 minutes

The cod must first be kept in a deep container with water for 24 to 36 hours before cooking (depending on the thickness of the fish). For this water to desalinate effectively, it must be changed frequently as soon as the fish has been desalted and before you begin cooking your meal. Boil it in 2 liters of water for no more than three minutes. Don't discard the liquid after removing it from the fire and letting it cool. Cod should be broken up into little pieces once the bones are removed. Leeks and garlic cloves should be sautéed in a lot of olive oil in a skillet until they start to brown but not burn. Stir a little after adding the potatoes before adding the reserved broth. Silently allow it to boil. If more salt is required, taste the food beforehand. Add the chopped fish once the potatoes are thoroughly cooked, simmer for an additional two minutes, and then turn off the heat. After 5 minutes, serve your cod porrusalda on a dish with drizzled olive oil.

Anchovies In Vinegar

Ingredients for 4 people

- ✓ 1/2 kilo of anchovies
- ✓ Salt
- ✓ 300 ml of white vinegar
- ✓ Water
- ✓ 150 ml olive oil
- ✓ 3 cloves of garlic
- ✓ 1 bouquet of parsley

Directions: 4 hours 5 minutes

We will mix white vinegar and cold water in a 4:1 ratio, or four parts vinegar to one-part water. We can begin by mixing 300 ml vinegar with 100 ml water. Place the anchovies in a large container that has a lip that will prevent fluids from flowingr The fish should be laid out in layers with the skin facing down. Salt is put on top of the fish. For each additional layer, you create, repeat the process. After that, thoroughly cover the fish in the marinade, covering every inch. The container should now be covered and placed in the refrigerator. Use aluminum foil if you don't have a lid. Give the fish three to four hours to relax. The marinade should have taken effect by then, and the flesh should be white. Due to a number of variables, such as the size of the fish, the refrigerator's temperature, and the vinegar's content, the cooking time should be closely monitored. The key is to ensure the anchovy flesh turns white and has the right texture—not firm or soft, like they're melting—for the anchovies to dissolve. During the lengthy cooking pause, you can peel the garlic and slice it into little pieces. There will be lots of time. After the anchovies have marinated and cooked in the vinegar, thoroughly drain them. Drain them, then top them with a generous amount of olive oil, garlic, and parsley. They will then return to the refrigerator. This time, it will last for a full day. Wash the parsley bunch and slice the leaves into little pieces before removing them. Take your anchovies out and serve them with some parsley on top.

Dogfish In 'Adobo'

Ingredients for 4 people

- ✓ 500 gr of dogfish
- ✓ 4 cloves of garlic
- ✓ Sweet paprika to taste
- ✓ Oregano powder to taste

- ✓ Cumin powder to taste
- ✓ 1 small glass of sherry vinegar 50 ml
- ✓ Flour for breading
- ✓ 3 bay leaves
- ✓ Salt to taste
- ✓ Water
- ✓ Vegetable oil

Directions: 25 min

They will then return to the refrigerator. This time, it will last for a full day. Wash the parsley bunch and slice the leaves into little pieces before removing them. Take your anchovies out and serve them with some parsley on top. Then, we will put them in the bowl together with the fish. We will also add a teaspoon of ground cumin, a tablespoon of salt, the bay leaves, a tablespoon of oregano powder, a tablespoon of sweet paprika, the vinegar, and 100 milliliters of water.

The ingredients will now be thoroughly combined in the bowl, covering the dogfish pieces with a kind of paste that is as homogeneous as possible. The dogfish should be marinated for whichever long you choose at this point. This step is necessary for the end product to be delicious. I advise marinating it for at least 8 hours, but the longer you can leave it, the better. Cover the bowl while it marinates in the fridge to prevent drying out. After the marinating period, we'll make a flat dish and coat it with a flour coatingr After that, take the bowl out of the fridge and drain the fish. To ensure that the excess marinade is removed, I prefer to put them on a plate covered with a sheet of absorbent paper. Next, we'll heat a sizable frying pan with significant oil. We'll turn the heat up high so that it becomes quite warm. The dogfish pieces will now be dredged in the flour while being well-covered on all sides. Only once we are certain that the oil is hot will we start to fry them. So that they are slightly crispy on the exterior but soft and juicy on the inside, only a brief amount of cooking will be required. As the fish cooks, we'll turn it over to ensure that it cooks evenly (although you may not need to do this if the oil is abundant enough). Remember that the dogfish pieces shouldn't be submerged in the oil for longer than one and a half minutes. You can drain the dogfish as you remove them from the oil by setting them on a rack or, even better, on a plate coated in paper towels. That's it. The marinated dogfish is now

prepared for consumption. It should ideally be consumed right away. Avoid needing to reheat the ingredients as much as possible because doing so will alter the dish's consistency.

Oxtail Recipe

Ingredients for 6 people

- ✓ 1 large red tomato
- ✓ 1 red bell pepper
- ✓ 3 carrots
- ✓ 4 cloves of garlic
- ✓ 2 white onions
- ✓ 1 branch of leek
- ✓ 4 tablespoons of flour
- ✓ 4 cups of red wine
- ✓ 1 1/2 kgs of oxtail
- ✓ 2 cups of beef broth
- ✓ Vegetable oil
- ✓ 1 bay leaf
- ✓ Salt
- ✓ Ground black pepper

Directions: 3 hours

To prepare the vegetables for later usage, let's start by taking care of them. The onions and carrots will be peeled. We shall cut them into pieces without much thought to size or shape. The leek, bell pepper, and tomato will then be washed and chopped. We will only utilize the leek's white portion and discard the bell pepper's head, seeds, and inner white portions. We'll leave the garlic's skin on as well. Our vegetables will be set aside for the time beingr We'll take care of the meat right away. The clean oxtail will first be cut into pieces and salted. Flouring it is the next step. To do this, we can distribute flour on a dish, roll the meat pieces over it, and hope the flour will stick to everythingr The slices of oxtail will next be browned in hot oil in a big frying pan. Each piece will be turned so that all of its sides are colored.

After the meat has been fried, take out all the pieces and add some of the already-prepared veggies, such as bell pepper, leek, carrot, garlic, and onion, to the frying pan. We'll turn down the heat a bit and, if required, add a little more oil. Give them around 8 minutes to fry.

After that, add the tomato and continue to cook for an additional ten minutes. After that, add the wine to the entire mixture and pour it into a sizable saucepan that has been prepared. Add the meat after stirring everything and cooking it for about five minutes. The preparation will then be seasoned as the next phase. The meat stock will be poured once we have added all the seasonings. Re-stir everything, cover the pot, and cook on low heat for two hours. To ensure that it cooks evenly and without sticking, mix the food occasionally instead of letting it go on its own. The oxtail ought to be prepared once the two hours have passed.

Meatballs In Sauce

Ingredients for 4 people

- ✓ 1 kg of minced meat
- ✓ 1 medium onion
- ✓ 1 can of crushed raw tomatoes
- ✓ 1 egg
- ✓ Bread crumbs
- ✓ Pepper
- ✓ Salt
- ✓ Fresh parsley
- ✓ Wheat flour
- ✓ Oregano
- ✓ Ground cumin

Directions: 1 hour

Put the minced beef in a sizable bowl that allows easy handlingr Mix in roughly 2 teaspoons of freshly chopped parsley. Salt, pepper, oregano, ground cumin, and garlic powder should be added. These amounts? I did it by sight. Use your senses to the fullest and always remember that it is preferable to have too little salt than too much when working with a pig because you cannot taste it uncooked. Add a medium or small whole egg and some breadcrumbs to the meat once you combine all the spices. Mix well. The goal is to achieve a texture, like dough, that is easy to work with with your hands, that you can shape, and that does not crumble. To achieve this, you might need to gradually add breadcrumbs to the meat, as we don't want the meatballs to taste like bread. Make balls a little smaller than a peach once you have a texture that you can "knead." Don't be concerned if they are not precisely

round or slightly adhere to your hands. The next step is to spread wheat flour on a plate or board and run each meatball through the plate until it is well covered on all sides. Just be careful not to have a coating of flour that is too thick. See the image? That's how your floured meatballs should seem. Once everyone is ready, heat a sizable pot or deep frying pan. Adding a generous amount of olive oil, sauté a sizable entire onion cut into small cubes. Remove the onion from the pan and set it aside after it has become transparent. Place the meatballs after adding a bit more oil. Let them fry while reducing the heat to half. They need to be regularly stirred so that they brown evenly. So that they don't disintegrate, do this cautiously. Recycle the previously cooked onion and add an 800 g can of smashed tomatoes. Stir well to distribute the sauce throughout the meatballs evenly. Reduce the heat, then cover. Remember to cook them on low heat for around 45 minutes, and ensure they never stick to one another. Periodically stir with a wooden spoon. Your meatballs in sauce ought to be prepared by then. Turn off the heat and give them a few minutes to recover.

Codfish Omelette

Ingredients for 4 people

- ✓ 1/4 kilo of desalted codfish
- ✓ 5 eggs
- ✓ 1/4 kilo of onion
- ✓ 2 cloves of garlic
- ✓ 1 bell pepper
- ✓ Olive oil or other vegetable oil
- ✓ Water
- ✓ Salt to taste
- ✓ Ground pepper to taste

Directions: 35 min

Let's begin by preparing the garlic for use. We're just going to peel it and chop it up into little pieces. After that, we'll put it aside. We are going to wash the bell pepper in this instance thoroughly. The branch's head or remaining portion will then be cut off, the seeds and vein (the internal, white sections) will be removed, and it will then be chopped into strips, ribbons, or julienne.

We'll reserve it as well. Peel the onion and cut it into strips or julienne strips if it is an onion. We'll reserve it as well.

The cod will now be taken care of. We will warm up some water in a big pot or pan. We will determine the amount of liquid by subtracting one and a half to two fingers from the pot's bottom. Place the slice of cod, skin side up, in the heated water. Let it simmer there for a few minutes, or until the water begins to bubble a lot. The fish will then be taken out of the fire, drained, and chopped up or crumbled. We now require a sizable frying pan. We can use the same one as for the fish, just wash it and then heat it with a splash of oil. We'll add the onion and garlic after the oil is heated. Add the diced bell pepper after they have cooked for a few minutes. Combine everything with a spatula or wooden spoon, then simmer the vegetables for eight minutes. To prevent the pieces from sticking together or cooking on just one side, cook over medium heat while stirring the food often. Add a little salt and pepper to taste while cookingr

Because there is generally some salt remaining on the fish, keep in mind to apply it sparingly. Add the cod pieces once the time has passed. Together with the remaining ingredients for cooking, combine them and let them sauté for a short while. Lower the heat after five minutes. Then, swiftly combine the egg's contents in a different basin. We'll lightly whip them, sprinkle a little salt and pepper on top (again, subtly), and combine them with the fish and veggies we've just cooked. Before adding the eggs, if more oil is required, add it to the pan. The omelet should be left to set before being turned over with a plate. We can fold it over on itself as well. Just that. It's time to serve the omelette.

Sacromonte Omelette

Ingredients for 4 people

- ✓ six eggs
- ✓ approximately 100 gr of lamb brains
- ✓ 150 gr of lamb shanks
- ✓ a bone from the marrow of veal
- ✓ a bay leaf
- ✓ a glass of white wine
- ✓ salt
- ✓ a spoonful of oil

Directions: 35 min

Cleaning the brains and spleens should be done initially. To clean them thoroughly, one must boil them in water. The white wine, bay leaf, and salt are then added. We wait for around five minutes after the water starts to boil before setting the offal aside once they are clean. Salt, water, and marrow are boiled in a pan. It must be reserved in the same manner after it is prepared. Cut the brains and criadillas into small pieces when they are cold, then combine them with the marrow in the previously beaten eggs. The omelet should be cooked after adding the oil to a frying pan.

Flamenquines with Frankfurter Sausages and Cheese

Ingredients for 4 people

- ✓ 4 frankfurters
- ✓ 4 slices of cooked ham
- ✓ 4 slices of cheese
- ✓ 2 eggs
- ✓ breadcrumbs
- ✓ extra virgin olive oil

Directions: 35 min

Pour the two eggs into a bowl and beat them well. Put the breadcrumbs on a plate. It is best to use a large plate, so the flamenquín does not stick out at the ends. Spread a slice of cooked ham, place a cheese on top, and place the Frankfurt sausage at one end so the slices of ham and cheese can be rolled up on the sausage. Repeat the process with the other three flamenquines. It is time to dip each flamenquín in the beaten egg, bathe it all over, even the ends, and pass it through the breadcrumbs, so it is well impregnated. Now in a frying pan pour the olive oil into frying them, as soon as the oil is hot, we are going to throw the flamenquines. We turn them over and leave them until they are golden brown but without burningr On a plate, we place a kitchen napkin and place the flamenquines already prepared; the napkin will serve us to absorb as much oil as possible. For a healthier recipe, you can also prepare them in a fryer without oil.

Recipe of gurullos with rabbit

Ingredients for 4 people

- ✓ One rabbit
- ✓ 75 gr of gurullos (a type of diamond-shaped pasta) per diner
- ✓ 1 red tomato
- ✓ 1 green bell pepper
- ✓ 1 onion
- ✓ 3 cloves of garlic
- ✓ Food coloring or saffron
- ✓ Olive oil
- ✓ Salt and pepper

Directions: 40 min

Clean, trim, and season the rabbit with salt and pepper. Pour a generous amount of oil into a frying pan and brown the meat pieces. Then, while the stew is still on low heat, add the onion, tomato, and garlic, all of which have been finely chopped. Roast the peppers to soften them in the interim. Peel it when it's done and cut it into strips to add to the pan. After the veggies have been well poached, cover the mixture with water, and when it begins to boil, add the gurullos, a pinch of saffron, and the coloringr The paste is cooked for about 10 minutes, or until it softens. It is salted-free and garnished with a small amount of parsley.

Lamb shoulder of one and a half kilo of lamb

Ingredients for 4 people

- ✓ Potatoes (3 or 4)
- ✓ Port wine
- ✓ White wine
- ✓ Honey
- ✓ Water
- ✓ Garlic
- ✓ Laurel
- ✓ Rosemary
- ✓ Olive oil

- ✓ A pinch of salt
- ✓ Parsley

Directions: 40 min

First, preheat the oven to 180 degrees. The shoulder should then be chopped into three or four pieces, salted to taste, and placed on the cooking tray. Mix one-half cup of white wine, a few drops of olive oil, three minced garlic cloves, some finely chopped parsley, and a few bay leaves in a bowl. Use a brush to apply this juice all over the meat. The item is then covered with half a glass of water and placed in the oven. Turn it over and sprinkle the remaining juice on it after 15 minutes have passed.

On the other hand, pour a glass of port into a saucepan and stir in three spoonfuls of honey when it is just heated. Ten minutes before the oven is turned off, top the lamb with the port, honey sauce, and some fresh rosemary. The meat must continue to brown in the oven until it is finished. Fried potatoes might accompany it.

Baked Pork Rib with Baker Potatoes and Vegetables

Ingredients for 4 people

Ingredients for the vegetables

- ✓ 2 large or 4 small potatoes
- ✓ 1/2 green bell pepper
- ✓ 1/2 red bell pepper
- ✓ 1/2 tomato
- ✓ 1/2 onion
- ✓ olive oil
- ✓ 1/2 glass of white wine
- ✓ 1/2 glass of water
- ✓ ground black pepper
- ✓ salt

Ingredients for the marinade for the ribs

- ✓ 2 cloves of garlic, peeled
- ✓ A little rosemary
- ✓ 2 sprigs of parsley
- ✓ 1 tablespoon of vinegar
- ✓ 1/2 teaspoon of hot paprika

- ✓ 1/2 glass of olive oil
- ✓ 2 tablespoons of white wine
- ✓ ground black pepper
- ✓ a little salt
- ✓

Directions: 1h 15min

The marinade for the ribs will soon be ready. To make this, combine all the ingredients in a blender and puree them (if feasible, the day before). Place the ribs in a freezer bag with the marinade, seal the bag, and move it around to coat the ribs with the marinade evenly. Place it in the refrigerator for up to 30 minutes before cooking, then remove it to bring the meat to room temperature. The potatoes should be peeled, cleaned, dried, and cut into one-centimeter slices before placing them in a bowl with a little olive oil. The tomato should be chopped and added after the onion and bell pepper have been julienned. Add water and white wine. Add salt and pepper to taste. Bake the rib for 45 minutes at 185° or until it turns golden brown by placing it on top of the veggies, bone side down, and in direct contact with the vegetables. The rib should be golden brown after 45 minutes of baking on the other side.

Chicken Cachopo

- ✓ One open chicken breast (both pieces)
- ✓ 1 or 2 slices of cheese, depending on size
- ✓ 2 slices of Serrano ham
- ✓ Provençal herbs
- ✓ Two eggs
- ✓ Breadcrumbs
- ✓ Oil
- ✓ salt

Directions: 20 minutes

You can ask the butcher to separate the chicken breasts into large fillets by slicing them in half on each side. Add salt and your choice of fresh or dried herbs. Place one of the open breasts with the herbs facing up on the work surface or a board. Put the ham and cheese on top. Salt and wooden toothpicks are used for sewingr After dipping the breasts in beaten eggs, they are covered in breadcrumbs. Our chicken cachopos are now ready for cooking after being prepared. Pour a lot

of oil into a griddle; we want to achieve a good golden hue. We place the chicken cachopos on it, brown one side of them, then flip them over and continue the process. Do not tell me that the cut in this picture, which I have included, is not lovely and delectable!

Greek main courses

Goat lamb oil and oregano

Ingredients for 4 people

- ✓ 1,200 g goat hand or leg, cut into portions
- ✓ 3 cloves of garlic, finely chopped
- ✓ 2 sprigs of thyme
- ✓ 150 ml of olive oil
- ✓ 1 glass of white wine
- ✓ 1 teaspoon oregano
- ✓ salt
- ✓ black pepper

Directions: 1h30min

The goat should be fried in olive oil in a flat pan over high heat, salting it as it goes. White wine, thyme, and minced garlic are added. Add two cups of water after letting the alcohol evaporate. Over low heat, simmer for one hour. Increase the heat toward the end to thicken the sauce and incorporate the oregano. Fresh French fries are the ideal pairing for it.

Kakavia

Ingredients for 5 people

- ✓ About 2 kg of fish for soup (scorpions, drakes, perch, cod and a few small shrimps)
- ✓ lemon juice
- ✓ 2 potatoes
- ✓ 1 large onion
- ✓ 1 large carrot
- ✓ 2 sprigs of celery
- ✓ 1 cup of olive oil
- ✓ black pepper
- ✓ Salt

Directions: 1h10min

Wash and clean the fish. Salt them and generously squeeze lemon juice over them. Put 8 to 10 glasses of water, an onion that has been roughly diced, potatoes that have been cut into large chunks, carrots that have been cut into rings, celery, olive oil, and 1 teaspoon of salt in a pot. 20 minutes of boiling is required. For a further 15 minutes, boil the fish uncovered. With a slotted spoon, transfer them to a plate. Strain the juice, and then add it to the pot with the veggies. Boil until there is practically no juice left in the pot, and the mixture has thickened and turned nearly white. A juice of one lemon may be added.

Fried crispy rabbit with lettuce sauce

Ingredients for 4 people

- ✓ 1 large rabbit in large 5 cm cubes (ask the butcher to fillet it)
- ✓ 1 liter of marouvas (Cretan aged wine, found in wine cellars)
- ✓ 3 cloves of garlic
- ✓ 4 cloves
- ✓ 1 cinnamon stick
- ✓ 4 bay leaves
- ✓ 5 grains of allspice
- ✓ 1 tablespoon of honey
- ✓ wild oregano
- ✓ sliced jalapeno pepper
- ✓ beef broth
- ✓ sunflower oil for frying
- ✓ zest of a lime
- ✓ coarse semolina

Directions: 22min

Add the rabbit, marouvas, bay leaf, garlic, spices, cloves, and honey to a deep metal pan. Give them three hours to marinate. Remove the pieces from the marinade and give them a thorough clean with paper towels. Stew the sauce by bringing the marinade liquid and a glass of beef stock water to a boil. Add a spoonful of oregano, along with the honey, at the very end. Semolina and lime zest are added before breading the chunks of rabbit.

Fry the rabbit pieces in a lot of sunflower oil in a frying pan until crispy and golden. Garnish with the jalapeño slices before adding the glazed sauce on top.

Lamb kebabs

Ingredients for 4 people

- ✓ 320 g minced lamb, minced twice
- ✓ 1 egg white
- ✓ 1 small bed of rosemary, leaves only, finely chopped
- ✓ 4 mint leaves, finely chopped
- ✓ Salt
- ✓ black pepper
- ✓ 20 ml milk, whole

For the spice mixture
- ✓ ½ teaspoon of cinnamon
- ✓ ½ small lemon, zest
- ✓ 3 grains of allspice
- ✓ 1½ teaspoon sweet paprika, powdered
- ✓ teaspoon of smoked paprika, powdered
- ✓ 1/3 teaspoon aniseed, ground

For serving
- ✓ 1 tomato, chopped
- ✓ 1 onion, finely chopped
- ✓ 2 tablespoons parsley, finely chopped
- ✓ 160 g boiled bulgur

119

Directions: 1h30min

Spices: Place the cinnamon, paprika, anise, allspice, and lemon zest in a food processor and mix until smooth. The cinnamon, lemon juice, lemon juice, and lemon juice were combined with the spice and beaten into a powder. Add the minced meat, egg white, mint, rosemary, milk, salt, and pepper to the deep bowl after adding the spice combination. The mixture should be smooth after kneadingr Form 50 g-sized kebabs after placing them in the fridge for an hour to firm up. Cook them on the BBQ for 8 to 10 minutes, flipping them frequently to ensure even cookingr Alternately, preheat a grill pan or frying pan, add a little olive oil, and cook the meat for 5 minutes on each side. When they are finished cooking, serve them hot with tomato, onion, parsley, and boiled bulgur.

Frittata with quinoa, vegetables and sausage

Ingredients for 4 people

- ✓ 2 tablespoons of olive oil, extra virgin olive oil
- ✓ 2 tablespoons Lurpak Soft salted
- ✓ 1 onion, finely chopped
- ✓ 280 g jarred asparagus, in 6 cm pieces
- ✓ 60 g peas, frozen, boiled for 10 minutes
- ✓ 150 g Arla Mozzarella, grated
- ✓ 120 g quinoa, boiled, well-drained
- ✓ 8 eggs, beaten
- ✓ 1 handful of dill, finely chopped and a little extra for serving
- ✓ 2 handfuls of baby spinach
- ✓ 1 handful of parsley, finely chopped and a little extra for serving
- ✓ 10 g mini sausages, cut in half, lengthwise
- ✓ Salt
- ✓ 1 clove of garlic, sliced
- ✓ 2 tablespoons of sherry vinegar

Directions: 55min

Heat the grill in the oven to a high settingr Heat 1 tbsp of the olive oil and all of the Lurpak in a nonstick frying pan with a removable handle that is 28 cm in diameter and fits in the oven. Over low heat, add a pinch of salt and sauté the onion for 5 minutes, or until it softens. The asparagus will then be added and cooked for an additional 5 minutes. For two minutes, toss in the quinoa and peas. Stir to thoroughly coat the vegetables in the eggs and half of the Arla Mozzarella. Stir in the spinach and the majority of the herbs. Cook the frittata for 5 to 10 minutes until the bottom is brown. After topping the remaining Arla Mozzarella, place the dish in the oven. Bake the frittata until the top is brown. When a frying pan is ready, add the remaining olive oil, and once it is hot, cook the sausages over medium-high heat until done and crispy.

30 minutes should pass after adding the garlic before the tarragon in the garlic begins to release. After adding the vinegar and stirring, turn off the heat. Serve the frittata topped with cooked sausage and some fresh parsley and dill.

Bamias with olives, sun-dried tomatoes and feta cream

Ingredients for 4 people

- ✓ 600 g okra, peeled
- ✓ 600 g of okra, cleaned, cleaned, cleaned, 600 g of okra, cleaned, cleaned
- ✓ 130 ml of olive oil
- ✓ 1 onion, dried, finely chopped
- ✓ 500 g butter
- ✓ 1 clove of garlic
- ✓ 1 onion
- ✓ 8 sun-dried tomatoes, thinly sliced
- ✓ 100 ml balsamic vinegar
- ✓ 150 ml vegetable stock
- ✓ 160 g feta cheese
- ✓ ½ bunch parsley, finely chopped
- ✓ ½ teaspoon of chili flakes (optional)
- ✓ 2 tablespoons drained yogurt
- ✓ 6 tbsp fresh milk
- ✓ Salt
- ✓ Black pepper

Directions: 60min

In a baking sheet, place the peeled okra, sprinkle with red vinegar, season with salt, and bake in the sun for 1.5 hours. Rinse. The dried onion and peeled olives should be sautéed in half the olive oil in a large skillet over high heat until they are just beginning to wilt. Add the sun-dried tomato, spring onion, and garlic as well. Pour all the ingredients into a baking dish after turning off the heat. Sauté the previously rinsed okra in the remaining olive oil and balsamic vinegar in the same pan over high heat. After adding the vegetable stock, simmer for 5–6 minutes.

Turn the okra into the baking dish with the olives, season with parsley, salt, pepper, and, if desired, red pepper flakes, and bake for 17–18 minutes at 220°C while covered. While waiting, create a thin cream by blending the feta cheese, milk, and yogurt in a blender. Add 1 tablespoon more milk if necessary. Bake the baking sheet for 7-8 minutes to brown it. The okra should remain whole, and the flesh should not rip. 10 minutes should be given for cooling before serving with the thin feta cream and olive oil.

Grilled picania with chimichurri sauce

Ingredients for 4 people

- ✓ 1 kg of veal piccani
- ✓ 1 tbsp. 1 pork chops 1 tbsp.
- ✓ 1 cup of flat-leaf parsley, finely chopped
- ✓ 2 cloves garlic, crushed
- ✓ 1/2 red chili pepper, diced
- ✓ 2 tablespoons of red wine vinegar
- ✓ 2 tablespoons of dried oregano
- ✓ 100 ml of extra olive oil

Directions: 35min

Place a grill close to the flames as the barbecue is heating up. To make the sauce, combine the parsley, garlic, red pepper, vinegar, oregano, and oil. Add salt and pepper to taste and set away. When the grill is heated, liberally season the spice with salt and pepper before placing it fat down. After 5 minutes of simmering, flip it over and cook until well browned. Stir the coals while raising the grill to the top. Cook the spice for 15-20 minutes on the cooler side (medium roasting).

Before slicing and serving with the chimichurri sauce, remove from the heat and let rest wrapped in foil for 20 minutes.

Bamias with tile cologne

Ingredients for 4 people

- ✓ 1 kg of okra, peeled
- ✓ 1 pork belly, cleaned, cleaned, 1 pork belly, cleaned
- ✓ 120 ml of olive oil
- ✓ 1 tbsp brown sugar
- ✓ 100 ml apple cider vinegar
- ✓ 2 onions, dried, finely chopped
- ✓ 500 g tomatoes, grated
- ✓ 2 cloves of garlic
- ✓ 1 tbsp tomato paste
- ✓ 100 ml vegetable stock
- ✓ 1 bunch of parsley, finely chopped
- ✓ 1 tbsp sweet paprika
- ✓ 1 teaspoon of smoked paprika
- ✓ 2 cabbages about 500-600 g
- ✓ 1 bay leaf
- ✓ Salt
- ✓ Black pepper

Directions: 60min

On a baking sheet, place the peeled okra, sprinkle with red vinegar, season with salt, and bake in the sun for 1.5 hours. Drain and rinse. Okra should be sautéed in olive oil for two to three minutes over high heat in a large saucepan. Add the vinegar and the sugar. Then incorporate the tomatoes, tomato paste, bay leaf, onion, and garlic. After 6 to 7 minutes, add the stock, followed by the sweet and smoked paprika and parsley. Turn the okra onto a sizable baking sheet, cover it, and bake for 15–17 minutes at 220°C. Once exposed, set the boneless legs atop the pedal (i.e. we have asked the fisherman to cut them in half horizontally). Serve with a splash of olive oil after baking for an additional 10 to 12 minutes.

Easy turkey meatballs with cheese sauce

Ingredients for 4-6 people

- ✓ For the meatballs
- ✓ 1 kg of minced turkey meat
- ✓ 2 egg whites
- ✓ 1 onion, grated
- ✓ 100 g toast, crustless, grated
- ✓ 1/2 bunch dill, finely chopped
- ✓ 1/2 bunch parsley, finely chopped
- ✓ 1 teaspoon of smoked paprika
- ✓ 1 good pinch of nutmeg
- ✓ 1 pinch of flower salt
- ✓ 1 pinch of black pepper
- ✓ 150 g of olive oil, for frying
- ✓ For the cheese sauce
- ✓ 1 teaspoon lemon juice
- ✓ 60 ml of olive oil
- ✓ 150 g flour, for frying
- ✓ 1-2 pinches of lemon zest
- ✓ 220 g cream cheese
- ✓ 1 tsp dill, finely chopped
- ✓ 1 teaspoon parsley, finely chopped
- ✓ 1 teaspoon basil, finely chopped

Directions: 45min

Cheese sauce: In a bowl, combine all the ingredients; chill until ready to serve. To make meatballs, combine all the ingredients in a big basin and knead them well. Then, place the bowl in the refrigerator for an hour to enable the flavors of the ingredients fully develop. Olive oil that is 34 full in a frying pan is heatingr In the meantime, form meatballs into the desired size, coat them thoroughly in flour, shake off the excess, and fry them over medium-high heat, tossing them frequently. To drain the oil, place them on paper towels. With the cheese sauce, serve them.

Baked pork chops with potatoes and bacon

Ingredients for 4-6 people

- ✓ 10 slices of bacon, coarsely chopped
- ✓ 50 ml of olive oil, extra virgin olive oil
- ✓ 2 cloves of garlic, coarsely chopped
- ✓ 2 bay leaves
- ✓ 1 large onion, sliced, finely chopped, finely chopped, finely chopped, finely chopped.
- ✓ 2 tablespoons of mild mustard
- ✓ 2 lemons, juice
- ✓ 1,200 g pork neck steaks, boneless
- ✓ salt, black pepper
- ✓ 4 large potatoes, sliced

Directions: 1h30min

The convection oven should be preheated to 160°C, and the frying pan should be heated to high. The bacon should be added to a nonstick pan and cooked until it begins to wilt. With a slotted spoon, transfer to a plate. In the same pan, add the onion and olive oil. Season with salt and pepper and cook until golden. Sauté for one minute after adding the garlic. Take out of the pan. Add the bay leaves, mustard, and lemon juice to a baking dish and stir until the mustard is completely dissolved. Mix well before adding the potatoes and bacon. Put the meat on top of the potatoes after thoroughly seasoning it with salt and pepper. Bake the meat and potatoes for an hour, or until done. Then increase the oven's temperature to 180°C and bake the meal for 10 minutes, or until it becomes red.

Pork pancakes with crispy green beans

Ingredients for 4-6 people

- ✓ For the pancakes
- ✓ 600 g boneless pancetta
- ✓ 1 liter of water
- ✓ 100 g salt
- ✓ 1 clove of garlic
- ✓ 200 ml dry white wine
- ✓ For the pepper cream
- ✓ 6 Florina peppers from a jar
- ✓ 30 g drained yogurt
- ✓ 1 clove of garlic
- ✓ 60 ml olive oil
- ✓ 200 g cream cheese

- ✓ 1 tbsp sweet paprika
- ✓ salt, freshly ground pepper
- ✓ For the beans
- ✓ 500 g broad beans
- ✓ 20 ml of olive oil

4 tablespoons of olive oil

- ✓ 1 tablespoon of salt, coarse salt,
- ✓ freshly ground pepper

Directions: 30min

Pancakes: Pour 1 liter of water and 100 g of salt into a large dish and mix to dissolve the salt. The pancetta should be added to the bowl and left for 15 minutes. Beans: In the meantime, boil some green beans in water for 15 minutes, then drain them. All cream ingredients should be blended in a blender for two to three minutes. The pancetta should be browned on each side for 3 to 4 minutes in a nonstick pan or grill pan with a bit of olive oil and 1 garlic clove. After removing the pancetta to a platter, use the white wine to clear them, and stir-fry the green beans for 2 minutes in the same pan. Serve with freshly ground pepper and pepper cream.

Goat in the oven with artichokes and fennel

Ingredients for 8 people

- ✓ 12 artichokes, fresh, cleaned
- ✓ 1 kg of baby potatoes or larger, cut and diced
- ✓ 2 kg of goat's leg and hand cut, in large portions
- ✓ 150 ml of olive oil, extra virgin
- ✓ 2 fennel, peeled, sliced
- ✓ 6 fresh onions, coarsely chopped
- ✓ 500 ml vegetable stock, fresh or refrigerated
- ✓ juice of 2 lemons
- ✓ 1 bunch of fennel, finely chopped
- ✓ 270 ml dry white wine
- ✓ black pepper
- ✓ salt

Directions: 2hs35min

Set the oven's air temperature to 180 °C. In a big bowl, combine the artichokes, potatoes, fennel, and onions. Sprinkle with salt and pepper, then add half the olive oil and half the lemon juice. Put the vegetables on a baking sheet. Put the chunks of meat in the same bowl and top with the remaining olive oil, lemon juice, and salt & pepper. Spread the meat over the veggies, top with the fennel, and then add the wine and vegetable stock to the baking dish on the side, keeping the meat and potatoes out of the liquid. Wrap in parchment paper, then foil, and secure. The potatoes and pork should be thoroughly softened after two hours in the oven. Remove the foil and parchment paper toward the end of cooking so the meat and potatoes can color.

Revithada with octopus

Ingredients for 4 people

- ✓ 1 octopus 2 kg
- ✓ 1 bay leaf
- ✓ peppercorns
- ✓ allspice grains
- ✓ 1 glass of wine
- ✓ 500 g chickpeas, soaked the night before
- ✓ 2 cloves of garlic, finely chopped
- ✓ 1 sprig of rosemary
- ✓ 1 onion, finely chopped
- ✓ 120 ml of olive oil, extra virgin olive oil
- ✓ 1 lemon
- ✓ pepper
- ✓ salt

Directions: 2hs

Put the octopus in a pot with the bay leaf, allspice, peppercorns, and wine. Cover the pot and stew the octopus in its juices for 35–40 hours over medium-low heat. Because the octopus releases a lot of liquid, take care not to let it stick and add a glass of water if required. At the same time, add the onion and garlic to a large pot of cold water and add the chickpeas. Boil for an hour over medium heat. Set the oven's fan setting to 180°C. Put the chickpeas and their juice in a pyrex or baking dish once they are soft. Octopus, rosemary, lemon slices, and olive oil should all be added. Make sure the liquid is covering the meal. Put the baking tray in the oven, season with salt and pepper, and bake for about 30 minutes.

Cuttlefish crostini with onions stew

Ingredients for 4 people

- ✓ 120 ml of olive oil
- ✓ 500 g stewed onions, peeled
- ✓ 3-4 garlic cloves
- ✓ 1 kg of fresh cuttlefish
- ✓ 1 teaspoon of tomato paste
- ✓ 1 bay leaf
- ✓ 1 cinnamon stick
- ✓ 1 glass of wine
- ✓ 2-3 grains of allspice
- ✓ 2-3 cloves
- ✓ 2 large ripe tomatoes, peeled, seeded and chopped
- ✓ salt flower
- ✓ black pepper, freshly ground

Directions: 2hs

The onions and garlic should be steamed in a skillet with half the olive oil until they are glossy and honeyed, around 15 minutes. After removing the bone, peel and cut the cuttlefish into thick slices. Put them plain in a pot and heat them gently so they will steam and the liquid will drain off. Add the remaining olive oil, the onions, and the garlic when they have drained their liquid. Add the tomato paste after sautéing them all together. The tomato paste should be well-browned before the spices are added. Keep on stirringr Put the wine in. Add the fresh tomatoes after the alcohol has had time to evaporate. Add a glass of water if necessary after seasoning with salt and pepper. Stirring often, the sauce should thicken, and the cuttlefish and spring onions should be soft after about an hour of cooking at low heat.

Chicken in the oven with red wine, cherry tomatoes and olives

Ingredients for 8 people

- ✓ 8 chicken thighs
- ✓ 3 red onions, thickly sliced
- ✓ 150 g pitted black olives
- ✓ 500 g cherry tomatoes
- ✓ 4 garlic cloves, broken, peeled
- ✓ 1 teaspoon of cumin powder
- ✓ 2 red peppers, in strips
- ✓ 4 tbsp olive oil, extra virgin
- ✓ 1 teaspoon sweet paprika
- ✓ 1 teaspoon of fennel seeds
- ✓ zest and juice of 1 lemon
- ✓ 1 small handful of parsley
- ✓ 1 tbsp fresh thyme
- ✓ 250 ml dry red wine

Directions: 1h10min

Set the oven's air temperature to 180 °C. In a big bowl, combine the peppers, onions, olives, cherry tomatoes, and chicken thighs. Mix in a bit of salt and pepper seasoningr Combine the spices, olive oil, lemon juice, and zest in a separate bowl. Mix well after adding the mixture to the bowl containing the chicken. A medium baking dish should be filled with all the ingredients. Add the thyme, wine, salt, pepper, and garlic cloves. After 20 minutes, flip the chicken over and bake for another 40 minutes. Drain, set aside for five minutes, top with parsley, and, if desired, serve with orzo or linguini.

Chicken with chickpeas and vegetables

Ingredients for 4 people

- ✓ 3 tbsp olive oil, extra virgin olive oil
- ✓ 4 large chicken thighs
- ✓ 3 cloves of garlic, sliced
- ✓ ½ dry onion, thickly sliced
- ✓ 1 teaspoon of smoked paprika
- ✓ 800 g chickpeas, boiled, drained

- ✓ 3 red peppers, cut into thick cubes
- ✓ coarse salt, black pepper
- ✓ 1 teaspoon cumin, powdered
- ✓ 400 g cherry tomatoes

Directions: 1h10min

Set the oven's internal temperature to 220 °C. Heat the oil to medium-high heat in a sizable frying pan that will fit inside the oven. Chicken thighs should be well-browned on all sides after being seasoned with salt and pepper and cooked in batches for 8 to 10 minutes. The chicken to a platter using silicone tongs. The onion and garlic should be added to the pan and cooked for 2-4 minutes while continually stirringr Add the peppers and stir-fry them briefly. When the paprika and cumin are added, simmer them for another minute while stirring to let the flavors come through. Stir in the chickpeas and cherry tomatoes before simmering for 5 minutes. Chicken should be seasoned with salt and pepper, placed in the pan, and baked for 30 minutes at 170 °C or until golden.

Moroccan main courses

Veal with Moroccan-style caramelized plums

- ✓ 1k of veal
- ✓ 2 onions
- ✓ 4 cloves of garlic
- ✓ 1 tablespoon of smen (or margarine)
- ✓ 2 teaspoons turmeric
- ✓ 1 teaspoon ginger
- ✓ extra virgin olive oil
- ✓ salt
- ✓ 1/2 teaspoon black pepper
- ✓ 2 pieces of cinnamon stick
- ✓ 2 bay leaves
- ✓ 1 teaspoon Ras el Hanout

For garnish:
- ✓ 200 g of raw peeled almonds
- ✓ 2 tablespoons of toasted sesame seeds
- ✓ Parsley

To caramelize the prunes:
- ✓ 1 teaspoon cinnamon powder
- ✓ 1 cinnamon stick
- ✓ 1/2k prunes
- ✓ 4 tablespoons sugar

Time spent: 1 hour, 25 minutes.

The meat should be cut into thick steaks and placed in a bowl with the pepper, ginger, turmeric, and ras al hanout. Without using any oil, preheat the crock pot and add the meat. Cook for 8 to 10 minutes on low heat. Peel, smash, and mix in 4 garlic cloves. The onions are added after being peeled and chopped into thin julienne strips. 100 ml of oil and the smen (traditional Moroccan butter) should be added. Cook for 10 minutes while partially covering the pan and sometimes stirring the meat. For around 15 minutes, season the meat, add 2 bay leaves, 2 cinnamon sticks, and water to cover. Put the sugar, 1 cinnamon stick, cinnamon powder, and pitted plums in a saucepan. Cook for 15 to 20 minutes after covering with water.

Almonds are added to a hot frying pan with a tablespoon of oil, briefly toasted, and then put aside. Place the stew, plums, and roasted almonds on 4 plates. Add a few parsley leaves as a garnish and scatter the toasted sesame seeds over the plates.

Tajine of veal with carrots

Ingredients for 4 people

- ✓ 1.2 Kg of veal (shank or knuckle)
- ✓ 700 ml of meat or vegetable stock
- ✓ 2 onions
- ✓ 8 carrots
- ✓ 2 teaspoons of Ras el hanout
- ✓ Salt
- ✓ Ground black pepper
- ✓ Olive oil

Directions: 2 hours and 50 minutes

The veal should first be chopped into bite-sized or medium-sized chunks. The onions were peeled and then sliced into julienne strips and placed in a basin. Five tablespoons of olive oil are heated to a medium-high fire in a tajine, and the meat pieces are added after it reaches that temperature. They are then fried for 4-5 minutes or until they are lightly browned on all sides. The meat should be drained and set aside on a platter. Reduce the heat to medium-low and sauté the onion for 5 minutes, or until it softens, in the same oil. Add two teaspoons of ras el hanout, whisk thoroughly, and then add the meat or vegetable broth. Stir in the leftover meat pieces and season with salt and pepper to taste. Stir to combine all the ingredients. With the lid on, cook the tajine for two hours on low heat while occasionally stirringr The carrots, which we will have peeled and cut into sticks, are added at the specified time. We re-cover the tajine and cook it over a medium fire for another 30 minutes. Now that the veal tajine is prepared, all that is left to do is check the salt, adjust it if required, take it off the heat, and serve it right away.

Lamb Stew (Tangia Dial Khuruf)

Ingredients for 4 people

- ✓ 1 kg lamb shoulder
- ✓ 1 onion
- ✓ 1 tablespoon ras el hanout
- ✓ 1 tablespoon of paprika
- ✓ 8 strands of saffron
- ✓ 1 tablespoon ground cumin
- ✓ 1 pickled lemon

Directions:

Pre-heat the oven first. One kilogram of lamb shoulder should be cut into large pieces and put in a sizable ceramic jugr Chop and peel 1 onion. Add the chopped onion, 1 tablespoon of ras el hanout, 1 tablespoon of paprika, 8 strands of saffron, 1 tablespoon of cumin, and a few pieces of finely chopped pickled lemon peel to the clay jar containing the meat. Wrap the jar in baking paper and secure it with a stringr In the oven, bake for one hour at 180°C. We remove it to inspect it before returning it for two more hours at 180°C. When ready, either place the earthenware jar on a dish or serve it that way.

Chicken Tajine with Apricots (Tajin Bel Djaj)

Ingredients for 4 people

For the apricots:

- ✓ 500 g dried apricots (dried apricots)
- ✓ 100 g powdered sugar
- ✓ 7 g ground cinnamon
- ✓ 100 g butter

For the chicken:

- ✓ 1.5 kg of chopped chicken
- ✓ 60 g peanut oil
- ✓ 5 g pepper
- ✓ Salt
- ✓ 7 g ground ginger
- ✓ 2 packets of saffron
- ✓ 10gr ground cinnamon
- ✓ 100gr toasted pine nuts
- ✓ 100gr onion

Directions:

Wash 500 gr of dried apricots or apricots first. Put a pot filled with a lot of water over the fire. Add 100 g of powdered sugar, 7 g of ground cinnamon, and 100 g of butter along with the apricots. Bring to a boil and continue to simmer until thickened. Get rid of the heat.

1.5 kg of chicken and 60 g of peanut oil should be placed in a separate pot. Add 2 sachets of saffron, 5 g of crushed pepper, 7 g of ground ginger, and 10 g of ground cinnamon. Stir. 100 g of washed, peeled, and chopped onion is added to the pot with the chicken. Submerge in water. Cook the saucepan for 20 minutes on low heat with the lid on. Serve the chicken, apricots, and 100 g of toasted pine nuts on top in a tajine.

Moroccan Sausage With Lentils

Ingredients for 4 people

- ✓ 1 kg of Merguez chorizo sausage
- ✓ Virgin olive oil
- ✓ 4 cloves of chopped garlic
- ✓ 500 g lentils
- ✓ 2 bay leaves
- ✓ 2 cinnamon sticks
- ✓ 8 strands of saffron
- ✓ 1 chopped onion
- ✓ 1 tablespoon of salt
- ✓ 1 teaspoon white sugar
- ✓ 1 teaspoon cinnamon
- ✓ 1 teaspoon pepper
- ✓ 1 bunch of fresh parsley
- ✓ Bread

Directions:

Set the oven to 180°C. Separate 1 kg of chorizos merguez, then put them in a baking dish with 3 minced garlic cloves and virgin olive oil. After cleaning the lentils, we put 500 g of them in a pot with water to cook. Olive oil, two bay leaves, two cinnamon sticks, and eight strands of saffron are added. One chopped onion, one garlic clove, one tablespoon of salt, and one teaspoon of white sugar are also added. For one hour, cook covered over low heat. Add 1 teaspoon of pepper to the baking tray containing the merguez and bake for 10 minutes at 180°C. When we remove the lentils from the pan, chop some fresh parsley and mix it in. Cut a loaf of bread to prepare a sandwich with the lentils and a small amount of chopped merguez. The remainder we plate and serve.

Kefta tajine

Ingredients for 4 people

- ✓ Half a kilo of minced meat (in Moroccan kefta, hence the name of the tajine)
- ✓ 4 tomatoes
- ✓ 1 onion (I used 2 because they were small)
- ✓ 3 cloves of garlic
- ✓ Salt to taste
- ✓ 1 teaspoon cumin
- ✓ 1 teaspoon paprika
- ✓ 1 teaspoon pepper
- ✓ 2 or 3 tablespoons of olive oil

Directions: 20 min

A handful of chopped fresh parsley and cilantro (if you don't have cilantro you can use just parsley). A tablespoon of tomato concentrate (optional). While the tajine is cooking up, julienne the onion and place it over low heat with the olive oil. Add the onion to the heated oil. The onion is usually sliced, but today there was time to cover it up, so I had to blend it. Add the diced tomatoes and garlic once the onion is halfway translucent. Add a glass of water and, if desired, the tablespoon of tomato concentrate once they have broken down. The process continues the same whether you used a blender now that the sauce is almost done. Salt, pepper, cumin, and paprika should be added.

Once the sauce has begun to boil, add the chopped parsley and cilantro and stir once more. Prepare the minced beef by forming small balls that are desired while it boils. I prefer to prepare little balls since, traditionally, the tajine isn't served on individual plates or eaten with cutlery; instead, everyone eats it with pieces of bread. Once the balls have been created, add them to the tajine and cook them covered for five minutes. Your kefta tajine is finished when you flip the meatballs over and cover them once again for five minutes to finish cooking on the other side. The tajine is served just as it is, and everyone eats it, as I previously stated (each one on his side, of course). The salads, however, come with utensils and are presented on individual plates.

Pork rib with lemon sauce

Ingredients for 4 people

- ✓ 1,200 g pork rib
- ✓ 4 lemons
- ✓ 4 cloves of garlic
- ✓ 1 meat stock cube
- ✓ extra virgin olive oil
- ✓ 4 sprigs of thyme
- ✓ 1 teaspoon ras el hanout
- ✓ 1 tablespoon of refined corn
- ✓ salt
- ✓ parsley

Directions

In a sizable casserole, heat 4 tablespoons of oil. The ribs are divided into ribs (sticks), seasoned, added to the pan, and nicely browned. Lemons should be cut in half, squeezed, and juice should be poured over the ribs. Peeling, chopping, and adding the minced garlic to the pan. Along with these ingredients, add the ras el hanout, thyme sprigs, 1 tablespoon of finely chopped parsley, half a lemon's zest, and the flavor cube, and cover with water. For 40 minutes, cook. A spoonful of refined maize flour diluted in a small glass of water can be added to the sauce if it is too light. When the sauce thickens, add a bit, boil, and whisk the mixture. Serve and add some to the dishes for decoration.

Veal Skewers (Kabab Al'baqari)

Ingredients for 4 people

- ✓ 1 onion
- ✓ 1 tablespoon chopped fresh coriander
- ✓ 1 dash of lemon juice
- ✓ 1 tablespoon paprika
- ✓ 1 tablespoon ground cumin
- ✓ Pepper
- ✓ Salt
- ✓ 1 tablespoon ras el hanout
- ✓ Virgin olive oil
- ✓ 1 kg of veal

Directions

One onion is first washed, peeled, and chopped. Then combine 1 tablespoon of chopped fresh coriander, 1 dash of lemon juice, 1 tablespoon each of paprika and ground cumin, pepper, salt, and 1 tablespoon of ras el hanout in a bowl with the chopped onion. Finally, top with virgin olive oil. 1 kg of cubed beef should be marinated in the mixture for an hour. Place in the fridge for two hours. For brochettes, skewer the meat and cook it. Serve.

Meatballs with mint and sesame

Ingredients for 4 people

- ✓ 750 g beef mince
- ✓ 100 g sesame seeds
- ✓ 1 bunch fresh mint
- ✓ 1 onion
- ✓ 4 pear tomatoes
- ✓ 1 teaspoon sweet paprika
- ✓ salt
- ✓ olive oil

Directions: 20 min

We cleaned and cut the menta leaves (only the leaves), picked them well, and reserved them. Additionally, we wash, remove, and throw away the tomato seeds before cutting them into pieces. We sautéed the tomatoes in a skillet with a little olive oil and salt. While combining the meat with freshly chopped cebolla, menthol, sweet pimentón, and sesame. We created little albedos. We added the albóndigas to the skillet with the tomato and sautéed for five minutes. The albondigas must be quite small.

Moroccan style roast chicken with raisins and pine nuts recipe

Ingredients for 4 people

- ✓ Halved chicken hindquarters
- ✓ Ras el hanout 2 teaspoons
- ✓ 1 onion
- ✓ Pine nuts 3 tablespoons
- ✓ Lemon juice
- ✓ Sultana raisins 3 tablespoons
- ✓ Extra virgin olive oil
- ✓ Salt

Directions: 1 h

Set the oven to 190°C to begin. We combine the lemon juice and the ras el hanout mixture in a bowl. Instead, warm the oil in a frying pan and sauté the onion slices in it.

Once finished, add the pine nuts to lightly toast before adding the raisins and adding half of the spice and lemon juice mixture. Get rid of the heat.

Put the chicken pieces and the previously sautéed mixture between the meat in an ovenproof dish that has been coated with oil. The remaining ras el hanout, lemon, and 50 ml of water are added after seasoning with salt and pepper. Bake the chicken for 40 minutes until it is cooked through and golden brown.

Recipe of lamb Tajine with zucchini, raisins and mint

Ingredients for 4 people

- ✓ 750 g Lamb meat in pieces
- ✓ 4 prunes
- ✓ Ras el hanout to taste
- ✓ Mint leaves
- ✓ 1 zucchini
- ✓ 1 onion
- ✓ 8 Manzanilla olives or any green olives
- ✓ 400 ml Orange juice
- ✓ 50 g Couscous for garnish
- ✓ 500 ml Meat broth

Directions: 1 h

To prepare the dish, sauté the finely chopped onion in a small amount of extra virgin olive oil. While it cooks, brown the lamb slices in a frying pan while

frequently tossing to keep the fire goingr Once the onion is cooked, add the meat to the tajine. Two spoonfuls of the Ras el Hanout spices are added to the meat, and the pieces are stirred in the tajine so that the spices toast. Bring to a boil after adding the beef stock, olives, and raisins. When it boils, cover the tajine and reduce the heat to the lowest settingr

After 30 minutes of boiling our stew, add the sliced zucchini and test the sauce to adjust the salt if necessary. 8 chopped mint leaves should be added, then combined with the soup to provide flavor. After 10 minutes of cooking, the zucchini will be done, at which point we may turn off the heat and let it rest while we take the opportunity to make the garnish. As seen in the first picture, the stew or tajine needs to have some broth. As we did when making the taboulé recipe, we create a couscous with orange juice and bring both dishes to the table to be served immediately.

Tajine of veal with carrots

Ingredients for 4 people

- ✓ 1.2 Kg of veal (shank or knuckle)
- ✓ 8 carrots
- ✓ 2 onions
- ✓ 700 ml of meat or vegetable stock
- ✓ Ground black pepper
- ✓ 2 teaspoons of Ras el hanout
- ✓ Olive oil
- ✓ Salt

Directions: 3 hs

The veal should first be chopped into bite-sized or medium-sized chunks. The meat is also available in supermarkets, already prepared in trays, or we can request it in our trusted butcher shop. The onions were peeled and then sliced into julienne strips and placed in a basin. Five tablespoons of olive oil are heated to a medium-high fire in a taijne. After it reaches that temperature, the meat pieces are added. They are then fried for 4-5 minutes, or until they are lightly browned on all sides. The meat should be drained and set aside on a platter. Reduce the heat to medium-low and sauté the onion for 5 minutes, or until it softens, in the same oil. Add two teaspoons of ras el hanout, whisk thoroughly, and then add the meat or vegetable broth. Stir in the leftover meat pieces and season with salt and pepper to taste. Stir to combine all the ingredients. With the lid on, cook the tayn for two hours on low heat while occasionally stirringr The carrots, which we will have peeled and cut into sticks, are added at the specified time. We re-cover the tajine and cook it over a medium fire for another 30 minutes. Now that the veal tajine is prepared, all that is left to do is check the salt, adjust it if required, take it off the heat, and serve it right away. Happy eating!

Moroccan turkey roast

Ingredients for 2 people

- ✓ 1 turkey (leg)
- ✓ 1 tablespoon cumin (ras de hanout)
- ✓ 1 glass of virgin olive oil
- ✓ 1 glass of white wine
- ✓ 1 tablespoon salt
- ✓ 1 tablespoon pepper
- ✓ 1 large garlic
- ✓ 1 glass of parsley
- ✓ 1 glass of mint
- ✓ 3 medium potatoes

Directions: 2hs 30 min

Correctly clean the leg by separating the cartilage and thoroughly clean it by rubbing it with water. When it is prepared, we will make a few shallow cuts to him so that when the ingredients are dispersed, the flesh will absorb the flavor. Ras el hanout, virgin olive oil, white wine, salt, pepper, garlic, and mint are combined in a mixer to create a homogenous mixture. If we don't have a mixer, it doesn't matter; we may use a whisk or even a fork. We will distribute this emulsion on both sides of the turkey leg to get through the surface cuts. In the interim, we turned on the oven. The garnish is the following stage, and we have here decided to use potatoes because they go perfectly with the chicken meat. You must first peel them before slicing them into about one-centimeter thick pieces. The same ingredient mixture we used to coat the turkey will also be applied to these potatoes.

Last but not least, we'll grab a baking dish. Before adding the potatoes, you can spread a little butter with your hands on the bottom. The leg will be placed on top, and theingredient mixture will be added if there are any leftovers. We place the dish in the hot oven and bake it for around two hours at 180 degrees. The fluids discharged at the bottom of the casserole might occasionally be served over the leg by opening the oven.

Additionally, if the outside of the leg appears quite tanned, silver foil can be placed on top to ensure that the inside is well-cooked. The only thing left to do is plate and savor this succulent Moroccan turkey roast. As you can see, the recipe is fairly straightforward, and you will have the ideal dish to surprise your guests with local cuisine from our neighboring nation.

Tajin Dial Hout

Ingredients for 4 people

- ✓ Virgin olive oil
- ✓ 4-5 potatoes
- ✓ 1 small onion
- ✓ 2 large tomatoes
- ✓ ½ Eggplant
- ✓ 2 zucchini
- ✓ 2 hake fillets
- ✓ Salt
- ✓ Pepper
- ✓ 2 cloves of garlic, minced
- ✓ 3 tablespoons cumin
- ✓ 1 teaspoon paprika
- ✓ Fresh parsley
- ✓ 1 dash of virgin olive oil
- ✓ 1 lemon

We first prepare the layers of seasoned veggies for our fish Tajine. We achieve this by rubbing virgin olive oil over the base of a Tajine. Four or five peeled potatoes are cut into slices and added to the Tajine. 2 large tomatoes, 1 tiny onion, and both have been washed and skinned. The tomato slices should be placed on top of the onion slices to form a new layer. Wash, peel, and slice two zucchini and one-half of an eggplant. We create a fresh layer of sliced eggplant and zucchini on top of the earlier layers. Two hake fillets should then be sliced and salted and peppered. Put the fish pieces on top of the base layer. 2 crushed garlic cloves, 3 tablespoons of cumin, 1 teaspoon of paprika, and a few handfuls of fresh parsley should be added on top. Splash in some extra virgin olive oil. We seal our Tajn and cook for 21 minutes on high heat. At this point, we rapidly serve the fish Tajin with a lemon.

Moorish soup

Ingredients for 4 people

- ✓ 500 gr of crushed tomatoes
- ✓ 1 grated onion
- ✓ 4 natural tomatoes
- ✓ 2 tablespoons chopped parsley
- ✓ 2 tablespoons of chopped celery
- ✓ 3 tablespoons chopped coriander
- ✓ 200 gr of veal
- ✓ 100 gr of flour
- ✓ 150 gr of chickpeas
- ✓ 45 gr of thin noodles
- ✓ 2 tablespoons lentils
- ✓ 1 teaspoon of turmeric
- ✓ 1 teaspoon black pepper
- ✓ 2 tablespoons tomato concentrate
- ✓ 1 teaspoon ginger
- ✓ 1 tablespoon salt

Directions: 80 min

Add the following ingredients to a pressure cooker: meat, chickpeas, lentils, turmeric, black pepper, ginger, 1/3 of the coriander, 1/3 of the celery, and chopped onion. For this quantity, 3 liters of water must be added to the ingredients. The pot is placed over medium heat until it begins to boil. In a separate pot, we chop the tomatoes, add water to cover them, and simmer them over medium heat for about 10 minutes with the lid on. Once the pressure cooker's contents have reached a rolling boil, cover it and continue cooking for another 20 minutes.

We add water if we see that it is lackingr To remove the seeds and skin leftovers, crush the tomatoes and run them through a sieve or strainer (we have not peeled them before to convert the intense red color). Add the strained tomato mixture to the pressure cooker after

20 minutes. Until the flour is thoroughly incorporated, we gradually dissolve it in cold water.

The mixture shouldn't be too thick. We must filter it through a sieve, just as we did with the tomato, to remove all lumps. We gradually add the dissolved flour while the pot's contents are still boiling, stirring thoroughly after each addition. Thickening the soup is the goal of this phase. Allow it to cook for another 30 minutes, occasionally stirring to keep it from stickingr Prepare the tomato concentrate by adding a little water to make it less liquid while it is boilingr

It is added to the simmering pot. Add the noodles, the remaining coriander, the celery, and the parsley when there are a few minutes left in the entire 30 that we had stated cookingr This is done to intensify the aroma and flavor of the herbs.

Moroccan lamb stew

Ingredients for 4 people

- ✓ 1 kgr and a half - 2 kgr of lamb
- ✓ 3 onions
- ✓ 2 cloves of garlic
- ✓ 80 gr. of peeled almonds
- ✓ 80 gr. raisins
- ✓ 80 gr. of prunes
- ✓ 1 tablespoon of honey
- ✓ 400 gr. basmati rice
- ✓ water
- ✓ extra virgin olive oil
- ✓ salt
- ✓ pepper
- ✓ 1 teaspoon powdered ginger
- ✓ 1 teaspoon cinnamon powder
- ✓ Parsley

Directions:

Ras al Hanout, ginger, saffron, pepper, and a little water are combined in a basin. Apply this mixture to the seasoned meat pieces and allow to marinade. The onion should be chopped and cooked in oil. Add the toasted almonds and the coated pieces to the pan with the onion. Cook for 25 to 30 minutes at a moderate temperature with a lid on, seasoning as needed. Honey and the remaining spice mixture should marinate the raisins and prunes. Brown the two garlic cloves in their skins in a skillet with oil. Add the rice and the same amount of water, then top with parsley that has been chopped. For 8 to 10 minutes, cook the food in the covered pan over medium heat. Add dried raisins, prunes, honey, and cinnamon once the lamb is soft. Allow it to simmer for a further five to ten minutes. Put the rice with the lamb in a serving dish.

Chapter 4 Desserts

Italian desserts

Tiramisù

Ingredients for 6 people

- ✓ 500 Gr Mascarpone
- ✓ 300 Gr Savoyards
- ✓ 5 Eggs
- ✓ 100 Gr Sugar
- ✓ Cacao
- ✓ Coffee

Directions: 1h30 min

Use the coffee maker to brew strong coffee, then set it away to cool. Prepare the syrup (pâte à bombe) in a small saucepan by heating the sugar with two tablespoons of water until it reaches 121°C 1, using a kitchen thermometer to check the temperature.

Separate the egg whites from the yolks. Whip the yolks while slowly drizzling sugar syrup over them as you whip. When finished, you ought to have a fluffy, airy mass. Gently stir the mascarpone into the mixture, working your way from the bottom to the top. Place the ladyfingers in an oval or round bowl, and slowly pour the coffee over them until they are thoroughly saturated. Fill a cream piping bag and add clumps to the top. You could choose to create one layer or two. Place the tiramisu in the fridge and give it an hour to chill. Dust it with a little unsweetened cocoa powder when it has firmed up. You can now serve up your tiramisu.

Caprese cake

Ingredients for 6 people

- ✓ 190 gr peeled almonds or almond flour
- ✓ 125 gr butter
- ✓ 130 gr seeded sugar
- ✓ 2 tbsp rum
- ✓ 120 gr 52% fonding chocolate
- ✓ 3 eggs
- ✓ powdered sugar
- ✓ orange rice

Directions: 1h

In a food processor, assemble the almonds. Then blitz to a reasonably uniform flour. The dark chocolate should be broken up and placed in a small saucepan. Then, place the saucepan over a second one filled with water to create a double boiler to melt the additional ingredients. The egg yolks and sugar should be combined in a clean, big bowl and whisked until light and fluffy. Add the rum and orange zest to taste, then whisk once more. Pour the melted chocolate and butter in slowly, incorporating them both. At this point, mix in the almond flour using a spatula. In a bowl, whip the egg whites until they are firm. They should be added in two batches, carefully stirred, and mixed from the bottom to the top. An 18–20 cm mold should have a disk of baking paper on the bottom. Fill the mold with the dough. Level the cake's surface and bake for 30-35 minutes in a static oven prepared to 180 °C. After removing the cake from the oven, cool it for at least an hour. Flip it over carefully onto a serving platter. Slice baking paper into strips, arrange them on the cake, and then liberally dust with powdered sugar. Slice the Caprese cake, preserving the decoration as you gently remove the strips.

Coffee panna cotta

Ingredients for 4 people

- ✓ Coffee 150 ml
- ✓ Fresh liquid cream 500 ml
- ✓ Gelatin sheets 8 g
- ✓ Sugar 100 g
- ✓ Coffee 80 ml

✓ Dark chocolate 100 g

Directions: 40 min

Start by making the coffee with the mocha using a fairly strong blend to make the coffee panna cotta. Put the gelatin in ice-cold water to soak. Once the vanilla bean has been sliced in half, and the inside seeds have been retrieved, pour the cream into a saucepan along with the sugar and bring to a simmer. The now-soft gelatin should be squeezed (or strained) and added to the cream. After a brief period of stirring, add 150 ml of coffee and pour the mixture through a fine-mesh filter. Fill 6 molds with a capacity of approximately 125 ml each with the resulting mixture, and place in the refrigerator for at least 3 to 4 hours. Prepare the sauce 15 minutes before removing the panne cotta from the form. Melt the dark chocolate in a bain-marie or microwave. Add 80 cc of hot coffee. Stir until the sauce is fluid but not liquid. By gliding a knife through hot water while keeping the blade from sinking too far, you may remove the panna cotta from the mold. The mold should be briefly submerged in hot water before being inverted onto a serving platter. Lightly insert the knife blade to release the vacuum if the panna cotta proves difficult to remove from the mold. Add some chocolate coffee sauce and, if you have them, a few chocolate coffee beans to the coffee panna cotta for decoration. Serve right away.

Apple strudel

Ingredients for 6 people

- ✓ 130 g Flour 00
- ✓ Seed oil (1 tablespoon)
- ✓ 30 ml Water
- ✓ Salt (1 pinch)
- ✓ 750 g Golden apples
- ✓ 1 egg
- ✓ 60 g Breadcrumbs
- ✓ 50 g Butter
- ✓ 50 g Raisins
- ✓ 60 g Sugar
- ✓ 25 g Roasted pine nuts
- ✓ 1 lemon peel
- ✓ Powdered sugar to taste
- ✓ Rum (2 tablespoons)

✓ Cinnamon powder (1 teaspoon)

Directions: 1h 10 min

Start making the dough by placing the sifted flour, salt, and water in a bowl. Add the egg and water, and then begin by kneading with your hands. When the dough is smooth, add the oil and knead the mixture. You can add no more than 10–20 g of flour if it is too sticky. The dough ball should then be moved to a surface and worked until it becomes elastic. When you're finished, shape the dough into a ball, transfer it to a bowl that has been lightly greased, wrap it in plastic, and let it sit for an hour in a cold location. While the breadcrumbs are toasting, soak the raisins in rum or if you'd prefer, warm water while melting 30 g of butter in a frying pan. Stirring often with a wooden spoon will prevent burningr After a few minutes of browning, remove the pan from the heat and allow it cool. The apples should be peeled, the cores removed, and sliced into four wedges, then thin slices. In a large bowl, combine the apples with the sugar, pine nuts, grated lemon peel, a dash of cinnamon, and the raisins that have been well-drained and squeezed. While the components should release their aromas, they shouldn't macerate too long to prevent the sugar from releasing excessive water. Put the remaining butter in a little pan and heat it gently. Then, using a lightly dusted tea towel, flatten the dough ball to create a 35 by-45-inch rectangle. This layer will absorb the fluids the apples will release during cookingr

Brush the surface, excluding the borders, with a little melted butter and sprinkle with the toasted breadcrumbs. With care to avoid breaking the dough (you can use the dishcloth on which it is placed as support), place the mixture with the apples on top. Roll the strudel starting from the most extended portion. Seal it well on the edges so the contents do not leak out when cookingr Place the strudel with the seal facing down on a baking sheet lined with parchment paper, and then brush it with melted butter before bakingr If vented at 180° for 30 minutes, bake the strudel in a static oven that has been warmed to 200° for about 40 minutes. When the strudel is finished cooking, you can top it with powdered sugar, serve it warm, and cut it into slices.

Cocoa strudel with pears and cinnamon

Ingredients for 6 people

- ✓ Bitter cocoa powder 20 g
- ✓ Eggs (large) 1
- ✓ Flour 00 125 g
- ✓ Extra virgin olive oil 10 g
- ✓ Fine salt to taste
- ✓ Water (at room temperature) 30 g
- ✓ Abbot pears 600 g
- ✓ Lemon peel 1
- ✓ Butter 50 g
- ✓ Sugar 60 g
- ✓ Cinnamon powder 1 pinch
- ✓ Breadcrumbs 50 g
- ✓ Butter (melted) 20 g

Directions: 1h 10 min

Start by making the dough for the pear and cinnamon-cocoa strudel. The 00 flour should be sifted into a big bowl. Sift the bitter cocoa powder and combine it with the flour that has been sifted. Add the water, oil, and eggr Add a dash of salt to the mixture to season it. Vigorously knead. Finish vigorously kneading the dough on the work surface once all the ingredients have been combined, ensuring that the dough is nice and smooth. Lay it down flat and cover it with plastic wrap. After that, leave the dough wrapped in foil to rest for 30 minutes at room temperature. Now toast the breadcrumbs in butter in a nonstick skillet over low heat. Breadcrumbs should be stirred with a wooden spoon until they turn golden. Making the filling is the next step. Pears should first be peeled once the stems are removed. Now divide each pear into four wedges after cutting it in half. Take each wedge apart at the leathery center. Slice each wedge into a thin circle that is 4 mm thick. Return the slices that were sliced in this manner to a bowl. Pieces of pear should be topped with granulated sugar, grated lemon zest, and cinnamon powder.

All the ingredients should be combined. Let the mixture sit wrapped in foil for a few minutes so the flavors can meld. Take care not to soak the components for an excessively long time. The strudel's preparation can now be continued. Take a dishcloth and sprinkle it with flour before rolling the strudel. With the use of a rolling pin, flatten the dough into an about 30x40 cm form. Spread the previously toasted breadcrumbs inside the dough that has been smoothed out. Leave no breadcrumbs on the dough's outer edges. The purpose of the breadcrumbs is to absorb the fluids that the pears will produce while bakingr Pears marinated in seasonings for a short while should be placed on top of the breadcrumbs. Using the tea towel to assist you, roll up the dough down the long edge of the rectangle. Don't break the dough, please. Some of the melted butter should be used to brush the dough's edges. Once the entire strudel has been folded up, tuck the ends under. After that, line a drip pan with baking paper. Reposition the strudel to the drip pan. Apply the remaining melted butter to the brush now. The strudel will next bake for around 40 minutes in a static oven that has been preheated to 200°. Before serving, generously dust your pear, cinnamon, and cocoa strudel with powdered sugar.

Graffe

Ingredients for 20 pieces

- ✓ Whole milk (warm) 120 g
- ✓ 00 flour 130 g
- ✓ Manitoba flour 400 g
- ✓ Flour 00 70 g
- ✓ Dry yeast 3 g
- ✓ Potatoes (yellow or white) 300 g
- ✓ Sugar 50 g
- ✓ Fine salt 8 g
- ✓ Medium eggs 3
- ✓ Butter (softened) 100 g
- ✓ Acacia honey 8 g
- ✓ Sugar 200 g
- ✓ Peanut seed oil 1 l
- ✓ Lemon peel 1
- ✓ Butter 30 g

Directions: 30 min

The potato is washed and boiled. Brewer's yeast that has been dehydrated should be mixed with sifted flour and heated milk in a bowl until smooth. The leaven should be covered with plastic wrap and allowed to rise for one hour in an oven with the light on (otherwise, cover with a woolen cover and leave to rise in a place away from drafts). Peel the potatoes, mash them using a potato masher, and allow them to cool after cookingr Place the two sifted flours and the honey in a planetary mixer with a leaf mixer. Add the grated zest of an untreated lemon that has been thoroughly cleaned and dried, as well as the sugar and the now-warmed mashed potatoes. When the dough is hard and has gathered on the leaves, replace the paddle with the hook and add the yeast. After lightly beating the eggs and adding them, run the mixer. Once the yeast has been thoroughly combined, add the salt and include the melted butter one piece at a time. Wait until each addition has been completely absorbed before adding the next.

Transferring the dough to a work surface lightly oiled with melted butter, knead it with your hands until it is smooth. Please place it in a bowl covered with cling film, give it a spherical shape, and allow it to rise for two hours in an oven with the light on (or cover it with a blanket and left in a place away from drafts). 26 to 30 degrees is the perfect range for letting it rise. Once this time has passed, transfer the dough to a work surface still greased with the remaining melted butter, shape it into cylindrical, and then divide it into portions of about 60 gr Give each portion a spherical shape, flatten it slightly, and punch a hole in the center. Then, gently enlarge the hole to create 20 staples. The finished doughnuts should have doubled in size after being placed on a baking sheet coated with parchment paper, covered with cling film or a tea towel, and raised for an hour with the oven light on. Start heating the seed oil in a big pan once they've risen; it should be 160 degrees. To prevent carrying them by hand and running the danger of damaging their shape, construct support by cutting the parchment paper behind each staple. Dip the accompaniments with the baking paper gently once the oil reaches the specified temperature. Fry each one for a few minutes on each side. They ought should brown uniformly. Drain the staples from the oil with a skimmer after they are golden brown on all sides, and then set them aside to dry on a tray covered in paper towels. Put the caster sugar in a basin and roll the doughnuts while they are still hot to cover them in

sugar completely. Your graffe are ready; serve them steaming hot!

Rum baba

Ingredients for 25 pieces

- ✓ Eggs (12 medium) 600 g
- ✓ Fine salt 10 g
- ✓ Manitoba flour 600 g
- ✓ Fresh brewer's yeast 25 g
- ✓ Sugar 30 g
- ✓ Butter at room temperature 200 g
- ✓ Water 1.5 l
- ✓ Rum 300 g
- ✓ Sugar 600 g

Directions: 180 min + the hours of rising

Start with the dough to make the rum baba. Place the yeast in the planetary mixer's bowl after adding the flour. Allow the ingredients to start mixing while running the mixer on medium-low speed with the paddle attachment. One at a time, add the eggs; make sure they are thoroughly cold. Add the sugar and let it mix in once they have combined. It will take a total of 10 minutes. After that, add the salt and let it work for a few more minutes until it is absorbed. In the following step, switch the leaf for the hook, restart the robot at a medium-low speed, and then add the butter to the flakes. Before adding the next piece, you must wait for the previous one to completely absorb. Allow the machine to run for a few more minutes after the butter has been produced. Knead the dough for 10 to 15 minutes at this point. The dough will be smooth and soft when it is finished. Move the dough to a bigger basin if your planetary mixer's bowl doesn't have a minimum capacity of 2.5 liters. Cover the bowl with foil and allow the mixture to rise at a temperature between 26 and 28 degrees for approximately 3 hours. Once the time has passed, generously butter the molds. After the dough has had time to rise, take it out and carefully peel the foil-attached portion off. Utilize a wet metal spatula to assist yourself. Deflate the dough gradually using your hands. Squeeze roughly 50 to 55 gr of mozzarella-style dough with a damp hand, and drop the piece directly into well-buttered aluminum molds. Let the dough rest until it reaches the rim while covered with foil. When ready to bake, transfer the babas to a drip pan and bake them for 20 to 25 minutes in a static oven set to 200°, being careful to keep them reasonably apart from one another.

Then allow them to cool for about 10 minutes before removing them from the mold and allowing them to cool completely, leaving them outside overnight so that the inside and outside can completely dry. Next, make the topping by adding the water to a small pot. Once the sugar has completely dissolved, add it and stir. When the water bath reaches 50 degrees, the optimal temperature for soaking, turn it off, add the rum, and then dip 1 or 2 babas. Turn them over and let them soak for approximately one minute. They should be gently squeezed 1–2 times with a forceful but gentle hand during this time to soften and thoroughly soak them. If you'd rather, you can also cease squeezing them after the final soak. Continue similarly with all the others before draining them on a rack with a plate below. Recover the extra dipping liquid as you go. Your rum baba is prepared for servingr You may simply eat them or top them off with custard, sour cherries, cream, and strawberries!

Savoiardi (Ladyfingers)

Ingredients for about 60 pieces

- ✓ Egg yolks at room temperature 125 g
- ✓ Sugar 185 g
- ✓ Potato starch 65 g
- ✓ Flour 00 150 g
- ✓ Powdered sugar 50 g
- ✓ Cornflour 5 g
- ✓ Egg whites at room temperature 190 g

Directions: 30 min

Separate the eggs before preparing the ladyfingers. Add 100 g of sugar to the yolks in the planetary mixer's bowl, and start the machine at high speed. The volume of the yolks should quadruple as they whisk. Turn off the machine and place it inside the bowl to see if the yolk sticks nicely to it and does not run, which indicates that the mixture has been thoroughly whipped. The egg yolk and sugar combination should be set aside while you whisk the egg whites. With the whisk still attached,

pour them into a different planetary mixer bowl and mix them on low speed. The texture will vary depending on when the sugar is added; adding it first, before the egg whites are whisked, will produce a thick, more compact, but less whipped mass.

On the other hand, when sugar is added to almost-whipped egg whites, the texture becomes more aerated, glossy, and full-bodied. In this instance, add the sugar sparingly, a bit at a time, after the egg whites have nearly tripled in volume. As soon as all of the sugar has been combined, speed up the planetary mixer and continue mixing the mixture until it is uniform, smooth, and takes on the shape of the traditional "bird's beak." Then, sift the flour and starch 10 separately, then resift them on a piece of baking paper. The more sifted they are, the less likely they will separate when added to the dough. Return the dish containing the yolks at this point and stir in roughly one-third of the egg whites. Gently fold them with a spatula while rotating from the bottom to the top. Add a third of the sifted powders before they are completely absorbed, again lightly sprinkling and mixing from the bottom up. Continue in this manner, incorporating the powders twice and the egg whites twice more, 16, until the mixture is foamy and stiff. Then, transfer it to a pastry bag with a smooth 13-mm nozzle and use it to make sticks on a baking sheet lined with parchment paper.

As they will expand while baking, the sticks should be about 5 to 6 cm long and spaced widely apart. When the first pan is done, combine powdered sugar and cornstarch and use the mixture to completely cover the ladyfingers' surface. This will create a vapor barrier, enabling the ladyfingers to expand and become fluffier. Place them at the top of a static oven prepared to 230° for 9 minutes. Insert a small ball of silver paper between the oven door and the oven frame to represent the open valve found in professional ovens. As soon as the first baking sheet has finished baking, you may add the second baking sheet. In the meantime, spread the remaining ladyfingers out on a baking sheet and sprinkle them as you did. After baking, let the ladyfingers cool completely before moving them to a serving plate.

Creme Caramel

Ingredients for 6 molds

- ✓ Whole milk 450 g
- ✓ Fresh liquid cream 150 g
- ✓ Sugar 120 g
- ✓ Egg yolks 1 medium
- ✓ Eggs 4 medium
- ✓ Sugar 150 g
- ✓ Vanilla pod 1

Directions: 70 min

To start, make the caramel: pour the sugar into a heavy pot and melt it over low heat, rotating the pan occasionally rather than stirringr When the caramel has taken on an amber hue, carefully pour it into the six 180 ml molds you have set inside a high-sided baking dish. Rotate the molds to distribute the caramel evenly over the base. Continue with the recipe after setting the molds aside. The seeds and vanilla pod should be added to the milk after pouring it into a bowl. The milk should then be simmered in a small pot. When it boils, turn off the heat and let the mixture sit for 30 minutes.

Remove the vanilla bean after this period, then stir in the cream and put aside for a while. To avoid integrating air, beat the eggs and sugar together in a separate basin without whipping them. After straining the milk and cream combination through a sieve, slowly add and whisk it once more to combine the ingredients smoothly. Return the baking dish with the molds, and spread the finished mixture using a ladle. Fill the pan with boiling water until the molds are covered by a third of the liquid. Then, bake for about 50 minutes in a bain-marie in a static oven that has been prepared to 180°. After being cooked, let the molds cool before putting them in the refrigerator to chill for at least four hours. After the required cooling period, remove the crème caramels from the mold, helping yourself with a small knife to take away from the corners more easily, and serve!

Coconut milk ice cream

Ingredients for 4 people (500 Gr)

- ✓ Coconut milk 300 g
- ✓ Dark chocolate 100 g
- ✓ Almond milk 100 g
- ✓ Brown sugar 50 g

Directions: 40 min

First, add brown sugar 1 to a saucepan with the almond milk and heat until the sugar has melted completely. Next, add the almond milk to the bowl of coconut milk and stir. Mix 4, wrap in plastic wrap 5, and put in the fridge for at least 30 minutes to solidify. Fill your self-refrigerating ice cream machine with the ice cream, cover it with the lid, and process it for at least 25 minutes. The chocolate should be roughly chopped and melted in a bain-marie or microwave. When the ice cream has thoroughly frozen, slowly pour in the chocolate as the machine keeps mixingr You will achieve a stracciatella-like effect in this manner. To achieve the ideal consistency, continue mixing the ice cream for an additional 10 minutes. Additionally, you may consume the coconut milk ice cream right away or freeze it in a container with high edges.

Chocolate coconut bars

Ingredients for 12 pieces

- ✓ Milk Chocolate 1 ½ cup (250 g)
- ✓ Shredded coconut 1 cup (200 g)
- ✓ Shredded coconut to taste
- ✓ Condensed milk ½ cup (150 g)
- ✓ Fine salt 1 pinch

Directions: 60 min + cooling time

Put the coconut shreds in a dish. With a spatula, add the condensed milk. Add the salt number three and mix once more. Form a 5.5 x 4 inch rectangle by placing the ingredients on a piece of parchment paper and manually pressing it into shape. It must have a thickness of 0.8 inches. Allow the food to chill for about an hour in the refrigerator. To create 12 bars, remove the mixture from the refrigerator and cut it into 6 pieces lengthwise after cutting it half lengthwise. Smooth the corners of each one by carefully shaping them by hand. As you shape each one, put them on a tray and put the tray in the refrigerator. Chop the chocolate finely and divide it into two bowls, one holding 7 ounces and the other 1.8 ounces. Melt the chocolate in a microwave or a bain-marie. To avoid burning the chocolate when using the latter, heat in brief bursts of a few seconds each; stir after every 30 seconds until completely melted.

Remove the bars from the refrigerator in the interim; they shouldn't be too cold, or the coating would cause the chocolate to crystallize right away. Add the piece you set aside and stir with a spatula once the chocolate has melted. Stir the chocolate constantly until it reaches 86°F (30°C). The simplest way of tempering chocolate is known as "seedingr" Line a grille with a piece of parchment paper in the meanwhile. Use a fork to dip the bars into the chocolate as soon as it reaches the proper temperature. After removing the bars from the chocolate, carefully tap them to get rid of any leftover chocolate. Continue drizzling chocolate over the remaining bars, then set them on the grills. Sprinkle some coconut shreds on top for decoration, then let the mixture sit at room temperature to crystallize. Place the bars in the fridge if it's too warm. You can serve the chocolate coconut bars as soon as the chocolate has dried completely.

Spanish desserts

Churros

Ingredientes for 2 people

- ✓ 250 gr all-purpose wheat flour
- ✓ 250 gr water
- ✓ 1 teaspoon of salt (about 8 gr)
- ✓ Sugar for sprinkling
- ✓ Sunflower oil
- ✓ A piping bag with a thin mouth
- ✓ Absorbent kitchen paper

Directions:

Organize the flour in a sizable bowl. In a saucepan, warm the salted water. Pour the liquid over the flour immediately after it begins to boil. We mix the flour and water together using a wooden spoon. We'll get a dough that is quite compact and sticky. We will now introduce this dough in a pastry bag or churrera. This step is crucial for the churros to turn out correctly and fry without any issues. The dough is compressed, and the air is removed by the churrera. This is a crucial step because it stops the churros from diving into the oil. Put the dough in your churro-making machine if you have one.

The ideal choice. If you don't have access to a churro machine, you may still make the churros using a pastry bag with a star-shaped nozzle. Because they are not the same as with a churro maker, it is not advised. However, some people have succeeded in producing tasty churros using piping bags. Disposable plastic can be used to create piping bags. They are available in places that sell baking supplies and online bakeware retailers. We prepare the churros parts using the uncooked dough on a tea towel on the counter. Chill the dough and stop it from popping or opening up while fryingr Plenty of light olive oil or sunflower oil is heated in a frying pan. We add the parts of the dough to fry when it is heated. Before frying, the oil's temperature must be measured (if possible) between 195° and 200°C for churros or 230°C. To keep the churros from being raw inside, cook over medium heat. Churros can leap when fried if you use a piping bag to create them. This issue won't arise with the churrera. Once fried, transfer to a tray lined with paper towels to absorb any extra oil.

Serve with icing sugar or white sugar sprinkles (powdered).

Pestiños with honey or sugar

Ingredients

- ✓ 260 gr all-purpose wheat flour
- ✓ 75 ml. sherry wine
- ✓ 400 ml. mild virgin olive oil or sunflower oil
- ✓ The peel of 1 lemon
- ✓ 1 tablespoonful of matalahúva seeds
- ✓ Salt (2 gr)
- ✓ 200 gr of honey (or sugar and ground cinnamon)

Directions:

In a frying pan, warm up all the oil (either sunflower or light olive oil). Add the lemon peel and the matalahva seeds after it is highly heated. After two to three minutes, remove them from the fire. Allow coolingr Put the flour, wine, 75 ml. of the oil spiced with the lemon and the seeds, and the fried matalahva seeds, in a bowl. Pour onto the kitchen surface after stirring with a wooden spoon. Make a tight ball out of the dough that doesn't stick to our hands. For 30 minutes, let the dough rest with a towel covering it. Cut chunks of dough approximately 5 x 5 cm in size after flattening the dough as thin as possible with a rolling pin. In theory, grease is unnecessary because the dough does not stick to the surface; however, if you'd like, you can sprinkle a few drops of oil on the counter before stretchingr Because the dough turns slightly fatty and flaky when fried, it is crucial to stretch them out as thinly as possible. To keep them from peeling off during frying, fold the opposing edges of each part in on themselves, coating them with a few drops of water and pressingr With the flavored oil, warm the frying pan over medium heat. The main challenge with this treatment is the oil's temperature; if it's not too hot, the dough will be uncooked and not crunchy. But if the oil is excessively hot, it will quickly brown and become raw within. The initial batch will enable us to test, and the subsequent batches will be delectable. A few at a time, add them to the frying pan. When they are golden brown, we remove the pesto to a paper towel to soak up the extra oil.

We have two choices for how to cover them: For every 100 gr of sugar, two teaspoons of cinnamon powder are added to a large bowl, and everything is thoroughly mixed with a fork. They can be dipped in this mixture while still heated. Having assistance at this stage is advantageous because doing everything at once is more challengingr Additionally, you can drop them in honey. To do this, we heat the honey with roughly 1/4 of its volume of water. We dip the pesto and remove it to a grid when it is hot and well-integrated. Allow them to dry, and drain the leftover honey.

Torrijas

Ingredientes for 10 people

- ✓ 1 loaf of bread from the day before
- ✓ 1 and a half liters of whole milk
- ✓ 5 medium eggs
- ✓ 1 cinnamon stick, 1 vanilla pod, the zest of half a lemon
- ✓ 100 ml port wine
- ✓ 300 g of white sugar and 1 tablespoon of ground cinnamon.
- ✓ 1/2 l of mild extra virgin olive oil

Directions: 25 minutes

Preparing the substances with which we will flavor the milk is the first stage. We thoroughly wash the lemon before peeling off as little white flesh as possible to make a bitter dessert. We have a component that will make a difference in the flavor of the milk as well as the cost because vanilla pods are not inexpensive. The entire open pod is required for this dish; the interior, or seeds, are optional and can be saved for another delicacy. I suggest freezing them in aluminum foil and using them gradually, based on the recipe, to save money on this component. To get the most out of it, use a knife to slit the largest area of the pod from one end to the other, opening it like a book. Cut the ends of the pod. To get the seeds, we intend to save and scrape the interior with a knife's blade (it works best to fully open it with your fingers and use only half of the edge). We will put the clean pod into the milk, and when the milk has been flavor-infused, we will remove it and dry it. It will be kept for future use.

For instance, we can produce our own vanilla sugar to flavor it. Near boiling point is reached by heating the milk at medium heat. Add the cinnamon stick, vanilla pod, and lemon peel after lowering the heat and turning off the burner. Allow everything to sit for 5 minutes so the milk can infuse. When we use the milk to soak the torrijas, it should be either warm or cold. Place aside. A small tip is to avoid adding sugar to the infused milk so that the torrijas don't come out overly sweet. However, we will add the sugar and cinnamon when preparing the syrup or before servingr We select a cozy vessel and fill it with the chilled infused milk that we have set aside to dip the bread we have chosen for the torrijas in. Add the port wine (optional step) to give the dessert its kick, and whisk the liquids together thoroughly. In another dish that is comfortable to dip the torrijas in before frying, beat the eggs until they slightly thicken. Add two teaspoons of the infused milk and mix again. Over medium heat, add a frying pan with extra virgin olive oil. Dip the bread slices in the infused milk while the oil is heatingr Sugar and cinnamon powder should be added to a large bowl. For every 100 gr of sugar, about two tablespoons of cinnamon powder are required. Mix thoroughly with a fork. To ensure that the torrijas are thoroughly coated in sugar and cinnamon, dredge them in this mixture.

Allow them to cool before enjoying them cold or at room temperature. Keep in mind that the torrijas get better over time. I allowed them to perspire, as you can see in the images. As a result, they are covered in a coating of sweet and creamy syrup, which elevates them to the top. Don't dispute it, exquisite; come on.

Papajotes

Ingredientes for 6 people

- ✓ 20 min.
- ✓ 250 g wheat flour
- ✓ 250 ml of whole milk
- ✓ 1 egg
- ✓ 1 soda or 1 tablespoon of baking soda or 1 tablespoon of baking powder
- ✓ Extra virgin olive oil
- ✓ Sugar
- ✓ A pinch of salt

✓

Directions: 20 minutes

The egg should be beaten in a big basin. Add the milk and continue beating until all of the ingredients are combined until it has reached the consistency of an omelette. Now it's the flour's time, which needs to be added gradually. Stir after adding a bit. At least three times should be performed again. Add the soda or teaspoon of commercial yeast (depending on what we have on hand) and a dash of salt after all the flour has been added. Stir the mixture once more until it resembles thick cream. Extra virgin olive oil in large quantities is heated in a frying pan. With a spoon, we scoop up bits of the dough and drop them into the hot oil. The papajotes should be turned so that each side browns equally. When the papajotes are done, drain the oil well before removing them from the pan. To make them less greasy, put them on a plate or dish covered with paper towels. When the sweet papajotes are prepared, they are dusted with sugar and served for consumption. If at all possible, serve with a cup of hot chocolate and serve right away. Enjoy!

Buñuelos de Calabaza (Pumpkin fritters)

Ingredientes for 4 people

- ✓ 250 g special wheat flour for baking
- ✓ 15 g fresh baker's yeast, at room temperature
- ✓ 1/4 sachet of baking soda
- ✓ 180 g pumpkin puree
- ✓ 130 ml water or pumpkin stock, lukewarm
- ✓ Vegetable oil for frying
- ✓ Sugar for coating
- ✓ A pinch of salt (3 gr)

Directions: 60 minutes

If we don't already have the pumpkin puree prepared, we do so and ensure that the required weight is available for the recipe. Peel the pumpkin, take out the seeds, and throw away the filaments as well. Chop and simmer till tender in a saucepan with lots of water. Drain, then mash with a fork or combine with a hand blender (we can save this liquid for the dough fritters or use water, to taste). Baker's yeast should be dissolved in water or the pumpkin broth after the pumpkin has been cooked. Make a hole in the center of the flour in a big bowl. Pour the previous mixture in and gently whisk while gradually incorporating more flour. Add a touch of salt and the pumpkin puree, then mix one more. After that, add the baking soda and stir once more for about 10 minutes or until the dough is thick and smooth. We have two options: we can stir slowly in a food processor, use our hands, a wooden spoon, or both (well-cleaned, of course). The dough should rest for 30 to 40 minutes, or until it doubles in size and begins to ferment, covered with a clean towel. We proceed to fry the fritters when the dough has fermented. To do this, prepare a plate with absorbent paper and heat up a frying pan with plenty of oil.

Along with the bowl of dough, we also put a bowl of water on the table because we'll need to wet our hands to shape each fritter. The manual and traditional method of making the fritters is pressing a tiny bit of dough into a fist with the left hand. The right hand, which had previously been immersed in water, extracts the dough as it bubbles out of the top of the container. After that, put it in the heated oil while poking a hole in the center with your thumb. Using three or four at a time, fry, flipping each batch halfway through to ensure even browning on both sides. Take off to a dish lined with absorbent paper, let the excess oil drain, and then roll in sugar. Along with a cup of hot chocolate or our preferred beverage, serve the pumpkin fritters. They are excellent and can even be eaten raw.

Arroz con Leche (Rice Pudding)

Ingredientes for 10 people

- ✓ 200 g of special dessert rice
- ✓ 200 ml of water
- ✓ 1 large lemon
- ✓ 2,5 l of whole milk
- ✓ 1 large cinnamon stick
- ✓ 1 generous pinch of salt
- ✓ 150 g white sugar
- ✓ 10 g cinnamon powder
- ✓ 100 g of sugar

Directions: 180 minutes

Preparing the substances with which we will flavor the milk is the first stage. We thoroughly wash the lemon before peeling off as little white flesh as possible to make a bitter dessert. The largest cinnamon stick you can locate is also required. Near boiling point is reached by heating the two liters of milk over medium heat. Remove from the heat and reduce the temperature. Then include the cinnamon stick and lemon peel. Allow everything to rest for five minutes (infusing the milk). Bring the rice, water, and a pinch of salt to a boil in a separate pan. The salt is crucial since it gives the dish a certain touch and is essentially the key to making it truly authentic rice puddingr Remove the rice as soon as it has soaked up all the water. Even though we just added a little water and the rice might still be a little firm, we managed to save close to 30 minutes using this method. My Asturian buddy Carlos Noceda adds the previously infused milk to the casserole to continue with his recipe.

Nevertheless, my mother advised me to put it in the milk casserole because that would be the wisest course of action. Moreover, the rice should always be cooked at a relatively low temperature. Therefore, I have always kept the temperature of my induction stove at 3, as per my mother's instruction of 10 points. Every 10 minutes, stir to prevent adhering to the pan and ensure that the flavors are well distributed. It will take about an hour for the milk and rice to evaporate, releasing the last starch. Add the reserved half-liter of milk after we have reached this point. For an additional hour, we maintain the low temperature while constantly stirring to get the appropriate level of creaminess. When the rice is creamy, keep in mind that it will become slightly fatty as it cools. Put the sugar in. The sugar is always added last to prevent sticking and to slightly thicken the cream. We fill some casseroles or chilled bowls from your home for the presentation. Give something 15 minutes to stand. We shall burn the surface before serving the rice puddingr On top, sprinkle a teaspoon of cinnamon-infused sugar. Use a kitchen blowtorch to burn. For this dish, a unique burner can also be used. Even though it is difficult to obtain and takes up a lot of room in a small kitchen like mine. I prefer the blowtorch that produces the infamous plate of crunchy sugar and keeps the rice pudding at the proper temperature.

Crema Catalana

Ingredientes for 4 people

- ✓ 1 l milk
- ✓ 200 g sugar
- ✓ 40 g cornstarch
- ✓ 9 egg yolks
- ✓ 1 cinnamon stick
- ✓ 1 lemon, peel only

To dissolve the cornstarch in the milk, we first separate a glass of milk from the rest of the milk. We then heat the remaining milk along with the cinnamon stick and lemon peel until it boils, at which point we take it off the heat. Mix the sugar and egg yolks together. Restart the fire, then add the milk that has been infused. Add the cup of milk with the cornstarch when it becomes hot (very hot), stirring continually. When it begins to boil, remove the heat and continue cooking while stirringr The cream should be divided into individual casseroles and left to cool. Put sugar on top right before serving, burn it so it caramelizes, and then? Time to eat!

Natillas

- ✓ 1/2 l cream
- ✓ 5 egg yolks
- ✓ 110 g sugar
- ✓ 2 vanilla pods

Open the pods, remove the seeds with a knife, and then put the seeds in a saucepan with hot cream for about 10 minutes to steep. On the other hand, whisk the egg yolks and sugar together in a bowl. Mix in the cream after adding the yolks. A bain-marie should be used to cook until 82°C is reached. Then chill for at least 20 minutes in the refrigerator. Serve the custard on a platter with some sugar sprinkled on top that has been caramelized with a blowtorch.

Flan

Ingredients for 6 people

- ✓ 4 eggs L.
- ✓ 2 egg yolks L.

- ✓ 500 ml of milk.
- ✓ 1 cinnamon stick
- ✓ 1 dessert spoon of vanilla essence or 1 vanilla pod.
- ✓ 150 g sugar
- ✓ 100 gr sugar
- ✓ 4 tablespoons of water plus 30-40 ml of hot water
- ✓ 1 dessert spoon of lemon juice

Directions: 90 min + 4 cooling hours

Over medium-high heat, add the cinnamon stick and vanilla bean to a saucepan with the milk. Once it begins to boil, turn off the heat, cover the saucepan, and allow the mixture to cool and steep for about 30 minutes. Infusing is done so that it will absorb much more taste than if the branches were removed right away. Place the sugar, 4 tablespoons of water, and lemon juice in a small skillet or pan over medium heat. Use a metal spoon to give it a quick stir so that it starts to dissolve (the caramel gets so hot that it is ideal to use metal tools).

Remove the spoon (and put it in a basin or something similar), and wait until the caramel turns golden brown without stirringr I'm sorry, but you cannot test it as I usually advise with everythingr Take it off the fire and use extreme caution while handling it because it is extremely hot and can result in severe burns. When the 40 ml of water is nearly boiling in the microwave, slowly pour it into your caramel while stirring with a spoon. If the caramel in the pan begins to firm while the flan is set, try adding more hot water until it stays liquid. The goal is to obtain a caramel that won't harden in the refrigerator. The caramel should be poured into 6 molds.

Crack the four whole eggs into a bowl, and then crack the two extra yolks into another bowl, leaving the white and yolk to come out with the rest of the eggs. In a bowl, combine the eggs, yolks, and sugar. Lay an oven rack in the center of the oven, where we will place the tray containing the flans, and preheat it to 160°C with heat up and down. The 4 whole eggs, 2 egg yolks, and sugar for the flan should all be whisked together until the mixture is uniform. Do not overbeat the mixture to avoid creating an excessive amount of froth. Beat the eggs and the sugar. Put the milk through a strainer and combine it with the sugar and eggs in a bowl. Place the molds with the batter on a baking sheet with a specific height. To cover the molds, fill the pan halfway with water, then place it in a medium-heated oven. For around 45 minutes, bake them in the oven in a bain-marie. After removing them from the oven and allowing them to cool, place them in the refrigerator to chill for three to four hours.

Moroccan desserts

Chebakia

Ingredients for 6 people

- ✓ 1 sachet of Royal baking powder
- ✓ 250 gr. of flour
- ✓ 100 gr. of toasted almonds
- ✓ 75 gr. of toasted sesame (plus whatever you consider sprinkling)
- ✓ 1 teaspoon cinnamon
- ✓ 50 ml. orange blossom water
- ✓ 1 teaspoon of aniseed
- ✓ 1 egg
- ✓ 1 tablespoon vinegar
- ✓ 25 gr. butter
- ✓ 50 ml. olive oil
- ✓ 100 ml. of water
- ✓ Sunflower oil
- ✓ 500 ml. of honey

Direction: 110 min

To prepare the ingredients for the dough, we blend the almonds (which we purchase roasted and skinless) until they are pureed because if there are any large bits, we won't be able to spread them out with the rolling pin effectively. The roasted sesame seeds are also made into a paste by blending them with a generous amount of oil and aniseed grain. Mix the mashed almonds with a fork in a bowl with an egg, cinnamon, and a small amount of vinegar. Then, incorporate the sesame paste, oil, and orange blossom water (the latter ingredient is optional if you don't have it at home but valuable if you want to add nuances). Mix everything in a bowl with a fork after adding the mashed almonds, an egg, cinnamon, and some vinegar. Add the sesame paste, oil, and orange blossom water next. All ingredients should be stirred. The dough should be placed on the counter, worked for at least 15 minutes, and water added gradually. I forewarn you that there may be occasions when you feel as though you are becoming sticky, but do not be alarmed; with love and patience, you will soon resume having a regular texture. People will take the initiative not to add water at this final step because they recognize how well the dough is already joined; if you make that choice, I can practically guarantee that it will be too crispy and dry when fried. Once prepared, we roll it into a ball, wrap it in plastic, and let it sit at room temperature for at least 30 minutes. To make it more comfortable, we increased the resting period after it and divided it into three parts. We keep the piece we will work with first and roll it out as thinly as possible with a rolling pin or a pasta machine. As shown in the illustration below, we cut four parallel cuts inside each rectangle that are approximately 6 cm wide but do not extend to the edges. Suppose you have a special cutter made just for chebakias. In that case, you may complete this process in a lot more comfortable and exact manner. The hardest part is now approaching—shaping it. We will need to be patient during this procedure, which will involve a lot of leftover chebakias.

We lay the rectangle on the palm of our hand and alternately separate the strips with our index finger (one above, one below, etc.). Afterward, keep the inner pieces folded inward like a sock while leaving the side strips in place. Finally, we flatten the ends and slightly widened the strips. The final form ought to resemble a rose. As we give the shape, we will heat the sunflower oil on a high heat source and the honey in a separate pot. We add them to the pan as we work on them. As soon as they are golden brown, we will remove them and immediately place them into the pan, allowing them to sit with the hot honey for at least five minutes. It is vital to leave them for just the appropriate amount of time so that they are not dry or too crunchy. They can now be served by placing them on a platter and topping them with toasted sesame seeds. The only options are to keep five or six and distribute the remainder to neighbors and friends, or to store them in a tupper on a visible shelf and give in to temptation at a rate of one chebakia every fifteen minutes. Which decision you make is up to your conscience, not mine.

Briwat

Ingredients for 35 pieces

- ✓ 250 grs ground almonds
- ✓ 100 g icing sugar
- ✓ 1 teaspoon cinnamon
- ✓ 40 g butter at room temperature
- ✓ 2 tablespoons orange blossom water
- ✓ 1 pinch of Arabic gum (optional)
- ✓ Brick pastry or filo pastry
- ✓ Melted butter
- ✓ Orange blossom honey
- ✓ Sesame

Direction:

The ground almonds, confectioners' sugar, cinnamon, room-temperature butter, two teaspoons of orange blossom water, and gum arabic should all be combined in a bowl. The latter can be found already powdered or in grains, so you must smash them before adding them. Mix everything thoroughly until it resembles a dough that can be formed into little balls, first with a spatula and then, in the final stages, with your hands. It only requires a little kneading; after 3 to 4 minutes, all the ingredients were well-integrated and compact. We shape little balls with all the dough after greasing our

hands with melted butter to help handle the dough easier. The balls will be modestly sized, roughly the size of a pin pon ball. Now, cut the brick dough or filo dough into about three fingers broad strips using a pizza cutter. It will be simpler if you like the rectangular dough. However, we can still get the same results using a circular one if necessary. Put a dough ball at the bottom of each strip of brick dough and slightly flatten it. Then, brush each strip with melted butter to help the bricks hold together. To construct a triangle, we are rotating the dough in both directions. Make sure they are well sealed to prevent opening while bakingr

Each triangle should be placed on a baking sheet lined with parchment paper. Bake each triangle for 10 to 15 minutes at 180 degrees (the oven will already be warmed with heat up and down). Pour the honey into a saucepan and set it over the fire two or three minutes before they are done bakingr Add a teaspoon of orange blossom to the honey. After we have finished baking, we run all of the briouats through the hot honey that will be on the stove, letting them pour the extra honey on a sieve before passing them to the dish. They can be embellished by adding sesame seeds on top of each one before servingr Allow them to cool. If you serve them with a fine Moorish tea, they'll be ideal.

Ghriba

Ingredients: 25 pieces

- ✓ 250 g All-purpose wheat flour
- ✓ 100 g sesame seeds
- ✓ 8 g baking powder
- ✓ 100 g icing sugar
- ✓ 80 ml oil
- ✓ 80 g unsalted butter
- ✓ 1/4 kg almonds
- ✓ 1 pinch of fine salt
- ✓ Cinnamon powder for sprinkling

Directions: 1 h 45 min

All the dry ingredients—almonds that have already been crushed; sesame seeds; yeast; flour; sugar; and salt—should be combined thoroughly in a big bowl. The dough should then be covered with plastic wrap and chilled for an hour. Make sure the melted butter is warm and liquid before adding it to the oil. After an hour, take the dough out of the refrigerator, knead it briefly to mix the liquid from the butter and oil, and then boléala a bit to remove some of the chills. The dough should then be weighed and divided into sections of 20 to 30 gr, depending on the desired cookie size. Place the balls on a tray that has been greased or lined with parchment paper with a centimeter of space between each one. Bake for about 15 minutes at 180 degrees, or until the tops begin to become golden. The snack is prepared for serving after cooling and being sprinkled with cinnamon.

Makrout

Ingredients:

- ✓ 125 gr medium semolina.
- ✓ 125 gr of fine semolina.
- ✓ 1 tablespoon of sugar.
- ✓ 1 pinch of salt.
- ✓ 100 g melted butter.
- ✓ 1 teaspoon orange blossom water.
- ✓ 125 ml of cold water.
- ✓ 125 g date paste.
- ✓ 1/2 teaspoon cinnamon.
- ✓ 1 tablespoon butter.
- ✓ 1/2 teaspoon orange blossom water.
- ✓ Honey
- ✓ 2 drops of orange blossom water.

Directions:

Mix the two types of semolina, sugar, and salt in a basin. After mixing everything, add the melted butter. The water and orange flower water should then be poured. Knead all of it. Combine the ingredients for the filling, knead them, and shape long sticks about 1 cm thick. Create additional sticks from the semolina dough, flatten them, and make a longitudinal slit in the middle with your fingers to create a groove for the date stick. Next, join the sides using weldingr If you don't have a mould, you can flatten the two sticks once they are made, cut them with a knife, and then decorate them however you like. At 180 degrees, bake the macaroni for around 25 minutes. After taking them out of the oven, cover them with honey flavored with orange blossom extract and let them cool.

Maamoul

Ingredients

- ✓ 250 g flour
- ✓ 135 g butter
- ✓ 40 g water
- ✓ 50 g sugar
- ✓ 1/4 tablespoon powdered milk (optional)
- ✓ 1 pinch of salt
- ✓ 1/8 cup homemade syrup
- ✓ 1 Filling
- ✓ Ground walnuts
- ✓ Amount of syrup needed
- ✓ Butter
- ✓ Sugar for sprinkles
- ✓ 2 Filling
- ✓ Date or fig paste
- ✓ Amount needed Butter
- ✓ Required quantity of syrup

Directions:

Due to the dough. Together with your hands, combine flour and butter until a very silky, crumbly, soft, and uniform dough is formed. Place aside. Combine water, sugar, and syrup in a glass. Pour the syrup concoction into a glass. Stir in the flour after adding the syrup mixture. It will initially look like there is too much water. Remain calm; it will absorb. When that occurs, put it away. If it's too warm, go to the refrigerator. To make the filling, combine the walnuts, syrup, and butter and work in your hands to form a workable dough. A marzipan-like texture, perhaps. Apply the date paste in the same way. It need to be soft and moldable.

for the stuffing of walnuts. Make ping pong ball-sized balls out of the dough. Similarly treat the walnut. The walnut ball ought to be more compact. Take a dough ball, and using your thumb, open it so that it may be filled. Place a walnut ball inside before sealing it off without letting it pass through to the opposite side. You can shape it as you like: with a fork, your hand, a mold, etc. Stretch it out as follows for the date filling (this should be very easy to prepare). Place aside. Take three little dough balls and combine them. To create a narrow strip, uselerear on plastic wrap. On top of the dough, spread the date paste. On top of the dough, spread the date paste. Close. Form it. It's wide and curved to my likingr Use a sharp knife that has been dampened. Take the buns and the pieces and bake them at 200 ° C in a preheated oven until the bottom edges are just starting to brown. 10 minutes or so. Their proper name is blanquitos. After removing from the oven, top with confectioners' sugar.

Kwirat Tlj

Ingredients for 12 servings

- ✓ 3 large eggs
- ✓ 1 cup (236 milliliters) vegetable oil
- ✓ 1 cup (200 gr) granulated sugar
- ✓ 1 teaspoon vanilla sugar
- ✓ 3 1/4 cups (400 gr) all-purpose flour
- ✓ 2 teaspoons baking powder
- ✓ 1/4 teaspoon salt
- ✓ 2 1/2 cups (200 gr) shredded unsweetened coconut
- ✓ 2 1/2 cups (625 gr) apricot jam
- ✓ 3 tablespoons orange flower water

Directions: 72 minutes

Assemble the components. Set your oven to 360°F/180°C for preheatingr Using parchment paper, line two or three baking sheets. Beat the eggs, oil, sugar, and vanilla until they are creamy and thick in a large bowl. Just long enough to create a soft, slightly sticky dough that can be formed into balls, add the flour, baking powder, and salt. Stir or knead the mixture with your hands. You can add a little more flour if you think the mixture is too soft and sticky, but be careful not to overmix it or add too much so that the dough turns firm rather than soft. Cherry-sized dough balls should be formed, and they should be spaced at least an inch (2.5 cm) apart on a baking sheet that has been prepared. For 10 to 12 minutes, or until gently brown, bake the cookies in batches in the center of the

preheated oven. Before garnishing, transfer to a rack to cool for roughly 5 minutes.

Decorate the Cookies

Prepare the garnish while the first batch of cookies bakes. Put the coconut on a pie plate or other deep, big dish. Place aside. Use an immersion blender or food processor to puree your apricot jam into a smooth consistency if it contains chunks of fruit. In a small saucepan, combine the orange flower water with the apricot jam. For a few minutes, cook the jam over medium-low heat until it is hot and syrupy. Get rid of the heat. Immerse a number of cookies at once in the hot jam. Remove two cookies, blot or drain the extra jam from them, then press the bottoms of the cookies together. Sandwiched cookies should be rolled in coconut before being placed back on the parchment-lined baking sheet to continue coolingr Reheat the apricot syrup to maintain its thin consistency before applying the garnish to the remaining batches of cookies.

Fekkas

Ingredients for 40 pieces

- ✓ 1 K (8 cups) all-purpose wheat flour
- ✓ 280 g (1 1/3 cups) sugar
- ✓ 6 eggs M
- ✓ 240 ml (1 1/8 cups) sunflower or neutral oil
- ✓ 1 tablespoon aniseed powder
- ✓ 15g baking powder or yeast
- ✓ 30 ml warm milk
- ✓ 30 ml orange blossom water
- ✓ 200 g (1 1/3 cups) of hazelnuts
- ✓ 300 g (2 cups) almonds
- ✓ 100 g (3/4 cup) pistachios
- ✓ 200 g (1 2/3 cups) walnuts
- ✓ 75 g (1/2 cup) sesame seeds, toasted and crushed
- ✓ 1 egg yolk
- ✓ 1 tablespoon of instant coffee
- ✓ 2 tablespoons of water

Directions: 60 minutes

Sift the flour first, then combine it with the salt and yeast in a separate bowl. Place aside. In a large bowl, whisk the sugar and eggs until foamy. Sunflower oil should then be added and thoroughly combined. The toasted sesame seeds and aniseed powder can then be added. Mix thoroughly. The dry ingredients you previously prepared should be added in many batches. Knead the dough until it becomes soft and slightly sticky. Add 1 tablespoon of flour if you need to add more. Depending on the sort of flour you use, the absorption will vary. Four parts of dough should be created. Roll out the dough with a rolling pin into a rectangle that is 1/2 cm thick after lightly flouring the work surface. 1 egg yolk, 2 tablespoons of water, and 1 tablespoon of instant coffee should be lightly beaten together. Place the almonds, walnuts, and pistachios on top of the dough after brushing the top with the egg mixture. To prevent the dough from breaking, carefully roll up and push down. Apply the egg yolk mixture to the roll's outside. Without preheating the oven, bake for 20 to 25 minutes at 160 °C on a baking sheet covered with parchment paper. Take the fekkas outside after the allotted time has passed so they can cool off a bit. Allow them to rest for four to five hours by rolling them up in a clean cloth. Slice them into 1/2 cm-thick pieces with a knife, being careful not to break them. The Fakkas should be baked on a tray in the oven until golden brown. At 160 °C, for 15 minutes. Enjoy your meals and cooking!

Mhancha

Ingredients for 8 people

- ✓ 8-9 sheets of filo pastry
- ✓ 20 pitted dates
- ✓ 100 gr walnuts
- ✓ 125 gr ground almonds
- ✓ 1 tbsp sugar
- ✓ 60 gr butter
- ✓ 1 tsp ground cinnamon
- ✓ 1 tsp ground cardamom
- ✓ 1 tbsp orange blossom water
- ✓ Honey
- ✓ icing sugar

Directions: 60 minutes

In a chopper, put the walnuts, dates and butter and chop them into a paste. We pass it to a bowl and mix it

with the ground almonds, cinnamon, cardamom, sugar and orange blossom water. We extend the sheets of pasta fila overlapping, joining them 2 cm one over the other and sticking them with melted butter. At one end, we distribute all the dough fillingr Carefully roll up to form a long cylinder. Roll up carefully to form a long cylinder. We roll up, careful not to break the sheets and to tuck the last end under a little of the spiral to make it as compact as possible. We put it in a removable mold with the base lined with parchment paper and the side with melted butter. We paint lightly with melted butter on top and bake at 190 ° until golden brown and crispy. When we take it out of the oven and it is still hot bathe with honey. And a couple more drops of orange blossom water. Let it cool completely and when serving, sprinkle with icing sugar.

Kaab el Ghazal

Ingredients for 50 pieces

- ✓ 1 1b./500 gr Blanched almonds, skinned
- ✓ 1 1/3 cups / 275 gr Sugar
- ✓ 1/3 cup / 75 ml. of orange blossom water
- ✓ 1/4 cup / 60 gr Unsalted butter, melted
- ✓ 1/4 teaspoon cinnamon
- ✓ Optional: 1 pinch of mastic or gum arabic powder
- ✓ 3 cups / 375 gr Flour
- ✓ 1/2 teaspoon salt
- ✓ 2 small eggs or 1 1/2 large eggs
- ✓ 3/4 cup / 170 gr Unsalted butter, melted
- ✓ 4 to 5 tablespoons of orange blossom water
- ✓ 1 egg
- ✓ 1 tablespoon orange blossom water
- ✓ Orange flower water for dipping (optional)

Directions: 2 hours and 30 minutes

To make a paste, repeatedly run blanched almonds through a meat grinder. Or, pulse the almonds in a food processor for at least five minutes, or until a workable paste forms. Until a smooth, moist paste is created, thoroughly combine the powdered almonds with the sugar, cinnamon, orange blossom water, and gum arabic powder using your hands. To taste, you can increase the amount of sugar, cinnamon, or orange blossom water. Shape miniature finger-sized sausage sticks out of a small amount of the almond paste mixture. Continue with the remaining almond paste, cover, and reserve. At this point, the made almond paste can be stored in the refrigerator for a few days. Construct the puff pastry dough.

After combining all the ingredients, the dough should be soft; knead it by hand for at least 20 minutes to make it smooth and elastic. Alternatively, you can use a stand mixer with a dough hook or a food processor attachment to combine the dough. The dough should be elastic and smooth after 5 to 10 minutes of machine kneadingr The dough should be divided into 4 to 6 sections, wrapped in plastic wrap, and let to rest for at least 15 minutes. The Kaab el Ghazal is shaped. Dust a work surface with flour very lightly. A dough sheet should be rolled out to a pretty thin consistency—roughly the same thickness as a very thin piece of cardboard. To make the dough easier to roll out, you should lift and reposition it multiple times while you work. Put a dough stick close to the dough's top. To conceal the almond paste, fold the top edge of the dough down tightly, leaving a small overlap. To tightly enclose the almond paste, press the folded dough. You might be able to fit two or more bars of dough in a row before folding the dough, depending on how wide the dough you've laid out is. When doing this, leave about 1 1/2 inches between each dough stick. Using your fingers, form the hidden almond paste into a letter-shaped crescent with the outside of the curve facing you.

Additionally, shape the crescent into the classic kaab el ghazal form with tapering tips and a broader base. Making the cookies seem a little thin is acceptable because they will puff up a little when baked. Use a pastry wheel or knife to carefully cut out the crescent; a fluted pastry wheel provides the most attractive edge. To properly enclose the almond paste, pinch the dough to seal the cut corners if necessary. Place the cookie on a baking pan without any grease. Use the leftover dough and stick to repeat. Put any leftover dough in plastic wrap. Scoop up any remaining dough as you go, roll them into balls, and put them back on the plastic

wrap before rolling them out again. Cook the cookies. Shaped cookies should be uncovered for at least an hour before bakingr 350 F/180 C oven temperature. The optionally beat egg gives baked cookies a lovely gloss. Beat one egg with one tablespoon of orange blossom water to make the beaten eggr Brush the wash very little over the cookies. Next, make two or three holes in the edge of the top of each cookie with a long pin or needle. One baking sheet at a time, bake the cookies in the center of the oven for 12 minutes, or until just beginning to turn golden brown. Do not overbake because this will cause the dough and almond paste to become tough. Before putting the cookies in a plastic container, move the biscuits to a wire rack to finish coolingr

Greek desserts

Kourobietes

Ingredients for 25 people

- ✓ 300 g sheep's and goat's milk butter
- ✓ 70 g icing sugar
- ✓ 1 vanilla
- ✓ 1 teaspoon of rose water
- ✓ 550 g soft flour (sifted)
- ✓ 1/2 tsp. cut baking powder
- ✓ 100 g small Greek almonds (with their skins on)
- ✓ A little bit of rose water
- ✓ 500 g icing sugar for steaming
- ✓ 1 vanilla

Directions: 45 minutes

Spread the small almonds with their skins out thinly on a small baking sheet, and bake them for about 10 minutes at 200 °C on the center rack of the oven or until they turn golden brown. Give them time to completely cool. You must use a knife to roughly cut the almonds if they are large. If the Greek almonds are small, either leave the skins on the whole or chop them in half. One hour before preparing the kourabiedes, remove the butter and allow it to warm up to room temperature. Allow the butter to sit in the refrigerator for 10 minutes to firm up and develop a body if the space you are working in is hot and it melts and becomes liquid. When you dip the spoon into the butter, it should come out solid and not runny. Add the butter to the bowl of an electric mixer, and whisk for 2 to 3 minutes at high speed to cream the butter. Add the powdered sugar and vanilla after lowering the mixer's speed. Beat the mixture for about 6 to 7 minutes, gradually increasing the speed to high or until it resembles whipped cream. It should be upright, bouncy, fluffy, white, and glossy. Place the butter and icing sugar in the refrigerator for a few minutes to allow the butter to start solidifying if your room is warm and the mixture begins to melt. Sift over the whipped butter before mixing in the rosewater and half of the flour. Using an electric mixer, beat briefly at low to low speed until the flour is mixed. Add the almonds that have been cold-roasted. 2 tablespoons of the remaining flour should be set aside. Sift in the remaining flour and use your hands to gently knead it into the dough. Your dough will now be visible; it should be as soft as plasticine while also being buttery and soft. Add the 2 tablespoons put aside gradually until the dough reaches the desired consistency if it is too soft and difficult to roll out.

Give the dough 10 minutes to rest. Shape the 30-35 g dough into classic kurabihis or crescents. Put the kourabies on a baking sheet that has been parchment papered over. Put them far apart from one another. After you've finished shaping them all, bake them for 30 minutes at 160 °C in a well-preheated oven. When baked, the currants ought to pop and brown nicely. After baking and while they are still hot from the oven, sprinkle a small amount of floral water on the quesadillas to quickly dry them from the heat. Add the counter after removing them. After letting the quesadillas set for ten minutes, combine the icing sugar and vanilla in a basin.

Sift powdered sugar liberally into a baking sheet to create a layer. Pick up a single pretzel with a spatula, then arrange it on top of the frostingr Sprinkle steaming powdered sugar on the baking pan once it has been full. Put the kourabies on a plate and steam some more icing sugar. When the traditional kurabiches have completely cooled, store them in an airtight container. Sprinkle steamed powdered sugar on top of the packed baking tin. The kourabies should be placed on a dish and steamed with more icing sugar. Once totally cooled, place the flaky and crunchy traditional kurabiches in an airtight container. Create a crescent form with the currabiades. Alternatively, spread the entire dough out on the counter and press it into a thick sheet. Use a cookie cutter to cut into any shape you like.

The kourabies must be steamed with icing sugar to pull the icing sugar in a while still hot. However, be careful not to overheat them since the icing sugar can cause them to become moist and mushy. The rose water should always be poured into the hot currants right before taking them out of the oven so that it will drip onto the currant's hot surface and evaporate. By doing this, you preserve just the fragrance of the rose water and not its moisture. The absence of an egg in the dough distinguishes these currants from others. Only high-quality goat butter or a blend of fresh cow butter and half and half can differentiate between flavors and textures. Kourabies is a year-round dessert offered as a special treat at festivals and gatherings in several regions of Greece, including Macedonia, the Peloponnese, and Sterea Greece.

Amygdalota Galaxidi

Ingredients

- ✓ 6 egg whites
- ✓ 1 pinch/s of salt
- ✓ 700 g granulated sugar
- ✓ 1 kg of peeled and ground almonds
- ✓ 150 g breadcrumbs, grated
- ✓ 3 tbsp lemon juice
- ✓ Monitor
- ✓ Almonds for garnish

Directions:

Combine the salt and egg whites in a fresh bowl. Use a hand mixer set to medium speed to beat ingredients until stiff peaks, or meringue, form. The sugar and ground almonds should be combined in a big bowl and well stirred with your hands so that the sugar melts from the heat of your hands and the mixture resembles dough. Add the breadcrumbs and lemon juice when the sugar and ground almonds have gotten soft. The meringue is then added after a light rosewater drizzle. Use a gentle spatula to whisk the mixture slowly and consistently in one direction. On a baking pan, spread non-stick paper. Press a whole almond into the center of the almond surface after molding the almonds into

the desired form (often the shape of a tiny burger). On shallow baking trays covered with non-stick paper, distribute the almond halves in a sparse layers after making them all in the same manner. They should be baked for about 20 minutes at 160 °C in a well-preheated oven. Due to the absence of egg yolk, which gives confections their color, almonds do not significantly brown and maintain their light color. They will be soft when you take them out of the oven, but the texture gradually hardens as they cool.

Be cautious during unmoldingr The almond cakes will gradually start to come off without breaking if you invert the baking pan onto a clean cloth and dab some lukewarm water on the back of the non-stick paper. After letting them cool, wrap each one individually in cling film or gelatin to preserve their freshness and aroma for a very long time. You can, if you'd like, sift some icing sugar over the warm almond halves.

Baklava with walnuts

Ingredients for 50 pieces

- ✓ 4 stacks of crust sheets (4x450 g)
- ✓ 50 nutmegs
- ✓ 1 cup vegetable butter (phytin)
- ✓ 1 cup olive oil
- ✓ 1 kg of walnuts
- ✓ 5 tbsp breadcrumbs
- ✓ 5 tbsp sugar
- ✓ 1/2 tsp cinnamon
- ✓ 1 pinch of cloves
- ✓ 900 g sugar
- ✓ 750 g water
- ✓ 1 stick of cinnamon
- ✓ 1/2 lemon
- ✓ 1/2 cup warm honey

Directions: 1 hour & 50 minutes

Use a large, deep baking pan that will fit the size of the sheets when they are opened. If not, you must calculate the pan's measurements and trim the protrude edges. After giving them a fine chop in a blender, put the walnuts in a bowl. Each filling component should be added. The last six sheets should be saved. The melted veggie butter and oil should be combined in a bowl. You may merely use oil. Spread six sheets on a baking sheet that has been generously buttered, and then liberally drizzle them with the veggie butter and oil. Ensure the leaves are stacked on top of one another without protruding or wrinklingr Add a layer of filling, making sure to cover the entire surface. Afterward, add another layer of filling and top with two greased sheets. Up until all the components are used, the process is repeated with 2 greased sheets and a layer of fillingr After buttering them by sprinkling them in between, cover with the six polenta sheets.

Use a sharp knife to cut the pastry into baclala-like pieces. Pour the remaining butter oil over the incisions and the surface. Place a clove of nutmeg in each piece. With your fingers, lightly mist the surface with water. Bake for about 1 hour and 30 minutes at 150°C on the bottom rack of the oven using the resistance. A clue that the baklava has cooked thoroughly throughout, from the bottom up, is when you hear it crackle. It must be well-browned. While finishing the baking, we make the syrup. As soon as the baklava is removed from the oven, we shall drizzle it with the hot syrup. The leaves will remain crisp and it will soak up all the syrup in this manner.

The syrup's components should be brought to a boil in a pan. Honey should be kept apart. Stir and boil for 4 to 5 minutes after it reaches a boil. Take the lemon out. Pour the hot syrup over the warm baklava as you remove it from the oven, a bit at a time. The sound of the leaf sizzling as it absorbs the syrup is what you want to hear. Slowly and steadily syrup it. When the syrup is done, warm the honey and drizzle it on top. Overnight cooling is recommended. Cut it, like other sugary treats, the following day. The ideal walnut baklava has been perfectly baked, syrup, and browned and thoroughly absorbed the syrup. When you bite into a slice of authentic classic walnut baklava, the syrup on the pan is gone since the pastry has absorbed it all.

Bougatsa

Ingredients for 12 people

- ✓ 1 drawer of crust (or Beirut)
- ✓ 150 g cow's butter (melted and cold)
- ✓ For the cream of the baguette

- ✓ 1½ lt fresh milk
- ✓ 200 g fine semolina
- ✓ 200 g sugar
- ✓ 2 vanillas
- ✓ 2 pinches of salt
- ✓ 60 g cow's butter
- ✓ For the topping
- ✓ Sugar
- ✓ Cinnamon

Directions: 55 minutes

For the cream baguette

A heavy-bottomed saucepan should include the milk, semolina, sugar, vanilla, and salt. Keep the butter till last. Over medium heat, bring to a boil while stirring continuously until smooth. The entire process takes a short while. Remove the pot from the heat when the sweet semolina sweet cream has boiled. Melt the butter into the cream after adding it and stirringr To stop the cream from boiling, pour it into a large bowl. Permit the semolina cream to cool and become more solid. The custard thickens as the temperature drops, stabilizing it. Kitchen foil must touch every surface of the custard to be covered entirely. A gap between the cream and the plastic wrap should not exist. This will stop moisture from accumulating while preventing unattractive skin development.

Use a 23 x 33 cm oblong baking pan for setup. Melted cold butter should be used to brush the baking pan. To ensure enough phyllo on all sides of the pan, spread out the 5 sheets, ensuring they are facing crosswise rather than in the opposite direction. Butter the baking sheet's edges that protrude from the pan. Over the sheets, spread the fillingr Turn the sheets that extend from the baking pan's sides inward onto the baguette's surface. Make sure to generously grease the turned sheets. After thoroughly buttering each sheet, place the final five sheets on top of the baguette. Push the top sheets that protrude from the baking sheet's edge into the tray that is underneath the baguette using a gentle spatula. Butter the baguette's exterior thoroughly. The pan can be wrapped in aluminum foil and kept in the refrigerator for up to four days when the bougatsa is done and the cream is cold. Alternatively, it can be stored in the freezer for a while. However, you must ensure that the phyllo utilized is brand-new because it is not permitted to defrost a sheet and then refreeze it.

When baking

Puff pastry should be fluffy and well-browned after about 35 minutes of baking at 180°C with the oven door open. Serve with cinnamon and icing sugar or granulated sugar. Make burekakia or triangles of Panorama using the leftover crust sheets.

The bugat's dark secrets

The bougatsa's sweet cream must be light, airy, and heavy. Because the liquid evaporates when the cream of bougatsa cooks on the fire for an extended period, the cream will end up thick after bakingr Place each ingredient in the saucepan with a thick bottom. Except for the butter, which is usually added after the bougatsa cream has boiled. In order for the semolina to bubble up and the cream to be thoroughly mixed as it cooks, the cream of bougatsa must be constantly stirred. Cover the bougatsa cream with foil that thoroughly touches the surface while it cools to prevent unattractive skimmingr Don't let any space exist between the cream and the plastic wrap. This will ensure that the custard stays frothy even after coolingr Melted and cold butter should be used for the sheets. The bougatsa will turn out particularly crisp if each sheet is thoroughly brushed. Make careful to butter the extra leaves and the leaf corners thoroughly. Turn your baguette carefully onto a larger baking dish in the final 10 minutes of baking for the prettiest result. Bake more until well browned. Carefully transfer the bougatsa out onto a cutting board after removing it from the oven. Give it ten minutes to stand. Then, cut into large or little pieces using a large knife and top with cinnamon sugar.

Melomakarona

Ingrediento for 50 pieces

- ✓ For the dough:
- ✓ 240 ml olive oil
- ✓ 240 ml sunflower oil
- ✓ 200 g granulated sugar
- ✓ 120 ml cognac
- ✓ Juice of 1 orange
- ✓ Zest of 1 orange

- ✓ 1 kg of flour, soft
- ✓ 2 teaspoons of baking powder
- ✓ 1 tsp baking soda, baking powder
- ✓ 1 teaspoon cloves, grated
- ✓ 2 teaspoons cinnamon, powdered
- ✓ Grated walnuts to serve
- ✓ For the syrup:
- ✓ 800 ml water
- ✓ 800 g granulated sugar
- ✓ 500 g thyme honey
- ✓ 2 cinnamon sticks
- ✓ 1 orange slice

Directions 45 minutes

Making the syrup: Combine all the ingredients in a saucepan, excluding the honey. Simmer for 4-5 minutes with the pot on medium-high heat. After the sugar has dissolved and cooked, remove the pot, whisk in the honey with a spoon, and then leave it to cool completely. Combine all the solid ingredients in a separate bowl except for the walnuts. Once the liquid and solid mixtures are blended, slowly transfer the liquid mixture into the solids-only dish while donning disposable gloves. WARNING: The oils will leak if you stir the mixture too much. The convection oven is preheated to 180°C. After that, roll the mixture into balls weighing 30 g each and bake them on a baking sheet covered with parchment paper. The top side of each dough should then be pierced with forks so that the melomakarona may bake more quickly and absorb the syrup more quickly. For 20 to 25 minutes, bake in a preheated oven set to 180°C with the fan. When everything is prepared, add the hot melomakarona to the chilled syrup and let them sit there for 10 seconds. Scoop the melomakarona out of the syrup with a slotted spoon, and then put them in a serving bowl. Before serving, top with chopped walnuts and let cool completely.

Kourabies

Ingredients for 50 pieces

- ✓ 250 g sheep and goat butter at room temperature
- ✓ 40 g icing sugar
- ✓ 500 g all-purpose flour

- ✓ 1/4 tsp. baking powder
- ✓ 150 g white almonds roasted at 160°C for 10 minutes

Directions: 45 minutes

Use the egg beater attachment to combine the goat butter and icing sugar in the mixer's bowl after it has sufficiently melted. It is prepared once thoroughly fluffed, doubled in volume, and transformed into a silky white cream with gentle peaks. It will require roughly 20 minutes of medium-speed hammering. Use the paddle attachment while switching out the mixer's attachments. Add the baking powder and flour. Crush the almond in the mortar and pestle. Add the smashed almond after the mixture has been blended.

Put on gloves made for cooking, then mold the kourabies into the desired size and form. To ensure consistent baking, ensure the kurabihis are all the same size. The kourabies should be put on a baking sheet covered with parchment paper. For about 20 minutes, bake in an oven preheated to 180°C with the middle rack in the air. Before they cool after baking, coat them thoroughly with icing sugar. Quesadillas should be presented on a decorative tray.

Kadaifi

Ingredients for 12 pieces

- ✓ 500 g cinnamon leaf
- ✓ 300 g chopped walnuts (or raw pistachios)
- ✓ 1 tsp cinnamon (chopped)
- ✓ 2-3 pinches of cloves
- ✓ 300 g melted goat and sheep butter (butter found in jars in the supermarket)
- ✓ A few chopped walnuts or Aegina nuts for garnish
- ✓ For the syrup
- ✓ 3 cups of sugar
- ✓ 2½ cups of water
- ✓ 1/2 lemon (juice)
- ✓ 2 tablespoons lemon peel

Directions: 1 hour & 30 minutes

First, open the cinnamon leaf and fluff it with your fingers. Finely chop the nuts in a bowl and sprinkle with the cinnamon. Stir. Make 12 melon rolls by mentally dividing the dough into 12 equal portions. To produce more, make the rolls smaller. Take some cinnamon roll sheets and spread them out into an oblong form for the wrappingr Roll it into its traditional shape, then spread 1 tablespoon of walnut, Aegina nut, or pistachio fillingr Make sure the sides are sealed. On a baking sheet that has been buttered, arrange all the rolls similarly. With a spoon, drizzle the melted butter gradually over the cantaloupes. Make sure the joint where they touch each other is well-greased. Bake for about 1 hour and 15 minutes, or until thoroughly browned, on the bottom rack of a preheated oven set to 170 °C. Alternatively, bake the food for 1 hour and 10 minutes at 150 °C on the middle rack in the air. Prepare the syrup while allowing the food to bake thoroughly. When it is thoroughly browned and all the cantaloupes move when you shake the pan, indicating that they are dry, transfer it to the counter and drizzle the hot syrup slowly over all the rolls. On the pan, let the cantaloupes stand and totally cool. Letting all baked goods overnight is recommended so the syrup can properly absorb. In a saucepan, combine the sugar, water, and lemon peel. Stir continuously till the sugar melts. Don't stir it again after it starts to boil; otherwise, the syrup will crystallize. Add the lemon juice at the very end after boiling for 3–4 minutes. On top of the warm cantaloupe, the syrup should drip hot and slowly. How to grow the ideal cantaloupe. A decent kadaifi is a simple recipe, but the few ingredients must be of the highest caliber to leave a lasting impression on everyone who makes it. The key to an unforgettable cantaloupe that makes you salivate is extremely nice butter with scents and rich flavors and very good and fresh almonds. To create a mountain of fluffy, fiber-splitting cantaloupe leaf, roll out the leaf very thoroughly with your hands as if you were scraping hair. To keep the leaf from drying out and to correctly wrap it into a roll, it must be handled swiftly in an area without any drafts. To keep the foil from drying out while you are preparing the cantaloupes, it is a good idea to cover the foil that has been fluffed but not opened with a damp towel. You should only use butter free of proteins since the cantaloupe would quickly burn during bakingr. Good baking is a prerequisite for well syruped cantaloupe. To fully cook it, bake it at a medium temperature for an extended period. A properly baked cantaloupe will take up the syrup and retain its crisp exterior and juicy interior without spilling any syrup. To do this, be patient and roast the food for an extended time at a low temperature. Nothing is worse than receiving a white cantaloupe softly leaking with juice. It must be allowed to stand overnight to draw out the syrup and thoroughly dry so that you may enjoy it and make it unforgettable.

Revani of Veroia

Ingredients

- ✓ 5 eggs
- ✓ 1 cup of sugar
- ✓ 1 spoonful of yogurt
- ✓ 1 baking powder
- ✓ 2 vanillas
- ✓ 1/2 cup flour
- ✓ 1 cup seed oil
- ✓ 1,5 cups of coarse semolina
- ✓ 1/2 cup fine semolina
- ✓ For the syrup
- ✓ 4 cups sugar
- ✓ 4 cups water
- ✓ 1 cup lemon peel
- ✓ cinnamon stick

Directions:

The flour, semolina, and baking powder should be combined in a bowl. Place aside. Separate the yolks from the whites after breaking the eggs. Beat the yolks and sugar in an electric mixer on medium-high speed until the sugar is dissolved and the mixture is frothy, puffy, and creamy. After that, incorporate the yogurt and continue beating. Add the seed oil and the mixer. When adding the flour, semolina, and baking powder, stop pounding and stir with a spatula until combined. The flavorings should be added last. Put a basin with the mixture inside. Add the egg whites after thoroughly cleaning the mixer bowl. They should be whisked at a medium speed until they stiffen into meringue. They should be gently incorporated into the remaining mixture using a spatula in a circular motion to preserve their volume. Butter the baking dish, then top with semolina. Place the mixture on the baking sheet (about 20 x 35) and bake for 30 to 40 minutes at 180 degrees,

or until golden brown. Cut into bits after being pierced with a toothpick for assistance. Boil all the ingredients for the syrup for 5 minutes. Pour it into the heated chickpea you just removed from the oven after allowing it to cool.

Melomakarona

Ingredients for 70 pieces

- ✓ 240 g sunflower or corn oil
- ✓ 240 g light olive oil
- ✓ 50 g cognac
- ✓ 160 g fresh orange juice
- ✓ 1 teaspoon of baking soda
- ✓ 200 g fine granulated sugar
- ✓ 1 teaspoon cut cloves
- ✓ 2 teaspoons chopped cinnamon
- ✓ 2 oranges unpeeled (zest)
- ✓ 900 g all-purpose flour
- ✓ 2 teaspoons of baking powder

For the syrup

- ✓ 400 g sugar
- ✓ 400 g water
- ✓ 400 g thyme honey
- ✓ 1/2 lemon (unpeeled)
- ✓ Ground pistachio or walnut (for sprinkling)

Directions 34 minutes

The procedure will go well if you weigh the ingredients and have them counted in front of you. To start, sift the baking powder and flour into a bowl. Put them apart. Combine the sugar, cinnamon, cloves, olive oil, sunflower oil, cognac, and orange zest in a separate basin. Whisk thoroughly to help the sugar melt and dissolve. Orange juice and baking soda should be mixed to dissolve the baking soda, then added to the mixture to begin the reaction. The materials are blended together. Finally, whisk the mixture briefly before gradually adding the flour. Fold the dough by hand gently once it begins to firm up. If you want them to be fluffy so they can adequately absorb the syrup, don't work the mixture for too long. The dough should be light, oily, and soft for gingerbread cookies. Leave the dough on the counter for 15 minutes if you have the time. The final shape is more exquisitely sculpted the longer it rests. Start rolling a piece of dough about the size of a walnut. On the baking sheet, distribute them out and space them far apart. The gingerbread cookies don't require non-stick paper because the batter is rather fatty and doesn't adhere to the pan after baking. With a fork, lightly push the surface to create patterns and holes. This will make it easier for them to properly absorb the syrup once they are baked. Place the first two pans in the oven after shaping them. For around 25 minutes at 160°C, bake on the middle rack in the air in a well-preheated oven. When they are nicely browned and crispy, they are prepared.

Additionally, their stench will make you sneeze. You'll know they're prepared when that happens. Allow them to fully and thoroughly cool down. I make many of these every year and add a little syrup whenever they run out. To prevent them from rubbing against one another, I layer sheets of non-stick paper between the baked gingerbread cookies and store them in a sizable airtight container. The syrup for In a saucepan, combine the honey and the remaining ingredients. Boil for three minutes. Remove the froth that accumulates on the syrup's surface by skimming. Reduce the heat to low once the syrup has reached a boil. Maintain a heat setting of 1 or 2, just hot enough to cause the syrup to bubble and simmer.

Several gingerbread cookies should be dipped into the syrup and sit there for about 20 seconds on each side. This will ensure they are correctly set, remain fluffy and honeyed, and melt on the tongue without becoming heavy or dripping with syrup. Spread them out tightly on a baking sheet and slowly pour the syrup over them if you want them to be more syrupy. Allow the syrup to thoroughly soak into the gingerbread cookies. I like them better with the original version. A small amount of syrup. Add chopped Aegina peanuts or walnuts after syruping them while they are still warm. The melomakarono is frequently topped with toasted sesame seeds and walnuts. By making them yourself, you may fill your house with delicious aromas and give your kids a sweet memory of the experience

Vasilopita Tsoureki Recipe (New Years Bread)

Ingredients for 10 pieces

- ✓ 110g sugar
- ✓ 75ml milk
- ✓ 80g butter
- ✓ 12g instant yeast
- ✓ 1–2 mastic teardrops
- ✓ 65ml tepid water
- ✓ 1 1/2 tsp ground mahleb
- ✓ 480g strong bread flour, plus extra for dusting
- ✓ 1/2 tsp salt
- ✓ zest of 1/2 large orange
- ✓ 2 large eggs
- ✓ seeds of 1/2 vanilla pod (optional)
- ✓ 20g flaked almonds (3/4 oz)
- ✓ 50g powdered sugar, sieved to remove any lumps
- ✓ 3/4 tsp water
- ✓ 1 tsp vanilla extract

Directions: 5 hours 10 minutes

Prepare the dough for Vasilopita Tsoureki

Make the dough first before preparing the Vasilopita tsoureki bread. In a small saucepan over medium-low heat, combine the butter, milk, and sugar. Until the butter has melted and the sugar has dissolved, allow to cook thoroughly while whisking frequently. Remove from the fire and give it some time to cool.

In the meantime, combine the yeast with the warm water and stir until foamy. Crush the mastic using a mortar and pestle. Add the mahleb and keep grinding until it is a fine powder to prevent sticking and to aid in the breakdown.

The flour, salt, orange zest, and spice mixture should all be combined in the bowl of a stand mixer before being set aside. Lightly whisk the eggs in the bottom of a large mixing jug. While continuing to whisk, add the sugar, butter, and milk mixture gradually; the eggs should now be cool enough for you to hold your finger comfortably inside without burning it. The yeast mixture and, if using, the vanilla seeds should then be whisked in.

Use a fork to incorporate the liquid mixture into the flour mixture, creating a loose dough. The dough should be smooth, taut, and stretchy after 15 minutes of kneading using the dough hook attachment. Scrape the dough with a dough scraper or spatula into a ball, cover the bowl with plastic wrap, and let it rise for about 2 hours, or until it has at least doubled in size.

Galaktoboureko with Kataifi

Ingredients for 15-16 pieces

- ✓ 500g kataifi dough
- ✓ 450g water
- ✓ 780g sugar
- ✓ 250g butter
- ✓ peel of 1 lemon
- ✓ 100g honey
- ✓ 220g sugar
- ✓ a cinnamon stick
- ✓ 10 drops of lemon juice
- ✓ 500g milk
- ✓ 160g finely ground semolina
- ✓ 4 eggs
- ✓ 70g butter
- ✓ 500g double (heavy) cream
- ✓ 1 tsp vanilla extract
- ✓ a pinch of salt

Directions: 2 hours

Prepare the syrup

Prepare the syrup first before beginning to create the galaktoboureko with kataifi recipe. Add the sugar, water, lemon peel, cinnamon stick, and lemon juice to a small pot, and then bring to a boil. Allow it to simmer until the sugar dissolves. After taking the pan off the heat, mix in the honey. Set the syrup aside to finish cooling.

Prepare the custard

To make the custard for this Galaktoboureko with Kataifi, combine the milk, cream, and half of the sugar in a saucepan, and bring to a boil without whisking. This is important because the sugar at the bottom of the pan prevents the milk from burning. Add the semolina and vanilla essence gradually while stirring as soon as it begins to boil and heat up. Reduce the heat to medium,

then whisk continuously until the mixture reaches a creamy consistency. Fold the ingredients after removing the pan from the heat and adding the butter and salt. While you are making the meringue, let it cool. Just keep in mind to whisk it occasionally to prevent the development of a skin on top. In a mixing bowl, combine the eggs and the remaining sugar. The eggs and sugar should be whisked with an electric mixer or hand whisk until the mixture is very frothy, foamy, and forms soft peaks. If using a mixer, run it for roughly 5 minutes on high speed. The two mixes from steps 3 and 4 should now be folded together. 1/4 of the egg-sugar mixture should be added to the custard mixture and blended using a spatula in a light, upward-moving circular motion. Fold after adding the entire mixture gradually. Set apart for cooling.

Koulourakia Ladiou

Ingredients for 30 cookies

- ✓ 130g olive oil
- ✓ 150g sugar
- ✓ 500g self rising flour
- ✓ 165g orange juice
- ✓ zest of 1 orange
- ✓ 1 tsp ground cinnamon
- ✓ 4 drops vanilla essence
- ✓ 80g sesame seeds for coating
- ✓ 1/4 tsp ground clove
- ✓ 1/3 tsp baking soda

Directions: 40 minutes

Orange juice and baking soda should be added to a big bowl to make these olive oil biscuits. Fork-whisk the mixture briefly until the baking soda dissolves and begins to froth.

Add the sugar to the same bowl along with the liquid components (cognac, if using, vanilla essence, and olive oil), and mix with a hand whisk until the sugar dissolves. Place aside. Add the dry ingredients—flour, salt, orange zest, ground cinnamon, and clove—to another bowl. Using a spoon, mix everything. In the dish containing the liquid components, combine all the dry ingredients. Use a spoon to briskly combine all the ingredients. At the end, gently knead the dough with your hands until the flour is incorporated. Avoid over-kneading the dough as this may cause the oil to separate. Preheating the oven to 170-180°C. From the dough, form 28–30 similar balls, each weighing 30–35g. Create circles or braids out of the cookies. Dredge the olive oil cookies in sesame seeds until covered on all sides. Place the cookies on 2 baking trays lined with parchment paper. Each tray should be baked for roughly 20 to 25 minutes, or until well browned and cooked through. Take them out of the oven and allow them to completely cool. Enjoy!

Made in United States
North Haven, CT
07 May 2023

36341118R10089